For Reference

Not to be taken from this room

THE ILLUSTRATED
HISTORY OF THE WORLD

VOLUME 11
SERIES INDEX

J. M. ROBERTS

Oxford University Press

The Illustrated History of the World

This edition first published in 2000 in the United States of America by
Oxford University Press, Inc.,
198 Madison Avenue, New York, N.Y. 10016
Oxford is a registered trademark of Oxford University Press

SERIES INDEX
Copyright © Duncan Baird Publishers 2000
Text copyright © Duncan Baird Publishers 2000

Produced by Duncan Baird Publishers, London, England

Series ISBN 0-19-521529-X
Volume 11 ISBN 0-19-521697-0

Indexer: John Noble
Editors: Hanne Bewernick, Ingrid Court-Jones, and Georgina Harris
Designer: Dan Sturges

Typeset in Sabon
Printed in Singapore by Imago Limited

NOTE
The abbreviations CE and BCE are used throughout this book:
CE Common Era (the equivalent of AD)
BCE Before Common Era (the equivalent of BC)

10 9 8 7 6 5 4 3 2

INDEX

References in this index refer to volume and page number, for example, 4:140 is Volume 4, page 140.
Page references to main text are in roman, to box text in **bold**, and to illustrations and captions in *italic*.

A

Aachen, Charlemagne's court 4:140, *4:140*,
    4:141, 4:145
    Carolingian Renaissance at 4:137, 4:139,
      4:140–43, *4:141*, 4:142
    intellectual life at 4:136–7, 4:139, 4:142–3
    Otto I at 4:148
    Otto III at 4:149
    thermal springs at 4:143
Abbasid caliphate 4:24, 4:32–41, *4:34*, 5:150
    architecture of 4:38, 4:39, *4:39*, *4:40*, *4:47*
    army of 4:43–4
    arts of 4:39–41
    Buwayhid dynasty 4:44
    Charlemagne, relations with 4:41, 4:140,
      4:140
    decline of 4:43–4, 4:96
    hereditary governorships of 4:34
    literature of 4:35–7
    mathematics and science in 4:37–8
    Mongols and 4:44, 4:107
    Persian influence upon 4:33–4
    Sunnite orthodoxy of 4:33
    vizier, office of 4:34
    see also Islam; Islamic civilization; Islamic
      science; Umayyad caliphate
Abbas the Great (c.1557–1629), Safavid shah of
    Persia 4:126–7, *4:126–7*
    Isfahan building programme and *4:126*,
      4:127
    religious intolerance and 4:127
Abd Allah (Abdullah el Taaisha) (1846–1899),
    Khalifa of Sudan 8:14, *8:57*
Abd-al-Malik, Umayyad caliph (685–705 CE)
    4:40
Abd-ar-Rahman I, emir of Córdoba (756–788 CE)
    4:39, **4:42**
Abd-ar-Rahman III, first caliph of Córdoba
    (912–961 CE) **4:42**
Abdul Hamid II (1842–1918), sultan of Turkey
    9:33, 9:34, **9:34**
Abgar VIII (or IX), Christian king of Osrhoene
    3:72
Aborigines, Australian 1:59, 6:168, *6:179*
    exploitation of 8:38, *8:39*
Abraham, Hebrew patriarch 1:163–4, 4:39
Abu-al-Abbas, first Abbasid caliph (749–754 CE)
    4:32, *4:33*
Abu-Bakr (573–634 CE), first caliph 4:24, *4:24*
Abu Simbel 1:104, 2:72
    temple of *1:112*, *1:128–9*
Academy of Athens, Plato's school *2:143*,
    2:145, 2:170
Acadia (Nova Scotia), French territory 6:159
    won by the British 6:160
Achaean peoples 1:150
    attacks on Egypt 1:152
    Siege of Troy 1:152, 1:155, **1:155**
Achaemenid dynasty in Persia 1:176–7, 2:76,
    2:78, 2:81, **2:111**, 2:112, 2:167, 4:8

Achaemenid dynasty in Persia (cont.)
    attacks by Scythians 4:15
    Empire of 3:108–9
Acheulian culture **1:27**
Achilles, Greek hero 2:94, 2:97, 2:162
Acre (Holy Land), taken in Third Crusade
    5:151
Acropolis, Athens *2:105*, 2:151, *2:153*, *2:172*
    Delian League and 2:129–30
    Persian attack on 2:82, **2:129**
    rebuilding by Pericles 2:82, 2:129–30, **2:129**
Acts of Parliament (Great Britain),
    Act of Union (1707) 6:69
    Act of Union (1801) 7:177
    Corn Laws 7:172
    Enclosure Acts 6:17, 7:49
    Factory Act (1801) 7:175
    Irish Land Act (1881) 7:179
    Quebec Act (1774) 7:75–6
    Reform Act (1832) 7:171, *7:171*, 7:172–3
    Reform Acts (1867 & 1872) 7:172
    Stamp Act (1765) **7:72**, 7:74–5, *7:74*
    see also Parliament, English
Aden,
    British strategic naval base 8:43–4
    Ottoman Turks and 4:122
    Soviet naval base 10:119
Adenhauer, Konrad (1876–1967), West German
    chancellor 10:11, *10:100*
Adjiki-Toffia, king of Dahomey *8:58*
Adoration of the Sacred Host by Charles II, The
    6:91
Aegas, capital of Macedonia 2:156
Aegean, the 1:129, 1:135, 1:142–56, *2:85*,
    2:90–02, **2:92**
    agriculture and 2:92, 2:125
    Dark Ages of 1:152–5
    depopulation of 1:154
    islands of 4:75, 4:116
    minerals and 2:92–3
    physical extent and population of 2:92–3,
      2:123–4
    topography of 2:84–5, *2:93*
Aeolians 2:90
Aeschylus (525–456 BCE), Greek tragedian
    2:136, **2:148**, 2:149, *2:150*
Aesop, Greek slave 2:98
Afghanistan 2:161
    Buddhism in 5:23
    civil war in **10:43**
    conquest of 5:10
    Marxist régime ousted in *10:127*
    Mujahidin and *10:127*
    Soviet intervention in 10:124, 10:127, 10:131
    Soviet troops withdrawal from **10:12**,
      10:127, 10:138
    Taliban in *10:132*
Afghans, revolt against Persia 4:128
Africa 2:57–62, 5:84–91, 6:122, **6:126**, **6:128**
    agriculture in 5:85, 10:53
    Arab trading posts in 6:127, 6:130

Africa (cont.)
    Azanian Iron Age culture of 5:89–91
    Bantu-speakers in 5:88–9
    Benin 5:89, *5:89–91*
    cave paintings in 1:42
    Christianity in 3:141–2, 3:144
    climatic change in 2:57–8, **2:58**
    colonialism in 8:57–8
    decolonization of 10:50–53, 10:55
    democracy and liberal principles in 10:56
    diseases in 5:85, 6:122, 6:127, 6:177
    Egyptian influence in 2:58–9, 2:62
    economy in 10:53, 10:57–8
    exploitation of resources in 8:59
    famine in 10:58
    German colonies in 8:57, 8:148–9
    Ghana 5:86–8
    gold in 5:86–7, *5:88*, 5:89–90
    as granary of the Roman Empire 3:127,
      3:133
    impact on Europe 8:59
    improved access to 8:53–4
    iron ores in 2:60, 2:62, 5:85, 5:89
    Islam and **4:42**, 4:43, **4:43**, 4:44–5
    Lagos, port of *8:13*
    Lake Chad 2:58, **2:59**
    legends of migration in 5:84
    Mali 5:86, 5:87–8, *5:88*
    metallurgical skills in 5:85, *5:85*
    migration from Europe 8:23
    Nigerian Ife culture 5:85
    Nile valley 2:58, 2:60
    opportunities for settlers in 8:59
    partitioning by European powers 8:57
    peoples of 2:58–9
    population growth in 5:85, 8:58, 10:53,
      10:58
    Portuguese trading posts in 6:127
    prehistory of 1:19–23, 1:27, 1:34–6, 1:38,
      1:40
    as a Roman province 3:126
    Sahara desert *see* Sahara desert
    Second World War in 9:75–7
    secure frontiers of 3:107
    slave trade in 6:23–4, 6:127, **6:147**, 6:162,
      6:165, 6:168–70, *6:169*, *6:170*, 10:56
    Swahili-speakers in 5:89
    trade with Asia 5:89
    urban growth in 10:53
    Vandals in 3:133
    see also British Empire; Oludavi Gorge; and
      under individual countries
African National Congress (ANC) 10:63
Afrikaners 10:59
Agamemnon, king of Mycenae 1:154
    tomb of *1:153*
Age of Reason *see* Enlightenment
Agilulf, king of the Lombards (590–616 CE)
    3:161
Agnese, Battista, cartographer *5:162*
Agni, Vedic god 2:15, *2:16*

Agra
    Akbar's court in *5:29*, 5:31, 5:35
    Taj Mahal in 5:32, *5:37*
agriculture 7:47–54
    Aegean 1:144, 2:92, 2:105, 2:125
    African 2:60, 5:85, 5:90, 10:53
    in the Americas 1:54, 1:59, 2:63
    animal breeding 7:49
    in Athens, specialization of 2:105
    Aztec 5:96
    Caribbean islands and 6:145–6
    collectivization in USSR 8:169
    commercialization of 6:28, 6:33
    Corn Sifters, The (Courbet) *7:51*
    cotton and 7:52, 7:158
    Cuban agrarian reform 10:69
    developments in 9:128–30
      chemical fertilizers 9:128
      climatic changes 9:158
      herbicides and insecticides 9:128
      mechanization 9:128, *9:129*
      production level disparities 9:129–32
      subsistence farming 9:129
    diffusion of **1:55**
    eastern European 10:140
    economic predominance of 6:13, 6:16, 6:19
    Egyptian 1:101, 1:108, *1:120*
    enclosures 6:17, *6:17*, 6:27, 7:49
    European 2:65–6, 4:170, *4:172*, 7:47, 7:50–2,
      7:53, 7:53
      agrarian societies 6:31, 6:35
      Common Agricultural Policy 10:100
      fifteenth-century advances in 6:15–18
      inefficiencies in 5:139–140
      innovations in 5:136–7
      land utilization increased in 5:133, 5:142
      productivity in 5:133, 5:137, 6:16, 7:47,
        7:169
      wage labourers in 5:134
    Chinese 2:32, 2:34, 2:36, 2:42
      improvements 10:27
      intensive farming 5:50
    Grape Harvest, The (Goya) *7:50*
    in Great Britain 7:47–50
    Harappan culture and 2:12
    imported crops 6:16, 6:172–3
    imported livestock 6:173–4
    improvements 5:93, 6:10
    in India 2:10–:11, 8:93
    invention of 1:52–3, **1:55**
    iron tools and 5:85, 5:137
    Japanese 5:77, 5:80, 8:84–5
    land ownership and 7:49, 7:51
    as major employer 7:60
    markets and 6:19
    Maurya empire and 5:14
    Maya 5:93
    medieval methods in 7:49, *7:50*
    in Minoan Crete 1:144
    Near Eastern 1:53–4
    North American 5:92, 7:47, 7:169

agriculture (cont.)
 population growth and 1:56
 rising food prices and 7:89
 the Roman economy and 3:15, 3:69, 3:104–7
 Russian 6:111, 8:136
 seasonal rhythms of 6:15
 self-supporting estates and 3:128
 slavery and 7:52, 7:73, 7:81, 7:158–7:160
 smallholdings and 3:28–9
 social effects of 1:56–8
 in Soviet Union,
  collectivization in 10:81
  failure of 10:81
 in Spanish colonies 6:142
 surplus production 1:56, 1:67, 1:71, 1:77,
  1:79, 1:108, 1:120
 in United States 7:47, 7:169
 wage labour and 6:17
 Wheatfield, The (Constable) 7:48
 Working in the Fields (Ferraguti) 7:50
 see also cereal crops; farming; ploughs and
  ploughing; vegetables
Agrippa, Marcus Vipsanius (63–12 BCE), Roman
 general 3:40, 3:53
Ahmed III, sultan of Turkey (1703–1730) 4:124
Ahmed, Muhammad "the Mahdi" (1848–1885),
 Sudanese leader 8:14, 8:57
Ahmose I, king of Egypt (1550–1525 BCE)
 1:105
Ahmose, Queen (18th dynasty) 1:116
Ahura Mazda, Zoroastrian creator god 4:8,
 4:10, 4:11
Ainu peoples of Japan 1:59, 5:69, 5:73–4
air warfare 9:71, 9:75, 9:76
 airships 8:150
 Battle of Britain 9:71
 Battle of Midway 9:75, 9:76
 bombing of Guernica by Germany 9:65
 bombing of Japan 9:28, 9:76
 Pearl Harbor 9:74, 9:74, 9:75
 strategic bombing in 9:78, 9:80–81, 9:80
 see also warfare
Ajanta caves 2:26–7
Ajmer, conquered by Akbar 5:28
Akbar (1542–1605), Moghul emperor 5:26,
 5:27–9, 5:31, 6:134
 religious tolerance of 5:28
 territorial conquests of 5:28, 5:28, **5:30**
Akhnaton (Amenhotep IV), king of Egypt
 1:105, 1:127, 1:127, 1:128, 1:128, 1:164
Akkad 1:90
Akkadian Empire 1:90–91
 overthrown by Gutians 1:91, 1:93
Akrotiri 1:137, 1:149
Alamanni 3:129
 defeat by Franks 3:153
 invasion of Rome 3:111
Al-Amarnah, tomb of Ay 1:128
Alaska, sale to United States 8:43
al-Aziz, Fatimid caliph of Egypt (975–996 CE)
 4:97
Albania 8:119
 communist state 9:88
 conquest by Ottoman Turks 4:122
 invasion by Yugoslavia **8:161**
 pro-China, anti-Soviet affiliation 10:96
Albert of Saxe-Coburg-Gotha (1819–1861),
 Prince Consort 7:177
Albigensian heretics, persecution of 5:111,
 5:111

Albuquerque, Affonso d' (1453–1515) 6:129
Alchemist at Work, The (Tenier the Elder) 7:16
alchemy 7:16, 7:16, **7:20**
alcohol 1:80, 1:89
Alcuin (735–804 CE), English scholar at
 Carolingian court 4:143
Alembert, Jean le Rond d' (1717–1783), French
 mathematician 7:28, **7:28**, 7:31, 7:31, 7:47
Aleppo, conquest by Mongols 4:113
Alexander I, king of Serbia 8:142
Alexander I (1777–1825), tsar of Russia
 7:140–1, 7:141
Alexander II (1818–1881), tsar of Russia 7:129,
 8:135
 abolition of serfdom 7:146–7
Alexander III (c.1105–1181), pope 5:155
Alexander III (1845–1894), tsar of Russia 8:143
Alexander the Great (356–323 BCE), king of
 Macedon 2:89, 2:160–64, **2:160, 2:163,
 2:164**, 5:8, 5:9, 5:10
 death of 2:161, **2:161**, 2:164
 march to the east **2:161**
 marriages of 2:162–3
 Persian Empire crushed by 2:161, **2:161**
 personal attributes of 2:162–3
 posthumous son of 2:164
 pupil of Aristotle 2:145, **2:160**
 sarcophagus of 2:164
 successor to Persian throne 2:161, 2:164
 Thebes (Grecian) destroyed by 2:159
 see also Macedon; Macedonian Empire;
  Philip II
Alexandria 2:140, 2:167, **2:169**, 9:32
 foundation by Alexander 2:161
 French community in 9:31
 Jewish colony of 3:77
 library at 2:169–70
 pre-eminence in science of 2:170
 unrest in 3:68, 3:77
Alexandrine Empire, fragmentation of 2:164–5,
 2:165
Alexeyev, Fiodor, Russian artist 7:141
Alexius I Comnenus (1048–1118), Byzantine
 emperor **4:74**
Alfonso II, king of Asturias (791–842 CE) 4:174
Alfonso X the Wise (1221–1284), king of Castile
 and León 5:170, 5:177
Alfred the Great (849–899 CE), king of Wessex
 and England 4:155–7, 4:155
 defeat of Norsemen (Danes) by 4:156
Algeria 9:108–109
 French colony in 8:8, **8:55**, 8:57
 French imperialism and 8:52–3, 8:52, 8:53
 independence of 10:47, 10:47, 10:51
 Islamic fundamentalism in 10:123, 10:132
 land law introduced in 8:53
 nationalism in 10:45
 rebellion against France 10:45–6, 10:52,
  10:100
 revolt in 8:57
al-Hariri, Maqamat, Islamic warrior 4:27
Ali, cousin of Muhammad, fourth caliph
 (656–661 CE) 4:24, 4:28
Alighieri, Dante (1265–1321), Italian poet 4:38,
 5:122, 5:122, 5:171, 5:173
Al-Khwarizmi (d:835), Islamic astronomer
 4:38
Al-Kindi (d:870), Islamic philosopher 4:38
Allahabad, Hindu sacred city **5:20**
Allenby, Edmund (1861–1936), British field
 marshal 9:39

Allende, Salvador (1908–1973), president of
 Chile (1970–1973) **10:72**, 10:73
Almagro, Diego de (1475–1538), Spanish
 conquistador 6:139
Al-Mansur (939–1002), Arab conqueror in Spain
 4:158, 4:159
Almeida, Francisco de (1450–1510), viceroy of
 Portuguese India 5:166
Almohads, Berber dynasty **4:42**
Almoravids, Berber dynasty **4:42–3**
alms-giving (*sadaqa*) **4:22**
al-Muizz, Fatimid caliph of Egypt (953–975 CE)
 4:97
Al-Mutanabbi, poet 4:28
Alsace 6:82, 6:92
al-Sahli, Ibrahim ibn Saud, instrument maker
 4:34
Altamira Cave, Cantabria 1:47
Alva, Ferdinand, duke of (1508–1582),
 Spanish general 6:60, 6:60, 6:61
Amalfi (city-state) 4:151
Amarna 1:127
Amaterasu, Shinto sun goddess 5:68, **5:71**
Amboyna, capital of Moluccas 6:131
Ambrose, St (c.340–397 CE), bishop of Milan
 3:137–40, 3:141
Amenemhet I, king of Egypt (c.2000–1970 BCE)
 1:125
Amenhotep III, king of Egypt (c.1411–1375 BCE)
 1:65, 1:127
Amenhotep IV *see* Akhnaton
American Civil War 7:163–6, **7:164**, 7:165, 8:121
 attack on Fort Sumter 7:164
 Confederate States of America in 7:163,
  7:164
 Reconstruction and 7:168
 see also United States of America
American Indians *see* Native Americans
American Revolution 7:77–8, 8:44
 British defeat in 7:78
 Declaration of Independence 7:77, **7:77**,
  7:161
 influence on French Revolution 7:85–7
 unrest prior to 7:73–7, 7:75–7
 see also North American colonies; United
  States of America
Americas, the 2:62–4, 5:91–9
 agriculture in 1:54, 1:59, 2:63
 discovery by Amerigo Vespucci 5:163
 discovery by Columbus 5:128, 5:162
 first human immigrations to 1:40, **1:40**
 South America 5:97–9, 5:162, 5:164
 see also Mesoamerican civilizations; North
  America; South America
Amon-hir-Khopshep, prince of Egypt 1:117
Amon-Re, Egyptian god **1:112**, 1:114, 1:125,
 1:127–8
Amorites 1:93–4, 1:98, 1:163, 1:169
Amos (8th century BCE), Hebrew prophet 1:171
Amritsar massacre 9:99, 10:117, 10:118
Amsterdam 6:132, 6:132, 6:159
 Bank of 6:20
 commercial development in 6:20, 6:94
 as international port 6:166
 merchants in 6:30
 population growth in 6:13
 stock exchange in 6:164
Anabaptists 6:50
Anabasis (Xenophon) 2:156
anarchists 8:110
 expulsion by Second International 8:111

Anatolia 1:54, 1:60, 1:67, 1:93, 1:98, 4:44,
 4:97, 4:100, 4:114
 absorption by Ottoman Empire 4:120
 Arabs removed from 4:62
 carts, first use in 1:136
 copper in 1:83
 Crete, links with 1:142
 Hittites move into 1:74, 1:159
 Medes invade 1:176
 Mesopotamia, links with 1:77–8
 Muslim settlement in 4:102
 ravaged by Huns 3:134
Anatomy Lesson, The (Rembrandt) 6:10
Anaximander (610–547 BCE), Greek philosopher
 2:140
ANC (African National Congress) 10:63
Ando Hiroshige (1797–1858), Japanese artist
 8:80
Angles, Germanic peoples 3:150
Anglican Church *see* Church of England
Anglo-Irish Treaty 8:162
Anglo-Japanese alliance 8:88–9
Anglo-Saxon kingdoms 3:150
Angola 8:57–9
 civil war in 10:60, 10:61
 Marxist régime in 10:60
animals
 domestication of 1:53, 1:53, 1:54, **1:55**
  in China 2:34
  in India 2:11, 2:20
 evolutionary development of **1:12, 1:14**
 see also mammals *and* individual names
Anna Ivanovna (1693–1740), tsarina of Russia
 (1730–1740) 6:114
Annam 9:107
 subdued by Han dynasty 5:41
 see also Vietnam
Anschluss 9:66, 9:66
anthropoid evolution **1:17**
Antigonid dynasty of Macedon 2:165, **2:165**
Antioch,
 principality of 4:62, 4:102
 Seleucid capital 2:165, 2:167
Antiochus IV, king of Syria (175–164 BCE)
 2:172, 3:75, 3:75
Antipodes *see* Australia; New Zealand
anti-semitism 5:123, 5:140, 6:19, 9:41, 9:61–3,
 9:63, 9:79, 9:79, 9:109–10, 10:47
 see also Holocaust; Jews
Antoninus Pius (86–161 CE), Roman emperor
 3:41
Antony, St (c.250–350 CE), Christian hermit
 3:170, **3:172**
Antwerp 6:6, 6:20, 6:25, 6:33, 6:59
 commercial development in 6:94
 as international port 6:166
Anu, Sumerian god 1:84, 1:98
Anubis, Egyptian god 2:73
Anyang, Shang capital 2:45
apartheid 10:58–9, 10:58, 10:61, 10:61,
 10:62–3
apes and monkeys 1:15–6, 1:16, **1:17**
Aphrodite, Greek goddess 1:148, **2:94**, 2:99
Apollo, Greek god 2:90, 2:96, 2:97, 2:134
 temples of 2:137, 2:134
Apollo moon-landing program 9:148–52, 9:150
Apollonius of Tyana (1st century CE), Greek
 philosopher 3:66
Appian Way 3:47
Aquinas, St Thomas (c.1226–1274) 5:147,
 5:168–9, 5:169, **5:169**, 5:171, 5:178

Aquitaine 4:146
conquest by Franks 4:136
Arabia 4:18–19, **4:20**, *6:95*, 6:97
Arabic 4:20, 4:31, 4:34, 4:38
Arab League 9:110
Arabs 6:127, 6:129–30, 6:165, 9:38–43
anti-western feelings of 10:44–5, 10:121–2
Ba'ath party of 10:44, 10:46
in China **4:25**, 4:26
communists, support for 9:42
conquest of Egypt *5:87*
conquest of Sicily 4:151
conquest of Sind (India) 5:23
conquests under Islam 4:24–6, *4:24*,
4:61
defeat by Franks at Tours (Poitiers) 4:25,
4:25, 4:135
in Europe 4:151–3
fundamentalism, opposition to 10:132–3
hostility toward Israel 9:110, **9:110**, 10:42,
10:49
invasions of Africa 5:86
as merchants and traders 5:87, *5:88*, 5:90
nationalism of 9:31, 9:38–9, 9:42–3, 10:42,
10:44, 10:49
as nomadic pastoralists 4:19–20
oil and 9:41–2, 10:43–4, 10:47–8
pan-Arabism 9:31, 9:38–9, 9:42–3, 10:42,
10:44, 10:49
political influence of 10:48
as polytheists 4:19
population growth of 10:123–4
press and 9:36
revolt of (1916) 9:39
as seafarers 4:19
in Sicily 4:102
Turkish empire and 4:98
see also Hussein ibn Ali; Islam; Islamic
civilization; Islamic science
Arafat, Yasser (1929–), Palestinian nationalist
politician *10:126*, *10:177*
Aragon, kingdom of **4:43**
Aramaeans 1:172
Arcadius, Flavius, Eastern Roman emperor
(383–408 CE) *3:134*
archaeological evidence 2:11, 2:14, 2:86–7
Archangel 6:100
archery 2:46, 2:176
Archilochus of Pirene, Greek sculptor *2:167*
Archimedes (c.287–212 BCE), Greek
mathematician **2:169**, 2:170, 3:26
architecture *3:62*, *3:143*, *3:164*
building materials 2:12–3
Byzantine **3:163**, 3:164, **4:69**, 4:130
Carolingian *4:142*
Chinese 2:52–4
Christian ecclesiastical 5:103, 5:108–9, **5:108**,
5:136
Gothic 5:108–9, **5:108**, 5:112, 5:174
Greek 2:151–2, **2:152**
Acropolis, the *2:82*, *2:105*, **2:129**, *2:153*,
2:172
Doric and Ionic orders of *2:120*, **2:152**,
2:153
Egyptian influence on 2:99
global influence of 2:151
Hellenistic *2:139*
military *2:158*
Parthenon, Athenian temple *2:82*, *2:105*,
2:128, *2:130*, *2:134*, 2:151, *2:153*
Temple of Concord, the *2:109*

architecture (cont.)
Indian
Gupta period 5:17
Moghul 5:26–8, 5:32, *5:37*
Islamic 4:39, *4:39*, *4:99*
Japanese, Buddhist 5:70
Lombard *4:151*
megalithic 2:67–9, *2:69*, *2:70–1*
monumental,
Egyptian 1:108–10
Mesopotamian 1:79
Persian *2:75*, 2:79–81, *2:79–80*
Roman technical skills in 3:51–5, *3:52*, *3:53*
Romanesque **4:165**
water supply infrastructure 3:59
see also art; buildings; Greek art; palaces;
temples; mosques; theatres
Ardashir I (Artaxerxes), Sassanid king of Persia
(224–240 CE) 3:108, **3:109**, *3:111*, 4:8–9,
5:16
Ardashir II, Sassanid king of Persia (379–383 CE)
4:8
Argentina
Falklands War and 10:104–105, *10:104*
food production and distribution in 7:52–3,
8:29, 8:149
human rights violations in 10:73
massacre of Indian population 8:27
military régime in 10:73, 10:105
Nazi sympathies of 10:65
nuclear weapons in 10:176
Arghun, Il-khan of Persia (1284–1291) *4:113*
Argos 1:153
Arian Baptistry, Ravenna *3:122–3*
Arianism, Christian heresy 3:122–3, *3:123*,
3:176, *4:55*, *4:135*
Germanic peoples and 3:141, 3:155, **3:157**,
3:159
Aristarchus of Samos (c.310–264 BCE), Greek
astronomer 2:170
aristocracy *see* nobility
Aristophanes (c.448–380 BCE), Greek comic
dramatist **2:148**, 2:151
Aristotle (384–322 BCE), Greek philosopher
2:104, 2:133, 2:143, 4:34, 4:167, 5:147,
5:168, 5:169, 5:171, 7:17, 7:22–3
city-states and 2:104, 2:145, 2:170
classification methods of 2:139, 2:145
concept of the Mean 2:145
logic and 2:145
Lyceum and *2:145*
Pythagoras and 2:141–2
Arius (c.260–336 CE), Christian heretic
3:122–3, *3:123*
Athanasius' opposition to 3:123
Ark of the Covenant *1:166*
Armada, Spanish 6:62, 6:86, 6:158, *6:158*
Armenia 2:164, 3:42–3, 3:108, 3:110, 4:62,
4:63, 9:43, 10:146
conquest by Arabs 4:61
conquest by Sassanids 4:9
partially absorbed by Russia 7:144, 8:43
Persian conquest of 3:109, **3:109**
Armenian Church (Monophysite) 4:54
Armenians 4:12, 4:114
armies (ancient and medieval) 2:18
Assyrian 2:157
Byzantine *see* Byzantine army
of Ch'in dynasty 5:44
Chinese 2:46
Greek 2:100–101, 2:121

armies (ancient and medieval) (cont.)
hoplites 2:100–101, *2:101*, 2:102, *2:106*,
2:117, *2:123*, 2:126, 2:173
Macedonian 2:157
mutiny of 2:161, **2:161**
reorganization of by Alexander 2:162
Mauryan 5:11, 5:14
Moghul 5:26
Persian 2:111–2, 4, **2:114**
Roman *see* Roman Army
Spartan 2:101, **2:114**, 2:120
armies (modern) *see* individual countries
Arminius (17 BCE–21 CE), German chieftain
3:42
arms and armour *see* armies; military techniques;
weapons
Armstrong, Neil (1930–), American astronaut
9:149, *9:149*
Arras 5:135
Arsacid dynasty of Parthia 2:177, 4:10
art 1:142
African, Benin bronzes *5:90*, *5:91*
avant-garde 9:51
Buddhist 5:15, *5:16*, 5:17, *5:23*
Bulgarian icons *4:81*, *4:90*
Byzantine **3:163**, *4:69*, **4:69**, 4:70, *4:72*,
4:116
in Iconoclastic period *4:67*, **4:69**
icons 4:63, **4:68**, *4:91*
influence on Carolingian court 4:142
influence on Christian Russian art *4:84*
paintings *4:71*
calligraphy 2:44
cave paintings 2:56–7
changing values in 9:50–51, *9:50*, **9:50**
Chinese
amateur work admired 5:64–5
bronze-working 5:42, *5:42*, 5:55
conservative nature of 5:64
painting 5:42, 5:55
pottery 5:41–2, *5:52*, 5:54–5, 5:64–5
Shang and Chou periods *2:37*, 2:52–3, *2:54*
decorated objects 1:42, 1:44, *1:46*, 1:53
disintegratory movements and 9:51
divergence from Christian mythology 5:174
earliest signs of 1:26
Egyptian *see* Egypt, art in
Etruscan *3:8*, *3:10*, *3:11*
Greek *see* Greek art
Greek influence on *5:9*, 5:11, *5:15*, 5:17
Hispanic *4:168*
idealization of artists 9:50–51
Indian 2:29
Gupta period *5:8*, *5:16*, 5:17, *5:17*,
5:19–20
Hindu *5:8*, 5:17
Moghul 5:28, 5:32
Irish *4:154*
Islamic 4:35, 4:39–40, *4:131*
calligraphy *4:38*
pottery 4:39, *4:131*
prohibition on figurative representation
4:23, 4:31, 4:38–9
Japanese
Edo period *5:83*
Heia period 5:76
imperial palace 5:76
Kamakura period 5:76–7, *5:76*
Muramachi shogunate 5:77
popular movement *5:83*
Lombard *4:151*

art (cont.)
Ludovisi sarcophagus bas-reliefs *3:130*
Mesoamerican 2:62, 2:63
Minoan *1:143*, 1:146–7, *1:146*, 1:149,
1:151
Neolithic *1:57*, *1:68*
Palaeolithic Venuses *1:44*, **1:45**
Persian *2:78*
Phoenician *1:156*, 1:157, *1:158–9*
Renaissance 5:173–4
rock *2:60*
Roman *2:87*
Russian icons *4:95*
Sassanid *4:10*
Sumerian 1:85–6, 1:91
Upper Palaeolithic, lack of 1:44–5
wall paintings *1:92*, *1:117*, *1:119*, *1:137*
see also architecture; bronze statuary; cave
paintings; Egypt: art; frescoes; Greek art;
jewellery; mosaics; rock art; sculpture; Upper
Palaeolithic art
Artaxerxes, *see* Ardashir I
Artaxerxes I, king of Persia (464–424 BCE) *2:77*,
2:80
Arthur (6th century CE), legendary Romano-
British king 3:150, 5:122, *5:123*, 5:143
Arthur, George (1785–1854), governor of
Tasmania *6:179*
Aryan culture 2:14–18
political systems of 2:17
religion of 2:15–16
Aryan peoples
in India 2:14–17
in Persia 2:75–6
Ashurbanipal, king of Assyria (668–626 BCE)
1:134, 1:157, **1:173**, 1:174, *1:174*, 1:175,
1:176, 2:75
Ashurnasirpal I, king of Assyria (883–859 BCE)
1:173
Asia
Central Asian nomads 4:13–8
diffusion of European culture 10:17
east-west division in 10:18
European influences in 10:18
Muslim provinces of 9:35–6
persistence of cultural traditions 10:17–18
resistance to manipulation 10:25–6
Tiger economies in *10:26*, **10:113**
Asia Minor 1:82–3, 1:159, 4:58, 4:62, 4:73
Achaean settlements in 1:155
in the Alexandrine Empire 2:161
Christianity in 3:126
conquest by Seljuk Turks *4:72*, 4:100
conversion from Christianity to Islam 4:100
Greek cities of 2:109, **2:138**, 2:146, 2:159
manpower reserves in 4:57
Mycenaean colonies in 1:152
Osmanlis in 4:116
return to Persian vassalage 2:122–3
Roman forces in **2:166**, 3:22
Asian-African Conference (1955) **9:131**
Asoka, Mauryan emperor of India (264–228 BCE)
2:19, 5:11, *5:11*, 5:13–4
conversion to Buddhism 5:11
religious tolerance of 5:12
Assassins, Islamic sect, destruction by Mongols
4:107
Assur, Assyrian god 1:175
Assur (city) 1:83, 1:172–3
Assyria 1:94, 1:98, 2:62, **2:72**, 2:79, 4:13–4
Amorite kingdom of 1:93

Assyria (cont.)
  collapse of **1:173**, 1:175
  conscription in 1:173, 1:175
  empire, extent of **1:174**
  expansion to create new empire 1:173
  Israel obliterated by 1:172–3
  mass deportations from *1:171*, 1:173–4
  Mesopotamia
    conquests in 1:173
    links with 1:77–8
  military techniques of *1:132*, *1:136*, *1:170*,
    1:175, *1:175*
  monarchy of *1:134*, 1:157, *1:169*, *1:172*,
    1:173, 1:174–5
  monuments of 1:174
  Samaria conquered by **1:168**, *1:170*
  subjugation in 1:174
  Syria conquered by 1:172–3
  war chariots in *1:133*, *1:174*
Astarte, Semitic goddess 1:148
Astrakhan, Tatars and 6:101, *6:101*
astrolabes *4:34*
astrology 2:173, 9:166
  Babylonian 1:97
astronauts *see* space exploration
astronomy 2:43, 2:142–3, *4:36*, 5:170, *5:171*,
    7:19
  Babylonian 1:97
  challenge of to Church 7:21
  Chinese 2:43, 2:52
  Egyptian 1:111–12
  Galileo and 7:23, *7:23*
  heliocentric model of 2:170
  heliocentric theory of Copernicus 7:22, *7:22*,
    7:23
  Kepler and 7:22–3
  megalithic monuments and 2:68
  Ptolemaic 2:142
  Pythagorean 2:142
  radio and *9:139*
  relativity theories in 9:141
  Tycho Brahe and 7:22, *7:22*
  see also Greek science
Asturias 4:158, *4:158*
Atatürk *see* Mustafa Kemal
Athalaric, Ostrogoth king (526–534 CE) *3:158*
Athanasius (c.295–373 CE), bishop of Alexandria
    3:123
Athene, Greek goddess *2:90*, **2:94**, *2:95*, *2:105*,
    2:128, *2:131*
  sacred olive tree and *2:130*
Athens 2:115, *2:118*, **2:121**
  Areopagus, the 2:96, 2:132–3
  boule **2:131**
  bureaucracy of 2:103
  Catalan duchy of 4:118
  coinage of *2:124*
  comedies of *2:99*
  commerce in 2:98
  Corinth, economic threat to 2:119, 2:121
  cultural and political dominance of 2:129–30
  defeat by Macedon 2:159
  defeat of Persians at Marathon 2:112
  Delian League and 2:118–19, 2:129–30
  democracy *see* democracy, Athenian
  dikasteria **2:131**
  divorce in 2:126–7
  drama festivals of **2:148**
  ecclesia 2:105, **2:131**
  economy of 2:104–5, 2:130
    export economy 2:100, 2:103, 2:105

Athens (cont.)
  education in **2:127**
  government of 2:104, *2:104*, 2:105
  Hipparchus, tyrant of *2:104*
  imperialism and 2:131
  Macedonian rule in 2:160, 2:165
  magistrates in **2:131**, 2:132
  navy of 2:112, 2:130–31
    destruction on Sicilian Expedition 2:122
    funding by Laurium silver mines 2:130
    role in Peloponnesian War 2:120–1
    at Salamis 2:115
    triremes **2:113**
  oligarchy of 2:122, 2:133, 2:160
  Panathenaea procession in *2:105*, *2:134*
  philosophical dominance of 2:170
  Piraeus and 2:121
  Pisistratus, tyrant of *2:104*
  politicians and 2:132
  poor soil in 2:103
  rebuilding of 2:122
  Roman Empire, as part of *3:22*
  settled by Achaeans 1:151
  Sicilian Expedition disaster and 2:122, 2:131,
    2:136, 2:177
  social institutions in 2:126–8
  Sparta, rivalry with 2:118
  women's status in 2:126
  see also Acropolis; Parthenon
Athos, Mount 4:69
Atlantic Charter 9:73, *9:73*, 9:80
Atlas of China (Martin Martini) 5:65
atomic bomb
  Hiroshima and Nagasaki 9:78, **9:78**, 9:88–9,
    9:89
  as last resort 9:90
  Manhattan Project 9:78, 9:138–9
  Russian development of 9:90–91
  see also nuclear weapons
Aton, Egyptian god 1:115, *1:127*
Attalid dynasty of Pergamum 2:165
Attica 1:150, 1:153, 2:92, *2:93*, 2:103–5
  abandonment of to Persians 2:115
  Laurium silver mines of 2:125, 2:130
Attila (c.406–453 CE), king of the Huns 3:134,
    4:16
  Leo the Great and 3:174
Augsburg, Diet of *6:49*, 6:50
Augustine, St (354–430 CE), bishop of Hippo
    3:141–8, *3:149*, *3:174*, 4:143, 5:173
  baptism by St Ambrose 3:143, *3:145*
  The City of God 3:144–7, *3:145*, 3:148,
    3:149
  Donatists and 3:143–4, 3:148
  influence on medieval political thought 3:144
  Manichaeism and 3:143, 4:11, *4:11*
  puritanism and 3:144
Augustine, St, archbishop of Canterbury
    (601–604 CE) 3:176
  missionary campaign of 3:176
Augustus (Gaius Julius Caesar Octavianus) (63
    BCE–14 CE), first Roman emperor 3:6,
    3:39–40, 3:42, 3:62, *3:71*
  administrative reforms under 3:46–7
  deification of 3:40
  pontifex maximus and 3:39, 3:63, 3:174
  republican forms maintained under 3:39,
    3:101
  rise to power of 3:38–40
  statesmanship of **3:42**
  successors of 3:40

Aurelian (Lucius Domitius Aurelianus)
    (c.215–275 CE), Roman emperor *3:107*,
    3:113
Aurignacian culture *1:42*
Aurungzebe (1618–1707), Moghul emperor
    5:30, *5:32*, 5:34–5, *5:34*, 5:35, *5:35*, 6:135
Australasia **3:152**, 3:154, 6:156
  discovery of by Dampier 6:177, **6:177**
Australia 7:170
  Aborigines 1:59, 6:168, *6:179*
    exploitation of 8:38
  colonized by *Homo sapiens* 1:41
  Commonwealth of (1901) 8:32
  European settlers in 6:122, 6:156
  food production and distribution in 7:52–3
  and Japan
    bombing by 9:76
    economic ties with 10:114
    threat to 9:74
    treaty with 10:39
  penal colony in 6:178
  White Australia policy 8:23
  wool and meat production in 8:37
Australopithecus **1:11**, 1:19–20, 1:23, 1:28
  afarensis *1:18*, **1:20**
  africanus **1:20**
  cranial development of **1:24**
Austria 4:148, 6:82, 6:91, 6:117–18
  Anschluss 9:66, *9:66*
  Congress of Vienna *7:114*, **7:116**, 7:117,
    7:117, 7:122–3, **7:134**
  defence of 6:94
  education in 7:14
  House of 6:78
  neutral state 10:15, *10:15*
  Poland and 6:119
  rebellions of (1848) *7:123*, 7:124–5
  religious toleration in 7:37
  serfdom abolished in 7:37
  territorial acquisitions of **7:116**
  Vienna 6:93, 6:94, *6:95*, 6:96, *6:96*, *6:99*,
    6:118
  Venice, absorption of 7:108, 7:117
  wars
    with France (1792–1801) 7:94, 7:102,
      7:102
    Napoleonic 7:105, 7:108
    with Prussia 7:130–1
    with Sardinia 7:130–1
  see also Habsburg dynasty; Habsburg empire
Austro-Hungarian empire 8:134
  annexation of Bosnia 8:141–2
  collapse of 8:155
  declaration of war against Serbia 8:145
  dual monarchy 7:131
  foreign policy of 8:141, 8:145
  nationalism in 8:119, *8:134*, 8:135, 8:142
  Russia and 8:141
  Serbian hostility to 8:142
  Triple Alliance and 8:143
  war seen as advantageous by 8:140
authoritarian régimes, post-1918 8:155, 8:174
Avars 4:58, 4:79
  in Balkans 4:12, 4:93
  conflict between Charlemagne and 4:138
  displacement from Mongolia 4:16
  as Sassanid allies 4:13, 4:17
  in south Russia 4:78
  stirrups introduced by 4:16, 4:175
Averroës 4:38
Avicenna (Ibn-Sina) 4:38

Avignon 5:140
  papal residence at 5:114–16, *5:115*, **5:115**
Ay, Egyptian ruler (1352–1348 BCE) *1:128*
Ayyubid dynasty in Egypt and Levant 4:103
Azerbaijan 10:146
  communist republic of 9:93
  Russian presence in 9:86
Azores **6:128**
  Portuguese established in 5:161
Aztec civilization 2:63, 5:95–7
  codices and *5:96*
  mythology of 5:96
  overthrow of Toltecs by 5:95
  prisoners–of–war in 5:97
  pyramids and 5:96
  solar calendar of *5:97*
  Spanish conquest of 6:139–40
  Tenochtitlán 5:96, *5:96*

B

Ba'ath régimes
  in Iraq 10:121–2
  in Syria 10:48, 10:50
Babeuf, Gracchus (1760–1797), French
    revolutionary 8:164
Babur of Kabul (1483–1530), founder of Moghul
    Empire 5:24–6, *5:25*, 5:31
Babylon
  Amorite kingdom 1:93
  conquered by,
    Assyrians 1:173
    Elamites 1:98–9
    Hittites 1:94, 1:98
    Persians (Medes) 1:178
  conquers Jerusalem 1:172
  cosmogeny 1:98
  defeat by Cyrus the Great **2:111**
  Empire of **2:72**
  first empire 1:93–8
  last empire 1:176
  legend of magnificence 1:96
  palace *1:178*, *1:179*
  Persian overthrow of 3:75
  religion 1:97–8
  revolt against Assyria 1:175
  ruled by Kassites 1:133, 1:172
Bacon, Francis (1561–1626), English philosopher
    7:18–19, *7:18*, 7:30
Bactria, Greek kingdom of 2:165, 2:176
  overrun by Scythians 4:15
Bactrians
  Artaxerxes and 5:16
  invasion of India by 5:15
Baghdad, centre of Abbasid caliphate 4:24,
    4:32–4, 4:43
  conquest by Turks 4:127
  sacking by Mongols 4:107
  Varangians 4:81–2
  see also Iraq
Bakunin, Mikhail (1814–1876), Russian
    anarchist 7:139
Balboa, Vasco Nuñez de (c.1475–1517), Spanish
    explorer 6:139
Baldwin I (1171–1205), Count of Flanders and
    Latin Emperor of the East 4:118
Balfour, Arthur James (1848–1930), British
    statesman 9:39
Balfour Declaration 9:39, **9:39**, 9:109

Balkans 5:158
 metallurgy in 2:66–7
 roads in 2:86
 Slavs and Avars in 4:12
Balkan states 8:15, 8:118–19, 8:148, 8:150
 see also Albania; Bulgaria; Greece; Romania;
  Yugoslavia
Baltic states 8:165
 authoritarian régimes in 8:174
 see also individual states
Baluchistan 2:1–11
 conquered by Chandragupta 5:10
Balzac, Honoré de (1799–1850), French writer
  8:109
Bandung Conference 10:22–3, 10:22, 10:44
Bangladesh (East Pakistan) 9:120, 9:124, 9:168
 independence of 10:20
 Islamic society in 10:119
 natural disasters in 10:21
banking 6:20, 6:20, 6:22
Bantu peoples 5:88–9
Baptists 6:65
Bar Kochba, Simon (2nd century CE), Jewish
  messianic claimant 3:90
Barbados 6:146–7, 6:159
barbarians
 assimilation into Europe 3:156–8
 civilizing influences acting upon 3:176–7
 cultural legacy of 3:158
 Euro-Asiatic nomads 4:14, 4:17
 Gaul threatened by 3:30
 incorporation within caliphates 4:44
 migrations of 3:126, 3:129, 3:132–3
 Roman army employment of 3:126, 3:129,
  3:132, 3:134–5
 tribes of 3:132, 3:134–5, 3:153
 tribute paid to 3:107
 Western Empire overcome by 3:127–136
 see also individual names of tribes
Barbarossa 5:151, 9:72–3
Barcelona
 county of 4:43
 destruction by Al-Mansur 4:158, 4:159
Bari, emirate 4:151
Basil I the Macedonian (c.812–886 CE),
  Byzantine emperor 4:71
Basil II (Bulgaroctonos) (c.958–1025), Byzantine
  emperor 4:62–3, 4:62
 as patron of the arts 4:69
Basil, St (c.330–379 CE) 4:91
Basle, Council of (1431–1449) 5:116
Basques 6:67
Basra 4:31, 6:129
 Indian-British army lands at 9:38
Basutoland 8:34
Batavia see Jakarta
Bath, thermal springs at 3:151, 3:151
Batista, Fulgencio (1901–1973), Cuban dictator
  10:69
battles 3:20
 Aboukir (1798) 7:105
 Actium (31 BCE) 3:38
 Adowa (1896) 8:57
 Adrianople (378) 3:132
 Adrianopolis (1205) 4:118
 Agincourt (1415) 5:125
 Almansa (1707) 6:92
 Arcole (1796) 7:102
 Atlantic (1939–1945) 9:70, 9:76–8
 Britain (1940) 9:71
 Cambrai (1917) 8:148

battles (cont.)
 Cannae (216 BCE) 3:19
 Crécy (1346) 5:125, 5:127
 Dien Bien Phu (1954) 10:34
 Edessa (260) 4:12
 El Alamein (1942) 9:77
 Eurymedon (467 BCE) 2:111
 Goliath Spring (1260) 4:107
 Hastings (1066) 4:177
 Horns of Hattin (1187) 4:102
 Issus 2:161
 Katzbach (1813) 7:105
 Lake Trasimene (217 BCE) 3:19
 Lepanto (1571) 6:85
 Leuctra (371 BCE) 2:123
 Lexington (1775) 7:77
 Manzikert (1071) 4:72, 4:100
 Marathon (490 BCE) 2:112, 2:116, 2:119,
  2:128
 Midway (1943) 9:75, 9:76
 Mohács (1526) 4:122
 Mohács (1527) 6:93
 Mycale (480 BCE) 2:115, 2:118, 2:123, 2:147
 Nehavand (642) 4:9
 New Orleans 7:153
 Omdurman (1898) 8:14
 Passchendaele (1917) 8:152
 Plassey (1757) 6:136, 6:137, 6:138
 Plataea (480 BCE) 2:115, 2:118
 Poltava (1709) 6:106
 Qadesh 1:129, 1:160
 Quebec (1759) 6:150
 Sakarya (1921) 9:45
 Salamis (480 BCE) 2:115–6
 Saratoga (1777) 7:78, 7:78
 Somme (1916) 8:147
 Stalingrad (1942–1943) 9:77
 Stamford Bridge (1066) 4:158
 Tannenberg (1410) 5:157
 Thermopylae (480 BCE) 2:114, 2:115
 Tours (Poitiers) (732) 4:25, 4:25, 4:135
 Trafalgar (1805) 7:105
 Verdun (1916) 8:147
 Waterloo (1815) 7:111, 7:111
 Yorktown (1781) 7:78, 7:87
 Zama (202 BCE) 3:19–22
Bavaria 6:118
Bavarians 4:147
Bayeux Tapestry 4:177
Bayle, Pierre (1647–1706), French philosopher
  7:26
Beatus of Liebana, 8th-century Spanish monk
  4:171
Beccaria, Cesare (1738–1794), Italian penologist
  7:33
Becket, St Thomas (1118–1170), Archbishop of
  Canterbury and martyr 5:107, 5:107
Becquerel, Antoine Henri (1852–1962), French
  scientist 9:140
Bede (c.673–735 CE), English scholar and monk
  3:154
Bedouin 4:18–19, 4:31
beer 4:169
Behaviourism 9:164–5, 9:165
Beijing see Peking
Belarus 8:165
Belgium 6:32, 6:92
 Africa and (Congo) 8:57, 8:59
 Frankish settlement of 3:152, 3:153
 Germans attack France through 8:145–6
 independence of 7:122

Belgium (cont.)
 industrialization of 7:137
 neutrality of 8:145
 rebellion against Dutch King 7:121
 urbanization of 7:60
 see also Low Countries
Belisarius (c.506–65 CE), Roman general
  3:161
Bellini, Gentile (c.1429–1507), artist 6:94
Belorussia 10:152
Belsen concentration camp 9:79
Belshazzar (6th century BCE), Babylonian prince
  1:177–8
Ben Bella, Mohammed (1916–), Algerian prime
  minister (1962–1965) 10:47
Ben-Gurion, David (1886–1973), prime minister
  of Israel (1948–1953, 1955–1963) 9:112
Benedict XII, pope (1333–1342) 5:115
Benedict of Nursia, St (c.480–c.544), monasticist
  3:171–3, 3:172
Benedictine monasteries 4:164
Benedictine Rule 3:172, 4:140, 4:142, 4:164,
  5:103
Bengal 2:20, 5:24, 6:135, 6:162
 East India Company and 6:137
 nawab of 6:136–7, 6:138
 partition of 8:94, 8:96–7, 8:98
Benin, kingdom of 5:89, 5:91
 bronze sculptures from 5:85, 5:90, 5:91
Bentham, Jeremy (1748–1832), British
  philosopher 7:33, 8:131, 8:131
Benz, Carl Friedrich (1844–1929), German auto-
  mobile engineer 9:134
Berber peoples 2:58
 as allies of Arabs 4:25
Berchère, Maurice, French artist 8:59
Beringia 1:40
Berlin 10:6, 10:9
 airlift to 10:10–11, 10:10
 Congress of (1878) 8:141, 8:141
 occupation zones 9:92–3, 9:93
Berlin Wall 10:6, 10:78, 10:79, 10:147
 demolition of 10:147–8, 10:149
Bermuda 6:173
Bernard of Clairvaux, St (1090–1153), Cistercian
  reformer 5:103, 5:113, 5:155
 advocate of First Crusade 5:151
Bessarabia 9:67, 9:72
Betrothal, The (Mikhail Shibanov) 6:110
Beveridge, Sir William (1879–1963), British
  economist 9:175
Bevin, Ernest (1881–1951), British statesman
  9:95
Bhagavad Gita 2:20, 5:13
Bhu, Hindu earth goddess 5:21
Bhutan 9:163
Bhutto, Benazir (1953–), president of Pakistan
  10:21
Bhutto, Zulfikar Ali (1928–1979), prime minister
  of Pakistan 10:21
Bibika Maqbara mausoleum 5:34
Bible 6:51, 7:14, 7:17
 chronology of 8:125
 copying by monks 4:142
 criticism of 8:124, 8:126
 diffusion of 1:162
 printed 1:162, 5:172, 5:174–6
 questioning of 8:123–4, 8:126
 translations of 7:14
 see also New Testament; Old Testament;
  Pentateuch

biological sciences 9:143–6
 DNA 9:144–5, 9:145
 genetic engineering 9:143, 9:144–5, 9:144,
  9:145
 milestones of 9:143
birth control 6:13, 8:106, 8:115–16
 see also contraception and family planning
Birth of Venus, The (Botticelli) 5:173
birth-rates 6:12–13, 6:155, 7:44–5
 effects of delayed marriage on 7:43, 7:44–6
Bismarck, Otto von (1815–1898), Prussian
  statesman 7:130–3, 8:118, 8:134, 8:141,
  8:142, 8:143
 foreign policy of 8:143
Bithynia 2:164
black Americans
 Civil rights campaign and 10:86–8, 10:87
 deteriorating conditions for 10:88–9, 10:95
 northward emigration of 10:86
 segregation of 10:86, 10:87, 10:87
 social and economic disadvantages of
  10:86–9
Black Death, bubonic plague epidemic 5:140–1,
  5:140, 5:141, 6:10, 6:14, 7:45
Black Sheep Turks 4:114
Blériot, Louis (1872–1936), French aviator
  8:128
Bloody Mary see Mary I (Tudor)
Blum, Léon (1872–1950), French prime minister
  9:59
Boadicea (d.62), queen of the Iceni 3:68
boats, earliest developments 1:137
Bodh Gaya 2:28
bodhisattvas 5:21, 5:22
Boeotia 2:119, 2:120
Boers
 concessions to 8:36–7
 Great Trek 8:33–4, 8:35
 grievances against British 10:58–9
 relations with Great Britain 8:33–7
 relations with non-whites 8:33, 8:34, 8:36,
  8:37
 Vaal River and 8:34
 war with Great Britain 8:35–6, 8:35–6
Boethius, Anicius Manlius Severinus
  (c.480–524 CE), Roman philosopher 3:155,
  3:155, 4:143, 4:157, 4:167
Bogomil heresy 4:72
Bohemia 4:92, 4:138, 5:129, 6:51, 8:119
Bohr, Niels (1885–1962), Danish physicist
  9:140, 9:142, 9:142
Bokhara 4:13, 4:14
 sacking by Mongols 4:105, 4:105, 4:108
Boleslav I, ruler of Poland (992–1025) 4:92
Bolívar, Simón (1783–1830), president of
  Republic of Colombia 8:26, 8:26
Bolivia
 expropriation of oil companies in 10:65,
  10:72
 failed Cuban-led revolution in 10:71
 land reforms in 10:68
 military government in 10:73
Bologna university 5:166
Bolshevik régime
 Allied hostility towards 8:154–5
 authoritarianism of 8:155
 Communist Party under 8:164
 economic policy of 8:168
 New Economic Policy of 8:168
 revolutionary propaganda of 8:154, 8:162,
  8:163, 8:167

Bolshevik régime (cont.)
  see also Russia
Bolshevik revolution 8:152–5, 9:17
Bolsheviks 8:112
Bombay 8:95, **8:96**
  European trading post 5:31, 5:35
Bonaparte, Louis-Napoleon see Napoleon III
Bonaparte, Napoleon see Napoleon I
Boniface VIII (c.1228–1303), pope 5:113–4
Boniface, St (680–754 CE), evangelist in Germany
  4:135, 4:164
books
  Book of Chess, Dice and Boards, The
    (Alfonso X) 5:170
  Book of Common Prayer 6:53
  Book of the Dead 1:67, 1:118
  Book of Marco, The (Marco Polo) **4:110**
  Book of the Thousand and One Nights, The
    (Haroun-al-Raschid) 4:35, **4:35**
  Book of the Wonders of the World, The
    (Marco Polo) 4:108, **4:110**, **4:112**, 5:59
  Diamond Sutra 5:55
  Domesday Book 5:124, 5:147, 5:178
  Little Red Book 10:34, 10:34
  prohibited books, index of 7:10, 7:15, 7:25
Booth, John Wilkes (1839–1865), American
  fanatical Confederate 7:165
Booth, William (1829–1912), British founder of
  Salvation Army 7:62–3, 7:62
Bordeaux 5:135
Borneo 10:25
  capture by Japanese 9:74
  see also Malaysia
Boru, Brian, mythical High King of Ireland
  5:122
Bosch, Hieronymus (c.1453–1516),
  Netherlandish artist 6:9
Boscoreale villa see frescoes; Pompeii
Bosnia–Herzegovina 10:151
  annexation by Austria 8:141–2, 9:35
  as base for terrorism 8:142
  conquest by Ottoman Turks 4:122
  independence from Yugoslavia 10:150,
    10:151
Boston Massacre 7:75, 7:75
Boston 'tea party' 7:75
Botha, P. W. (1916–99), president of South
  African Republic 10:62, 10:62, 10:63
Botticelli, Sandro (1444–1510), Italian artist
  5:173
Boucher, François (1703–1770), artist 6:37
Boudica, Boudicca see Boadicea
Bougainville, Louis de (1729–1811), French
  explorer 6:178
Boulton, Matthew (1728–1809), British
  manufacturer 7:56
Bourbon dynasty
  in France 6:55, 6:73, 6:80–1, 7:103, 7:105,
    7:111
    Habsburgs and 6:66, 6:87
    restoration of 7:118–20, 7:119
  in Spain 6:91, 8:23
Boxer movement (1900) 8:75–6, 8:76, 8:121,
  9:8, 9:14, 9:20
Brahe, Tycho (1546–1601), Danish astronomer
  7:22, 7:22
Brahma, Hindu creator god 2:23, 2:24, 2:24
Brahmanas, Indian texts 2:18
Brahmanical religion 5:21
brahmans
  Aryan priests 2:15–7, 2:23–6

brahmans (cont.)
  Hindu priestly caste 5:19
Brahmaputra River 5:20
brain size
  in hominids 1:19, 1:23–4, 1:34, 1:36
  in primates 1:16, **1:16**
  see also cranial development
Bramante, Donato (c.1444–1514), Italian artist
  7:8
Brandenburg, Electorate of 6:87, 6:116
  see also Prussia, Germany
Brazil 6:139, 6:145, 10:65
  discovered by Portuguese 5:162, 5:164
  human rights violations in 10:73
  military government in 10:73
  monarchy abandoned in 8:28
  nuclear weapons 10:176
  racial tolerance in 8:27
  resources in 8:29
  Rio de Janeiro 8:24–5, 8:29
  in Second World War 10:65
  slave trade and slavery 6:23, 6:24, 6:165,
    6:169, 8:12, 8:25, 8:27
  social divisions in 10:75
Brest-Litovsk, Treaty of (1918) 8:154, **8:165**
Brethren of the Common Life, followers of
  Thomas à Kempis 5:112
Brezhnev, Leonid (1906–1982), Soviet president
  10:80, 10:83, 10:129, 10:136, 10:140–42
  Brezhnev doctrine 10:140–1
Bristol 6:161, 6:162, 6:169
Britain, ancient
  Battle of see air warfare
  Celtic peoples of 3:150
  Germanic invasions of 3:150–52
  Hadrian's Wall 3:42, 3:43, 3:125, 3:151
  reconnaissance of by Caesar 3:42
  Roman conquest of 3:42
  see also Great Britain
British Commonwealth of Nations 9:98, 10:46
  see also British Empire
British Empire 8:6, 8:23
  in Africa 8:57–9
  in Burma 8:45, 8:59, 8:74, **8:91**, 8:100,
    8:100, 8:104
  Dominions 9:70, 9:82, 9:98–100, 9:102
    status created 8:33
    World War I 8:149
  "Dual Control" and 8:45
  in Egypt 8:57, 8:144
  extent in 18th century 6:161–2
  extent in 1914 8:64
  foreign policy of 8:44
  in India see India
  in Malaya 8:44, 8:59, **8:91**, 8:100
  naval bases of 8:43–4
  North American colonies of 7:73–7
  shift toward the East 8:44–5
  slave trade in **6:147**, 6:160, 6:162,
    6:169–70
  in South Africa 8:33–7
  trading bases of 8:51
  treatment of native populations by 8:38–40,
    8:39, 8:45
  War of Independence and 7:78
  see also Great Britain
Brittany 4:146
bronze 1:58, 1:58, 1:135, **1:135**
  armour 1:155
  castings 1:59
  in China 2:36–7, 2:45

bronze (cont.)
  in Egypt 1:118
  in India 2:20
  statuary 1:59
    Chinese 2:35–7, 2:47, 2:53–4
    Greek 2:90, 2:99, 2:99, 2:104, 2:107,
      2:135, 2:154
    Indian 2:24
    in Sumer 1:88
  see also Greek art; sculpture
Bronze Age 1:39, 1:58, 1:107
  Iron Age fades into 1:135, 1:150
  metal currency of 1:138–9
  societies 2:16
    Egyptian 2:74–5
    European 2:65, 2:67
Bronze Horseman, The (Pushkin) 7:143
Brown, Ford Madox (1821–1893), British artist
  7:150
Brueghel the Elder, Pieter (c.1520–1569),
  Netherlandish artist 6:15, 6:18
Bruges 5:135, 5:139
Bruno, Giordano (1548–1600), Italian
  philosopher 7:25
Brutus, Marcus Junius (c.85–42 BCE), Roman
  statesman 3:12
bubonic plague 5:140–1, 5:140, 5:141, 6:10,
  6:14, 7:45
Buchenwald concentration camp 9:79, 9:79
Buddha, the (Siddhartha Gautama)
  (c.563–c.483 BCE) 2:26–9, 2:26, 2:27–8,
  2:28
  as deity 5:16, 5:21
  Kushana depiction of 5:15, 5:23
  sculptures of
    Burma 5:13
    China 5:47
    India 5:15, 5:15–6, 5:17, 5:20–1, 5:23
    Japan 5:70, 5:72, 5:77
Buddhism 2:21, 2:23, 2:27–9, 2:52, 4:105,
  8:85, 8:99
  in Afghanistan 5:23
  in China 5:47, 5:48, 5:59
  Eightfold Path 2:27
  at the Great Stupa, Sanchi 2:6, 2:29
  in India 2:21, 2:23, 2:27–9, 5:10–13, 5:16,
    5:19, 5:20, 5:21–2
    Asoka converted to 5:11, 5:11
    decline of 5:23
    Kushana people of 5:15–16, 5:23
    Mahayana version of 5:21–2, 5:22–3,
      5:48
    manuscripts of 5:18
    spread of 5:13, 5:13, 5:22, 5:47
    Varanasi 5:20
  Japan 5:70, 5:70
    Shintoism and 5:71, 5:72
    Zen 5:77
building materials
  brick 1:67
  mud 1:77, 1:88, 1:108, 1:143
  stone 1:108–10, 1:118, 1:143
buildings
  Egyptian 1:108–110
  Minoan Crete 1:142–3, 1:145–6
  Neolithic 1:57, 1:60–62, 1:143
  religious 1:71
  Solomon's Temple, Jerusalem 1:157, 1:166,
    1:170, 1:172
  Sumerian 1:71, 1:88
  see also architecture; churches; mosques

building skills
  Maya 5:93–4
  technological advances in Europe 5:136–7,
    5:138
  at Teotihuacán 5:93, 5:93
  in Zimbabwe 5:90–1
Bulgaria 8:119
  communist state of 9:93
  conquest by Ottoman Turks 4:120
  as first Slav state 4:79, 4:84
  free elections in 10:149
  independence of 9:35
  invasion of Greece 8:161
  joins Central Powers in Great War 8:146–7
  relations between Byzantium and 4:79, 4:114
  Treaty of Versailles and 8:158
Bulgars 4:58, 4:61–2, 4:78, 4:78, 4:79–80,
  4:79, 4:87
  conversion of to Christianity 4:62, 4:79
  defeat by Basil II 4:62–3
  priests in Kiev Rus 4:88
  revolts of 4:72, 4:75
  siege of Thessaloniki and 4:78
bureaucracies (ancient world),
  Chinese 2:43
  Greek and Hellenistic 2:103–4, 2:169, 2:173
  Persian 2:79
  see also Roman Empire and civilization
Burgoyne, John (1722–1792), British general
  7:78
Burgundians, Germanic peoples 3:129
  defeat by Franks 3:152, 3:153
Burgundy, duchy of 5:124, 5:129, **5:129**
burial rituals 1:36–8, 1:85, 1:151, 2:36–7, 2:36,
  2:38, 4:14
  in Egypt 1:113–14, 1:113
Burke, Edmund (1729–1797), British political
  philosopher 7:38, 7:100, 8:45, 9:173
Burma (Myanmar) 5:13, 5:13, 6:130,
  10:18
  conquest by Manchus 5:63
  conquest by Mongol China 5:59
  independence of 9:102, 9:108
  occupation by Japanese 9:76, 9:104
  reconquering by Britain 9:83
  rice production in 9:129
Bushido, creed of the samurai 5:79
Buwayhid dynasty, Abbasid caliphate 4:100,
  4:44, 4:97
Byblos 1:91, 1:157
Byron, George Gordon (1788–1824), British poet
  7:115, 7:140
Byzantine army 4:56, 4:57, 4:61, 4:65, 4:66,
  4:67, 4:72, 4:84
Byzantine Empire (Byzantium) 3:163, 4:17,
  4:48–95
  alliance between Umayyad caliphate and 4:43
  Arab conquests within 4:25–6, 4:60–61
  architecture of 3:163, 3:164
  art of 3:163
  Christian heritage of 4:51
  clerical intransigence in 4:118–19
  confinement to Anatolia 4:44
  Constantinople regained by 4:116
  decline and extinction of 4:114–20
  declining economy of 4:70–71
  defeat by Turks at Manzikert 4:72
  divergence from West 4:51–2
  dynasties of
    Comneni 4:72–3, 4:73
    Isaurian 4:62–3

Byzantine Empire (Byzantium), dynasties of (cont.)
  Macedonian 4:63, **4:69**
  Palaeologus *4:116*
  Phrygian 4:63
  expansion under Justinian 3:160
  Hellenistic influences on 4:56
  imperial court in 4:70
  internal power struggles of 4:72
  Islam seen as heresy in 4:51
  medieval characteristics of 4:56–60
  naval power of 3:163
  Orthodox Church in 4:51–2
  Osmanli Turks and 4:116, 4:120
  papal primacy accepted in 4:118–19
  resources of 4:57–8
  Roman Catholic Church, union with 4:118–19
  sale of offices in 3:165
  Sassanid conflict in 4:8, **4:9**
  Serbian attacks on 4:116
  splendour of 4:70
  territorial extent of in 600 CE 4:58
  territorial losses of 4:60–61, 4:116–18
  Trebizond and 4:116
  Western assistance sought by 4:116–19
  see also Constantinople; Roman Empire
Byzantium 2:157, **3:119**, 3:168, 5:135
  see also Constantinople

C

Cadiz 1:157
Caesar, Gaius Julius (c.102–44 BCE), Roman general and dictator 3:6, 3:31–6, *3:34*, *3:36–7*, *3:44*
  assassination of 3:35, 3:38
  Britain and 3:41–2
  The Conquest of Gaul 3:32
  deification of 3:36, 3:40
  dictatorship of 3:34
  Gaul and 3:31–2, **3:32**, 3:42
  Octavian and 3:38
  Pompey defeated by 3:34
  Rubicon, crossing by 3:32
Cairo, seat of Fatimid caliphate 4:43, *4:43*
Calais 5:125–6
Calas, Jean (d.1762), French Protestant, execution of 7:36, *7:36*
Calcutta
  Black Hole of 6:137
  capital of India 8:94, *8:98*
  capture by nawab of Bengal 6:136
  as English trading post 5:35, 6:135
calendars 5:92
  Aztec *5:97*
  Chinese 2:43, 5:61
  Egyptian 1:111–112
  Julian 3:35
  Mayan 5:94, *5:95*
  Muslim 4:23, *4:23*
Calicut (Kozhikode) *5:31*, 6:123, *6:123*, 6:125, 6:129, 6:132
Caligula (Gaius), Roman Emporer (37–41 CE) 3:41
caliphs 4:24, *4:24*
calligraphy see art; writing
Callimachus, Greek sculptor 3:26

Calvinism 6:50–1, *6:50*
  in Netherlands 6:60–1
  in North America 6:150
  Puritanism and 6:64
Calvin the Younger, John (1509–1564), Protestant theologian 6:50–1, *6:50*, 6:56
Cambodia, French protectorate 8:100, 9:107
Cambodia (Kampuchea) 10:34, 10:93, 10:112
  communist victory in 10:94–5
  Khmer Rouge in *10:36*, 10:95, *10:95*
  Vietnamese invasion of *10:95*
Cambrian period **1:12**
Cambridge University 7:10
Cambyses, king of Persia (529–522 BCE) **2:111**
camels *1:136*
Canaan
  Hebrew destruction of 1:167
  Hebrews in 1:163–4, 1:166–7
  Philistines settle in 1:161
Canada 7:73, 7:170
  conquest by British 6:152–3, 6:161
  food production and distribution in 7:52–3
  French rule of 6:151
  frontier with United States 7:153–4
  granted dominion status (1867) 8:32
  increased food production in 8:37
  NATO and 10:11
  Quebec 6:149, *6:150*
  Quebec Act (1774) 7:75–6
canals see industrialization; irrigation; Panama Canal; Suez Canal
Canary Islands 6:128
cannibalism 1:38
Canossa 5:106
Canterbury Tales, The (Chaucer) **5:123**, 5:174
Canton 6:122, 6:125, *6:174*, 6:176, 8:67
Canute I (c.995–1035), king of England 4:157, *4:157*
  see also Denmark
Cape Colony 8:33–4, 8:37
Capet, Hugh (c.938–996 CE), king of France 4:147, 4:155
Capetian dynasty 4:147, 4:150, 5:124–6, 6:38
capitalism
  development of 6:20–2
  effect on standard of living 8:111
  industrial conservatism and 8:113
  Marx's views of 7:138
  opportunities for women 8:115
  philosophical justification of **8:131**
  unemployment and 8:108
  in United States 7:166–7
Cappadocia 1:138, 2:164, 3:118
Caracalla (186–217 CE), Roman emperor 3:103, *3:103*, 3:104, *3:104*
Caravaggio (1571–1610), artist *6:28*
caravanserais *4:13*
Caribbean islands,
  agricultural economy in 6:142, 6:145–6
  British acquisitions in 6:159–2
  disease and deaths in 6:168
  English and French settlements in 6:146
  piracy in 6:145, 6:148
  plantation crops in 6:145–7, *6:146*
  slave trade in 6:23, 6:147, **6:147**, 6:148, 6:165, 6:169
  see also West Indies
Carinthia 4:138
Carnac, megalithic monument 2:69
Carolingian dynasty 4:136–47, *4:147*

Carolingian Empire **4:149**
  decline of 4:146–7
  legacy of 4:150
  partitioning of 4:145–6
  territorial expansion of 4:137–8
Carolingian Renaissance 4:140–43, *4:141–2*
  copying of the Bible during 4:142
Carter, James Earl (1924–), United States president 10:121, 10:124, 10:127
Carteret, Philip, English marine cartographer **6:177**
Cartesianism 7:25
Carthage 2:109, *2:110*, 2:164, 2:177–8, **2:178**, *3:128*
  capture by Vandals 3:133
  conquest by Arabs 4:25
  defeat by Syracuse 2:109, 2:177
  destruction by Scipio Aemilianus *2:110*, 2:177, *3:19*, *3:20*, 3:23
  new city of *3:19*
  Phoenician foundation of 1:157
  Pyrrhus, campaigns of 3:18
  religious rituals at *3:142*
  in Second Punic War 3:19
  treaty between Rome and *3:10*
cartography 5:65, *5:65*, 5:160, *5:161–2*, 5:163–4, *5:163*
  Islamic 5:170
Caspian Sea, Russian naval power in 8:43
caste system in India 2:8, 2:16–17, 2:24, 2:28, 5:11, 5:19, **5:19**, 5:38
  economic costs of 5:14
Castile and León, kingdom of **4:43**
Castillo Cave, Cantabria *1:46*
Castlereagh, Robert Stewart (1769–1822), British Tory politician 7:117
castles *5:120*, 5:123
Castro, Fidel (1927–), Cuban dictator 10:69–71, *10:69*
catacombs
  of Domitilla (Rome) *3:85*
  in Naples *3:96*
  of Priscilla (Rome) *3:77*, *3:89*, *3:94*
  of St Ermite (Rome) *3:100*
  of Via Latina (Rome) *3:74*
Catalonia 6:67
Çatal Hüyük, Anatolia
  brick buildings in *1:60*, 1:67
  copper at 1:58
  sculpture of *1:61*
cataphracts, Parthian heavy cavalry 3:42
cathedrals, Gothic 5:108–9, *5:108*, *5:112*, 5:136
Catherine II "the Great" (1729–1796), tsarina of Russia 6:73, *6:74*, 6:114–16, *6:114*, 6:118–19, 7:34–5
Catherine of Aragon (1485–1536), wife of Henry VIII 6:53
Catholicism
  Henry VIII's break with *6:52*, 6:53
  in Latin America 6:143, 6:144–5
  sale of indulgences in 6:47, 6:56
  see also papacy; religion; Roman Catholic Church
Cato, Marcus (234–149 BCE), Roman statesman 3:22
Caucasian people 1:73–4, 1:93
  in Sumer 1:78
cavalry 1:133–5, 2:77
  Assyrian 1:175, *1:175*
  in Greek warfare *2:101*, 2:157, **2:159**

cavalry (cont.)
  in Persian army 2:114
  Scythian 1:175
cave paintings and etchings 1:42–4
  in France *1:43*, *1:49*
  in Italy *2:66*
  in Namibia *2:57*
  in the Sahara desert *2:56*
  in Spain *1:47*, *1:50*, *1:51*
  see also art; rock art; sculpture
Cavendish Laboratory, Cambridge 9:138
caves 1:27, 1:35, *1:37*, *1:43*, *1:46*, *1:47*, *1:49*, *1:56*
Cavour, Camillo Benso di (1810–1861), Italian statesman 7:130–1, *7:131*, 7:132–3, *7:132*
Ceauçescu, Nicolae (1918–1989), president of Romania 10:148
Celestine V (d.1296), pope 5:113–4
Celtic Church, the 3:173, 4:155
Celtic peoples 2:66, 2:165
  Christianity preserved by 3:152
  incursions into Gaul 3:27
  invasion of Macedonia 2:165
  location in Britain 3:150
  wheeled transport of 2:66
Cenozoic era **1:12**, **1:17**
censorship 7:36, 7:90
  Catholicism and 7:10
  in France 7:93
  hindrance to growth of journalism 7:15
  Napoleonic 7:103
  in Russia 7:143
  in the Soviet Union 10:83, *10:83*
censuses 6:9, **6:10**
Central America see Mesoamerican civilizations; Spanish Empire *and individual states*
Central Asia
  caravan route to 2:175–6
  nomads from 1:175
Cephren (Khafre), king of Egypt (2555–2532 BCE) **1:105**, *1:110*, *1:111*
cereal crops 2:66, 9:128, 9:129
  barley 1:89, 1:108, 2:60, 2:85
  corn 2:86, 2:100
  in Crete 1:144
  in Egypt 1:108
  emmer 1:54, 1:108
  in the Fertile Crescent 1:53–4, 1:77
  grain 5:133–4, *5:135*, 5:137
  in international trade 6:23
  maize 2:63, 5:36, 5:77, 5:92, 5:99, 6:172
  in Mesopotamia 1:76–7, 1:89
  millet 1:53, 1:89, 2:36, 2:60
  rice 1:53, 2:13, 2:18, 2:60, 2:81, 5:10, 5:50, 5:56, 5:64, 5:80–81, 6:16, 6:145–6, 6:152, **6:155**, 8:84–5, 8:101
  in Russia 6:112
  storage of **1:138**
  tariff system (Corn Laws) and 7:67
  wheat 1:89, 2:60, 2:85, **6:155**, 6:173, *7:48*, 7:53
  wild barley 1:54
  see also agriculture
Cerularius, patriarch of Constantinople 5:102
Cervantes, Miguel de (1547–1616), Spanish writer 7:14
Cetewayo (c.1826–1884), king of Zululand 8:33, 8:39
Ceylon (Sri Lanka) 5:13, 6:173
  British replace Dutch in 6:137
  Dutch replace Portuguese in 6:132

Ceylon (Sri Lanka) (cont.)
   independence of 9:108
Chadwick, Sir James (1891–1974), British
   physicist 9:140
Chalcedon, Council of 3:166
Chalcolithic era 1:51
Chaldea, conquest of by Islam 4:24
Chaldeans (Chaldees) 1:173, 1:175, 1:178
Challenger space shuttle disaster 9:155, 9:156
Champlain, Samuel de (1567–1635), French
   explorer 6:149
Chandra Gupta, first Gupta emperor (4th
   century CE) 5:17
Chandragupta, Maurya ruler of India (c.321–296
   BCE) 5:10–11, 5:12
Ch'ang-an, T'ang capital 5:52, 5:54–5
Ch'an school of Buddhism 5:47
La Chanson de Roland, epic poem 4:138
chariots 1:89, 1:107, 1:135
   Achaean 1:150–51
   Aryan 2:14
   Assyrian 1:133, 1:175
   Chinese 2:36, 2:46
   Egyptian 1:107, 1:107, 1:125, 1:126, 1:128
   European 2:65
   Hittite 1:159
   Hyksos 1:125, 1:125
   Israelite 1:169, 3:60, 3:60
   Saharan 2:58
   Sumerian (war wagons) 1:91, 1:133–4
   use in warfare 1:133–4
   see also transport, wheeled
Charlemagne (742–814 CE), king of Franks and
   emperor 4:136–45, 4:136, 4:137, 4:137,
   5:122
   Alcuin, tutor of 4:143
   Byzantium and 4:139–40
   Church and State under 4:138–140, 4:142,
   4:161
   code of law and 4:137
   coronation by Leo III 4:136, 4:138–9, 4:162
   cultural renaissance under 4:137, 4:140–43,
   4:141, 4:142–3, 4:142
   death of 4:145
   defence against Norse raiders 4:155
   Denmark and 4:138
   as Frankish warrior-king 4:136, 4:139,
   4:142
   Haroun-al-Rashid and 4:41, 4:140, 4:140
   imperial title and 4:138–9
   personality of 4:143–5
   reformation of the Frankish Church by 4:135,
   4:140, 4:143
   Saxon March and 4:137–8
   Spanish March and 4:138, 4:158
   successors to 4:145–6
   sword of 4:138
Charles I (1600–1649), king of Great Britain and
   Ireland 5:131, 6:64, 6:64, 6:66
Charles I and V (1500–1558), king of Spain and
   Holy Roman Emperor 6:57–9, 6:81–5,
   6:84, 6:93, 6:129, 6:142
   abdication of 6:85
   conquest of Tunis by 6:84
   Diet of Augsburg and 6:49, 6:50
   dynastic ambitions of 6:81–3
   election as Emperor 6:81, 6:83–4
   Habsburg-Valois wars and 6:84–5
   Italian wars and 6:83–4
   Luther banned by 6:49
   Netherlands and 6:60

Charles I the Bald, king of the Franks and
   emperor (840–877 CE) 4:144, 4:146, 4:155,
   4:166
Charles II (1630–1685), king of Scotland and
   England 6:64, 6:66, 6:66, 6:68, 6:133,
   6:160
Charles II (1661–1700), king of Spain 6:91, 6:91
Charles III (1716–1788), king of Spain 6:140
Charles III the Simple (879–929 CE), king of the
   Western Franks 4:146
Charles IV (1316–1378), Holy Roman Emperor
   5:145
Charles VI (1685–1740), Holy Roman Emperor
   6:77
Charles X (1757–1836), king of France
   7:119–20, 7:120
Charles XII (1682–1718), king of Sweden 6:106
Chartism, British radical movement 7:176
Chartres Cathedral 5:108, 5:108
Chaucer, Geoffrey (c.1340–1400), English poet
   5:122, 5:123
   The Canterbury Tales 5:174
   treatise on astrolabe 5:170
Chaumette, Pierre (1763–1794) 7:98
Chauvet Cave, Ardèche valley 1:43
Chavin culture 2:64
   pottery 2:62
Cheibanid khanate 4:107
chemical industry 8:107, 8:129
chemistry 7:16, 7:20, 7:21, 7:44, 8:129–30
   see also scientific revolution
Cheng Ho (c.1371–1435), Chinese admiral 5:60
Ch'en Tu-hsiu (1879–1942), Chinese
   revolutionary 9:12–13, 9:17
Cheops (Khufu), king of Egypt (2552–2528 BCE)
   1:105
   pyramid of 1:109–10, 1:110
Chernobyl nuclear disaster 9:154–6, 9:156
Chiang K'ai-shek (1887–1975), Chinese
   statesman 9:19, 9:20, 9:21, 9:21, 9:22,
   9:104–105, 9:105, 9:106
   exile of 9:106
   leadership style of 9:26
   United States and 9:28
Chichen Itza, Maya city 5:95
childbirth 1:24, 1:25
Childeric I, Merovingian king (460–481 CE)
   3:129
children
   allowances for in France and Belgium 7:46
   child labour
      abuse of 7:64–5, 7:64
      in China 10:27
      in factories 7:67
   infant mortality 1:119, 7:45, 8:150, 9:119,
   9:120, 9:120, 10:70
   marriage of 5:21
Chile
   American copper company 10:72
   civil war in (1891) 8:28
   European style architecture in 8:29
   Falklands war and 10:104
   military coup in 10:73, 10:74
   nitrate deposits in 8:29
   Pacific War against Peru and Bolivia 8:26
   Spanish conquest of 6:139
China
   administrative élite in 5:38, 5:46
   agricultural privatization in 10:111
   agriculture in 2:32, 2:34, 2:36, 5:56
   ancestor worship in 2:41, 2:50, 2:53

China (cont.)
   art of
      ceramics 2:54
      terracotta figures 2:52, 2:55
   Boxer movement in 9:8, 9:14, 9:20
   bureaucracy 2:43
      Confucian values of 5:44–5, 5:46–8
      conservative nature of 5:47
      entry into 5:44–6, 5:58
      Manchu cooperation and 5:62
      persistence of 5:44–6, 5:51–2
   Canton 6:122, 6:125, 6:174, 6:176, 8:67
   census in 5:45, 5:54
   Ch'in dynasty 2:38–9
   Chinghis Khan and 4:104
   civilization
      conservative nature of 5:57
      continuity of 2:30, 5:38
      earliest period 1:61, 1:68, 1:69
      influence on Japanese 5:69, 5:70
      prestige of 5:42
      T'ang dynasty and 5:52
   clan structure in 2:36, 2:40–42
   coal 5:57
   collectivization in 10:27, 10:27, 10:30, 10:30,
   10:31
      abandonment of 10:154
   colleges and universities in 9:15
   communes in 10:30, 10:30, 10:31
      replacement by family farms 10:154
   Communist Party in 9:12, 9:26, 9.88, 10:30
      formation of 9:17, 9:17, 9:18
      Kuomintang and 9:19–20, 9:21, 9:27
      Long March of 9:26–7, 9:26
      nationalists and 9:22, 9:26, 9:104–106
      peasants and 9:20–21
      persecution of 9:21, 9:22
      proscription of 9:22
      split with Soviet communists 10:29–31,
      10:31
   Confucian administrators in 5:38–9, 5:44,
   5:47
   Cultural Revolution in 10:32–4, 10:33,
      10:110–11, 10:111, 10:112, 10:154, 10:155
   cultural traditions threatened 8:66–7,
   8:69–70
   currency 2:46, 2:47
   defence against Huns 4:15
   dialects of 2:45
   disillusionment with western liberalism in
   9:16–7, 9:19
   Dutch trade centred on Formosa 6:132
   dynastic rule in 5:39–44
      decline and fall of 8:60, 8:62, 8:78, 8:79
   dynasties 5:41, 5:43, 5:48–50
      Ch'in 5:39, 5:40
         administrative innovations under 5:40
         completion of Great Wall under 5:44,
         5:49
         persecution of scholars in 5:44
         Shih-Huang-ti, First Emperor of 5:39,
         5:44
         unification of China under 5:40
      Ch'ing (Manchu) 5:61–6, 8:66, 8:66, 8:70
      Chou 2:37–8, 2:37, 2:40
      Han 5:40–2, 5:44, 5:48
      Later Han 5:41–2, 5:47, 5:70
      Manchu see Ch'ing
      Ming 5:50, 5:60–61, 5:67
      Shang 2:35, 2:36–7, 2:36–7, 2:39, 2:41,
      2:44, 2:45, 2:53

China, dynasties (cont.)
      Sung 5:51–2, 5:55–6, 5:57
      T'ang 5:39, 5:43–6, 5:43–4, 5:47, 5:49–51,
      5:55
   economy 4:109, 5:55–7
      foreign debt 10:154
      growth of 10:16, 10:111–12
      inflation 10:154
      liberalization of 10:15–4, 10:154, 10:156
      non-communist countries and 10:110
      silver inflation in 8:68
      special economic areas of 10:111–12
   educational reforms in 10:112
   eunuchs 5:46
   examination system in 8:77
   famine in 5:50–51
   female infanticide in 9:118, 9:122
   foreign influences, assimilation of 5:38, 5:42
   foreign policies of 10:28, 10:110–12
   foreign relations of
      attitude to foreigners 8:67, 8:69–70, 8:71,
      8:73–6
      Boxer movement 8:75–6, 8:76, 8:90
      France, conflict with 8:100
      Japan, war with 8:86, 8:87
      opium trade in 8:17, 8:68–9, 8:73
      Westernization movement in 8:76
   Foundation of People's Republic 9:106
   Great Leap Forward 10:30, 10:31, 10:111,
   10:112
   Great Wall of 2:30, 2:31, 4:15, 5:44, 5:49,
   5:54, 5:62
   growth of cities in 1:69
   Hong Kong and 10:39, 10:41, 10:112
   Hundred Days of Reform, The (1898) 8:75–7
   Hundred Schools era 2:47
   imperial China ends 8:78, 8:79
   India, conflict with 10:21
   India, relations with 10:28
   industrialization 9:15–16, 10:27, 10:110–12
   influence on eastern Asia 10:18
   innovation, lack of 5:48, 5:57, 5:64, 5:65
   intellectual impact on European
      thought 6:167
   isolation of 2:32, 5:38, 5:39
   and Japan
      attacks on China 9:12, 9:24, 9:25, 9:27–8,
      9:104
      cultural influence 5:69, 5:70
   Jesuits in 8:66
   K'ang-hsi (1654–1722), Manchu emperor
      (1662–1722) 8:66
   Korean War and 10:13, 10:26, 10:28
   Kuomintang (KMT) see Kuomintang (KMT)
   land reform in 9:105–6, 10:27, 10:27
   land-owning gentry in 5:45–6, 5:52, 5:60,
   5:62
   legal system in 9:11
   literacy in 5:57
   literature in 5:55
   Macao and 8:74, 10:112
   Manchu empire (1644–1912) 5:61–6, 8:66,
   8:70
   Maoist cult in 10:32–4
   maritime expeditions and 5:57, 5:60
   Marxism 2:35, 2:48, 8:20, 9:106
      sinicization of 10:30–31, 10:154, 10:156
   May 4th Movement in 9:15–17, 9:104,
   10:112, 10:154
   military rebellions in 5:51
   military techniques of 2:44, 2:46

China (cont.)
modernization in 9:171, 10:153–4
monarchy of 2:43, 2:47
mysticism in **2:50**
nationalist movement in 9:11–13, 9:22–3, 9:25, 9:104–106
Neolithic culture in 2:32–34, *2:34*
nobility in 2:46–2:47
privileges of 2:40–41
oracles in 2:42, 2:44, *2:44*
parliamentary government in 9:11, 9:14
peasantry in 2:40–41, 2:47, 5:42, 5:54, 8:68, 8:70–73, 8:74, 8:78
barred from clan structure 2:40–42
conscription of 5:49
land hunger and 8:71
magic and superstitions and 5:48
rebellions by 5:48–51, 5:54, 5:60–61
secret societies and 5:48, 5:60
standard of living of 5:48, 5:50, 5:57
worship of nature gods by 2:42, 2:45
philosophy in 2:47–51, **2:50**
population
control of *9:118*, 9:122, **9:122**
density of 9:124
growth 8:68, 10:32, 10:112
pressure 5:49–50, 5:66
printing in 5:55, **5:55**, 5:57
punishments in 2:40–41
Red Guards 10:32
Red Turbans 8:71
religious tolerance in 5:57, 5:59
Republic of 8:77–9, **8:78**, 9:13, 9:18–22, 9:26, 9:103, 9:105–106, 10:26, 10:30, 10:32–4, 10:40
origins of 8:68, 8:69, 8:76–78, **8:78**, 8:79, 8:89, 8:101
effects of 9:9, 9:11, *9:13*, *9:21*
respect for authority in 10:33–4
Russia and 6:102, 7:144
science and technology in
astronomy 2:43, 2:52
calendar 2:43, 5:61
cartography 5:65, *5:65*
early technologies 2:44–5
fire, early use of in 1:27
hydro-electric power *10:171*
iron, early use of 1:71, 2:44–5
nuclear weapons in 10:31, 10:176
scientific stagnation 7:20
secret societies in 5:48, 8:68, 8:71, 8:77, 9:11, **9:24**
Shang dynasty *1:69*, *1:71*
Shih-Kai, Yuan (1859–1916), President of China **8:78**, 8:79
silk trade and 5:39, 5:42, 5:52
social distinctions drawn in 2:40–42, 2:46–7
socialist economy *see* China, economy of modern China
society and social organization in 5:46, *5:46*, 5:48
Soviet Union, relations with 10:29–31
student protests and demands 10:154–6
Sung dynasty 4:112
Taiping rebellion (1850–1864) 8:71–3, **8:72**
Taiwan (Formosa) 6:132, 10:26, 10:28, 10:110, 10:112
T'ang dynasty 4:98
terracotta army in *5:39*
territorial losses of 8:74–5

China (cont.)
Tiananmen Square incident 10:155–6, *10:155*, *10:157*
Tibet, occupation of 10:28, *10:29*
topography of 2:31–4
traditional values in 10:154, 10:156
Twenty-One Demands and 9:14
United Nations and
entry to 10:93
exclusion from 10:28
Security Council and 9:85
United States and
end of relations with Kuomintang 10:110
support of for Kuomintang 10:28
withdrawal of forces from Taiwan 10:110
universities closed in 10:32
urban developments and urbanization 2:45–6, 5:54–5, 9:15–16
Vietnam 10:34, 10:93, 10:112
warlords in 9:11, 9:16–17, 9:19–20, **9:21**, 9:22–3, 9:25
Warring States period 2:38–40, 2:47, 5:39, 5:40
wartime economic boom in 9:15–16
war with Germany 9:14
Western powers in 9:18–19
world trade and 8:16, 8:51, 8:73
written records in 5:38
Yellow River **2:31**, 2:32–4
see also Chou dynasty; Formosa; Japan; Kuomintang; Mao Tse-tung; Mongol China; Shang dynasty; Taiwan
Chinese Soviet Republic 9:26
Ch'ing dynasty *see* Manchu dynasty
Chinghis (Genghis) Khan (c.1162–1227), Mongol conqueror and emperor *4:104*, 4:105–106, **4:105**, *4:106*, 5:51, 5:58
Chioggia, War of *4:74*
Chionites *see* Hsiung-Nu
Chios 2:100, 2:157
Chittor, conquest of 5:28
Chlotar I, king of the Franks (511–561 CE) *3:153*
chocolate *6:153*
cholera 7:45
Cholula people, massacre by conquistadores *6:142*
Chou dynasty 2:37–8, *2:38*, 2:40, *2:40*, 2:46–7, 5:44
clan structure of 2:41
displacement by barbarians 2:38, *2:38*
end of 2:44, 2:46
influence on Yangtze River valley 2:40
Shang dynasty and 2:37, 2:42–3
Christ *see* Jesus of Nazareth
Christendom 6:39, 6:82–3
Western
geographical extent of 4:131, 4:134–5
insecurity of 4:159–60
Norse influences on 4:153–5
Christianity 3:6, 3:12, **3:91**, **8:99**, 9:49
in Africa 3:141–3, 5:85–6
Donatists, heretical sect 5:86
in Asia Minor 3:126
Augustine and 3:144–8
Byzantine emperors and 4:50–51
Constantine and 3:122
conversions to
Abgar, king of Osrhoene 3:72
Augustine, St 3:143, *3:145*

Christianity, conversions to (cont.)
Clovis, king of the Franks **3:152**, 3:153, **3:157**, 3:177
Constantine 3:120–22
Paul, St 3:86, *3:116*
Visigoths **3:157**
differences between Eastern and Western Church 3:140, 3:143, 3:168–9
declining force of 8:122
doctrinal divergences in 3:166–8
early puritanism 2:144
Easter festival and 4:155
in the Eastern Empire 3:166–8
in the eastern Mediterranean 2:84, 2:86
in Egypt 5:87
in Ethiopia 5:85–6, *5:87*, 8:13
Europe
Albigensian heresy 5:111, *5:111*
autonomous criticism 5:178
crusades and 5:150–1
developing mysticism 5:112, 5:117
dualism of 5:178
heresies in 5:111, *5:111*, 5:112, 5:117, *5:117*
impact on 3:72
importance in 5:102–3, 5:118–19
military orders 5:155–7, **5:155**
popular religion 5:117
spread of 5:150
evangelism and social service in cities 7:62
Greek philosophy and 3:116–17, 3:123
heresy and *see* heresies
hierarchical structure of Church in 3:88, **3:91**
India and 5:16
Islam 4:103
Japan and 5:77, *5:78*, 5:79
Jewish origins of 3:73–80
Judaism and 1:171, 3:77, 3:87
Julian the Apostate and 3:135–6
links to economic penetration of China 8:74
Manichaeism *see* Manichaeism
martyrdom in 3:85, 3:90–91, *3:92*, *3:94*
medieval life and 5:178
Muhammad and 4:23
mystery cults and 3:66
in North American colonies, dominance of 6:154
origin and development of 3:80–78
pagan rites assimilated into 3:177–8
in Persia 4:11–12
as a philosophy 3:95
Plato's influence on 2:144
Roman Catholic Church *see* papacy; Roman Catholic Church
Roman reaction to 3:87, 3:91, 3:115–18
in Scandinavia 4:153
sense of superiority of 6:124
Slavs and 4:76–7
soul-body schism and 2:144
in Spain 4:158–9
spread of 3:87–8, **3:91**, *3:99*, 3:115, 3:118
symbolism of *4:131*
Zoroastrian influence on 2:81
see also Catholicism; Christendom; Christian missionary activity; Christian sects; Christians; papacy; religions; Roman Catholic Church; Roman religions
Christian missionary activity **3:88**, 3:115, 3:118, 3:140, **3:172**, 4:52, 4:162, *8:10*, 9:36
in Africa 8:56
Anglo-Saxon 4:164

Christian missionary activity (cont.)
in Bulgaria 4:79
Catholic 6:171, **6:172**, 8:123
in China 8:70, 8:73
crusading zeal of 8:39–40
cultural contamination and 8:13, 8:20
encouragement of by bishops 4:164
in European cities 7:62
in European colonies 6:124, **6:172**
expansion of 8:13
French mission in Siam 6:132
in Germany 4:135
in India 6:135–6, 8:47, 8:49
invigoration of by Counter-Reformation 6:171
Irish 4:155
by Jesuits 6:57, 6:171
mendicant orders 5:110–11
and Muslims 5:154
in New Zealand 8:32
in northeastern Europe 5:156
Portuguese 5:28, 5:61, 5:77–8
Protestant 6:171–2, **6:172**
in Scandinavia 4:153
Slavs and 4:79–80, *4:80*, 4:93
in Spanish Empire 6:141, 6:143–4
Spanish in North America 6:148
in Tahiti 6:178
see also missionary activities
Christian sects
Anabaptists 6:50
Calvinism 6:50–1, *6:50*
effects on native cultures 6:172
humanism 6:44–6, *6:50*
Lutheranism 6:49–51, *6:51*
Quakers 6:172
Unitarianism 6:65, 6:70
Christians
diaspora (dispersion) **3:76**, 3:90, 3:95
persecution of 3:85, 3:90–93, *3:91–2*, 3:94, 3:117–18
property of, restored under Edict of Milan 3:120–21
Christina (1626–1689), queen of Sweden (1632–1654) *6:98*
Christy, Howard Chandler, American artist *7:81*
Chrysippus (3rd century BCE), Greek philosopher *2:171*
Ch'u civilization 2:40
Chun Tsai-Feng, Chinese prince *9:10*
Church of England 6:52–5
Book of Common Prayer 6:53
dislike of extreme Puritanism by 6:66
Royal Supremacy in 6:53–4
Church and State **3:125**, 3:126–7, 3:140, 5:105, *5:106*
see also Church of England
in Byzantine Empire 4:50–53
under Charlemagne 4:138–40
clerical marriages and 5:104–5
combination of in Western Christendom 5:111
enlightenment and anti-clericalism in 7:37
established religion in Europe upheld by 7:10
in Habsburg empire 6:75
Investiture Contest and 5:104–7
Lateran treaties (1929) 8:172, *8:172*
in Latin America 8:28
linking by Constantine 3:124, **3:125**, 3:143
under Lombards *4:151*
under Otto I 4:148–9

Church and State (cont.)
  papacy, loss of temporal power 8:122–3, *8:122*
  papal supremacy and 5:113–14
  rejection of papal authority 6:52–5
  resistance to improvement 7:36
  in revolutionary France 7:94, 7:98–9
  in Russia 6:104
  simony and 5:105
  in Spain 6:57–9
  see also Protestant Reformation
churches
  Arian baptistry (Ravenna) *3:122–3*
  desecration during French Revolution 7:99
  in Dura Europos *3:121*
  enriching by Charlemagne **4:136**
  Neonian baptistry (Ravenna) *3:81*
  Nôtre Dame, Paris *7:98*
  St Apollinare the New (Ravenna) *4:58*
  St Apollinaris basilica of Classe (Ravenna) *3:159, 3:163*
  St Clement (Rome) *4:80*
  St Dmitri (Vladimir-Suzdal) *4:88*
  St Eugene (Trebizond) **4:69**
  St Irene (Constantinople) *4:75*
  St Isadore (León) *4:168*
  St John (Ephesus) *4:75*
  St Laurence (Rome) *5:118*
  St Maria Novella (Florence) *5:169*
  St Mark (Venice) *4:75*
  St Martin Fromista (Spain) *4:165*
  St Mary (Llugo de Llanera) *4:131*
  St Mary of the Valley (Cividale) *4:151*
  St Michael (Avila) *5:138*
  St Peter (Monteno) *7:8*
  St Peter (Rome) *3:86, 7:9*
  St Saviour, Chora Monastery (Istanbul) *4:91, 4:116*
  St Simeon basilica (Qalaat Semaan) *3:115*
  St Sofia (Constantinople) **3:163**, *3:164, 3:164*
  St Sophia (Kiev) *4:85, 4:93*
  St Sophia (Novgorod) *4:87, 4:93*
  St Vicente basilica (Córdoba) *4:39*
  St Vitale (Ravenna) *4:49, 4:51, 4:67*
  St Vitus (Prague cathedral) *4:92*
  San Lorenzo (Milan) *3:143*
  San Pedro de la Nave (Zamora) *3:157*
  San Vitale (Ravenna) *3:146, 3:159, 3:161*
  Santa Costanza (Rome) *3:85*
  Santa Croce (Florence) *5:110*
  Sts Cosmas and Damian (Rome) *3:72*
  Theodolinda chapel (Monza) *4:151*
Churchill, Sir Winston Spencer (1874–1965), British prime minister 9:71, *9:72, 9:79,* 10:11
  Iron Curtain speech *9:94*
  resignation of *9:38*
  Roosevelt and *9:73, 9:73*
  as war leader 9:71, *9:72, 9:79*
  at Yalta Conference *9:81, 9:83, 9:85, 9:92*
Chu Yan-chang (1328–1398), first Ming emperor of China (1368–1398) 5:60
Cicero, Marcus Tullius (106–43 BCE), Roman orator *3:28*, 3:62, 3:143
Cilicia 1:173
cinema 8:150, **10:163**
Cisneros, Francisco Ximenez de (1436–1517), Spanish cardinal 6:57
Cisterian order 5:103
cities 2:14, 7:60–64, *7:61*, 7:175
  atheism and irreligion tendencies in 7:62

cities (cont.)
  Chinese 2:45–6, 2:54
  development of 1:69, 1:89
  ghettos 10:88
  Harappan **2:8**, 2:12, *2:15*
  Hellenistic 2:167–9
  as industrial centres 7:54, 7:175
  see also industrialization; urbanization
citizenship
  Greek 2:102–4, 2:107, 2:126, 2:128
  Roman, 3:14, 3:15–16, 3:28, 3:29, **3:33**
    subjects 3:16, 3:28, 3:30, 3:47
The City of God (St Augustine) 3:144–7, *3:145,* 3:148, *3:149*
city-states 2:101–8, 2:118, 2:153, 2:160
  absence in Egypt 1:103
  after Peloponnesian War 2:170
  Aristotle on 2:104, 2:145, 2:170
  Athens 2:129–36
  Carthage 2:177
  citizen body of 2:102–3, 2:106
  coinage of *2:124*
  constitutions of 2:103–4
  decline of 2:123
  Etruscans and 2:70
  government and administration in 4:77, 4:151
  Greek 2:101–8, 2:129–36
  Italian 4:151, 5:117, 5:130–31, *5:135, 5:135,* 5:139–40, *6:14*, 6:83–4
  law and legal institutions of 2:103
  origin of politics in 2:101
  polis 2:101–2
  in Sumer 1:89
  topography of 2:102–3
civilization
  in China
    Ch'u 2:40
    initial spread southward of 2:31, *2:31*
    long duration of 2:30
    in Shang and Chou dynasties 2:36–8
    unique nature of 2:52–4
  in classical Mediterranean 2:86–8, *2:87, 2:89,* 2:124–5
  definitions of 1:67–8
  development of 1:70–71
  diffusion of 1:157–9
  in Egypt 2:62
  in Europe 2:65–6, 5:102, 5:117–19, 5:177–8
  first appearances of 1:59–60, 1:64, 1:66–7, **1:66**, 1:68–9, *1:72*, 1:78
  in Greece *see* Greek civilization
  in India 2:11–12
    Hindu, Gupta period 5:17–21
    Indus valley **2:8**, 2:12
  integration in Near East 2:72–3
  modern 7:63
  Olmec 2:63–4
  variation in 1:71–2
  see also Greek civilization; Greek culture
Civil Rights Movement in USA *see* United States of America
civil service (Japan), aristocratic 5:73
Civil War, American *see* American Civil War
Civil War, English 6:63–4, *6:64, 6:65,* 6:66, 6:67
class structure
  aristocracy 7:171
  in Europe 5:142–7, 6:27–33
    bourgeoisie and 5:144, *5:149*
    English nobility 6:28–9

class structure in Europe (cont.)
    merchant class and 5:143–5
    mobility within 5:143–4
    nobility and 5:142–3, *5:143*
    in Poland 6:99
    serfdom and 5:134, 5:141
    social mobility 6:27–8, 6:29
    social status 6:29
    waning support from religion for 6:30–1
  industrial proletariat 7:138
  in Japan 5:78–9
  middle classes 7:176
  peasants 7:49, 7:52, 7:89
  ruling classes 7:170
  in Russia *6:103,* 6:104–5, 6:109, 6:116
  in Spanish Empire 6:142–3
  working class 7:138, 7:139, 7:176
Claudius (Tiberius Claudius Nero) (10 BCE–54 CE), Roman emperor 3:42, **3:54**, *3:64*
clay tablets in antiquity 1:80, 1:117, 1:174
  in Ebla palace archives *1:99*
  at Knossos **1:147**, 1:148–50, 1:151, *1:151*
  in Mari palace archives 1:96
  at Pylos 1:151–2
Clemenceau, Georges (1841–1929), French president 8:147, 8:162
Clement V (c.1260–1314), pope 5:115
Clement VI (c.1291–1352), pope 5:115
Clement VII (1478–1534), pope **5:115**
Clement of Alexandria, St (1st century CE), Christian Platonist 3:96, 3:117
Cleopatra (c.68–30 BCE), queen of Egypt 2:164, 3:34, 3:38, *3:38*
clergy
  anti-clericalism and 6:45, 6:66, 6:145, 8:28, 8:123, *8:123*
  celibacy and 5:104, 5:108, 6:52
  legal immunities of 5:107
  resistance to reform 5:104
  separation from laity 5:105, 5:107
  universities and 5:166
  see also clergy; Christian missionary activity
climate
  Aegean depopulation and 1:154
  in Africa 2:56, 2:57–8, **2:58**, *2:59*
  in China 2:31–2
  demographic patterns and 1:73
  evolution and 1:11–16, 1:35, 1:46
  glaciation **1:13**
  in India 2:10
  Nile floodplain and 1:101
  in the Palaeolithic *1:8*, 1:40, 1:45, 1:52
  recent relative stability of 1:64
  social developments and 1:40
Clinton, Bill (1946–), United States president *10:177*
Clive, Robert (1725–1774), British imperialist *6:136, 6:137,* 8:46
clocks 5:65, 7:19
clothes 1:36, 1:41, *1:50, 1:82, 1:86, 1:122*
Clouet, Jean (c.1485–c.1541), artist *6:83*
Clovis (465–511 CE), king of the Franks 3:152, 3:153–4, 3:156, 3:157, 3:158, 4:135
  conversion to Catholicism *4:135*
Cluniac monasticism 4:164–7, *4:168*
  influence on Romanesque architecture **4:165**
Cluny, Abbey of **4:165**, 4:167, 5:103, *5:103*
coal 7:55, 7:56, 7:59
Cobden, Richard (1804–1865), British statesman 7:67

Cochin China (south Vietnam) 8:100, *8:101,* 9:107
Codex Constitutionum **3:54**
coffee 6:35, 6:133, 6:145, *6:153,* 6:166, 6:173
coinage 1:138–9, 2:18, *2:164, 2:174, 3:38,* 5:9
  Anglo-Saxon *4:155*
  Arabic 4:31, *4:31, 4:34*
  Bactrian 5:15
  Byzantine *4:54, 4:63, 4:70, 4:70*
  Chinese *2:47*
  Greek 2:100, **2:103**, *2:124, 2:125*
  Han dynasty monopoly on 5:44
  Japanese 5:77
  Merovingian *4:169*
  of Ottoman Turks *4:120*
  Parthian 3:108, *5:14*
  reformation of under Charlemagne **4:137**
  in Roman Empire 3:107
  silver 2:100, **2:103**
  Sparta, resistance to 2:100, 2:106
  Venetian **4:74**
Cold War 9:96–7, *9:97,* 9:110, 9:127, 10:8–9, 10:11–16, **10:12**, 10:161
  Asia and 10:20, 10:22–3, 10:26, 10:39–40
  China and 10:28
  economic systems during 10:15–16
  Islam and 10:119
  Latin America and 10:68, 10:70, 10:79
  Middle East and 10:42, 10:131
Colombia 10:66
  American intervention in 8:30, 8:63–4
  insurrection in (1781) 8:24
colonialism
  abuse of native populations by colonizers 6:124, 6:168–70, 6:172
  animal importation during 6:173–4
  benefits of 6:141–2, 6:153, 6:158
  British 8:31–4
    impact on primitive societies 8:38–9
    and loss of American colonies 8:31
    responsible government by colonies 8:32, 8:34, 8:36
    see also British Empire
  British and French in Caribbean 6:146–8
  British in North America 6:149–54, *6:149, 6:150,* **6:155**
  consequences of 6:153–4
  crop importation 6:172–3
  decolonialization 9:25
  Dutch in Java 6:131–2
  Dutch in North America 6:149
  economic theories 6:142, 6:153, 6:158
  French in North America and Canada 6:149
  Greek 2:93, 2:100, 2:105–6, 2:108–9
  nationalist rebellions and 9:23
  Phoenician 1:156–7, 2:109
  Portuguese in Africa and Asia **6:126**, 6:127–30, **6:128**
  Spanish and Portuguese in Americas **6:126**, 6:139–46, **6:141**
  Swedish in North America 6:148
colonial territories,
  anti-colonial movement 8:59
  Christianity in 8:10
  demands for independence by 8:6
  enlightened administration of 8:11
  European emigration to 8:21–2
  nationalism of 8:6, 8:32, 8:58

colonial territories (cont.)
native troops and European officers *8:14*,
8:43
see also British colonialism; imperialism;
nationalist movements
Colossus of Rhodes **2:174**, 2:175
Columbus, Christopher (1451–1506), explorer
and navigator *5:128*, 5:160–62, 6:139,
6:141
COMECON (Council for Mutual Economic
Assistance) 9:96, **10:12**, *10:76*, 10:96,
10:98
Cominform 9:95–96, 10:77
Comintern (Third International) **8:164**, 8:165,
8:166, 9:17, 9:20, 9:22, 9:27
international class-struggle by 9:59
revived as Cominform 9:95–6
Commodus, Lucius Aelius Aurelius (161–192
CE), Roman emperor 3:41, 3:101, *3:102*
Commonwealth, the *see* British Commonwealth
of Nations
Commonwealth, 17th century England 6:65–6,
6:159–60, 6:162
navy and 6:159, 6:162
Commonwealth of Independent States (CIS)
10:146, 10:153
see also Russia (Russian Federation); Soviet
Union (USSR)
communications
cinema **10:163**
isolation reduced by 8:18
newspapers 8:54, 8:83, 8:110, 8:118, 8:124
postal services 7:173
telegraph 7:133, 8:18, 8:92
telephone 8:129
television 10:144, **10:163**
see also railways; shipping
communism 7:136, **7:139**, **8:164**
in Azerbaijan 9:93
in China 2:35, 2:40, 9:17–23, *9:17*, **9:21**,
9:26, **9:26**, 9:27, 9:88, 9:104–6
early proponents of **8:164**
in eastern and central Europe 9:82, 9:88,
9:93
fears of 8:164–6, 9:59, 9:60
in France 9:59, 9:60, 9:87
in Germany 9:60–61
in Indonesia 9:106
in Malaya 9:108
nationalist rebels and 9:23
revolutionary parties 8:165
Russian support for Arab communists 9:42
in Southeast Asia 9:106–108
in Spain 9:60
Taiping movement and 8:72
in Vietnam 9:107–108
in western Europe 9:59–60, 9:94
see also Bolshevik régime; Russia
Communist Manifesto (Marx and Engels)
7:138, **8:164**
Communist Party **8:164**
compass, magnetic 5:57, 5:65, 5:160, 5:170
computers 9:129, 9:136, *9:136*, 9:137, *9:140*
Comte, Auguste (1798–1857), French
philosopher 8:131, **8:131**
concentration camps *9:79*
Conditions of the English Working-Class, The
(Engels) 7:61–2
Confederate States of America (Confederacy)
7:163–4
Confederation of the Rhine 7:108, 7:134

Confessions of a Child of the Century (de
Musset) **7:120**
Confucianism 2:48, **2:50**, 2:51–2, 5:43, *5:44*,
5:45, 5:48, **8:99**
in China 5:38–9, 5:44–5, 5:46–8, 8:70, **8:72**
conservative nature of 5:47, 5:65
formalization of doctrine of 5:44
in Japan 5:70, 8:83, 8:85
pragmatic nature of 2:50–2:51
Thirteen Classics 2:50–51
views on rebellion of 5:50
Confucius (551–478 BCE), Chinese philosopher
2:46, 2:47–51, *2:48–9*, *5:44*
conservative teachings of 2:48
influence on Chinese civil servants 2:48, 2:50
precepts of 2:48, 2:52
Congo (Zaire)
Belgian colony 8:57, 8:59
civil war 10:55
Congregationalists 6:65
Congress *see* North American Colonies; United
States of America
Congress of Vienna (1815) *7:114*, **7:116**, 7:117,
7:117, 7:122–3, *7:134*
conquistadores 6:139–40, *6:139*
brutality of 6:140, *6:142*
as models of Christian superiority 6:168
Conrad I, king of Franconia (911–918 CE)
4:147
conservatism 7:99, 7:100, 7:125–6
in eastern Asia 10:26
growth in Soviet Union 10:32
industrialism and 7:66–8
see also liberalism
Constable, John (1776–1837), English artist
7:48
Constance, Council of (1414–1418) 5:116
condemnation of Hus 5:117
Constantine I the Great (Flavius Valerius
Constantinus) (c.274–337 CE), Roman
emperor 3:118–24, *3:118*, **3:119**,
3:120–21, *3:123*, 4:49, *4:50*, **4:51**, *4:70*
Caesaropapism 3:121
conversion to Christianity 3:119–22, 3:123
Council of Nicaea and 3:122, *3:123*
foundation of Constantinople by 3:124
tax reforms and 3:119
Constantine V (718–775), Byzantine emperor
4:63, 4:65, **4:67**
Constantine XI, Byzantine emperor (1448–1453)
fall of Constantinople and *4:48*, 4:120
Constantinople 3:119, **3:119**, 3:124, *3:137*,
3:160–61, **3:163**, 4:12–13, 4:17, *4:17*, 4:87
besieged *4:17*, 4:120, 4:26, 4:41, 4:57, 4:61,
4:62
defences of 4:57
emperors restored in 4:75
Fourth Crusade and **4:51**, **4:74**, 4:75–6, *4:76*,
4:94
Latin Empire of 5:153–4
Norsemen penetrate defences of 4:79, 4:81
Ottoman building programme in *4:129*
Ottoman Turks' conquest of 4:48, *4:48*, **4:51**,
4:53, 4:120, 5:158
raided by the Rus 4:80–81
sacked by crusaders 5:153
see also Byzantine Empire; Byzantium
Constantius, Flavius Valerius (c.225–300 CE),
Roman emperor in West 3:118
constitutions *see individual states*

consuls (Roman) 3:14, 3:16, 3:25, 3:34, 3:39
Augustus 3:39
Caesar 3:31
Marius 3:29
contraception and family planning 7:44–5,
9:118, *9:118*, 9:122–3, **9:122**, 9:170
see also birth control
Cook, James (1728–1779), British explorer
6:157, 6:176, 6:178
Copernicus, Nicholas (1473–1543), Polish
astronomer 7:22, *7:22*
copper **1:135**
from Anatolia 1:83
copper working 1:58, 1:102, **1:135**
from Cyprus 1:136
in Europe 2:66–7
in India 2:11, 2:20
ingots 1:137, 1:138, **1:138**
refinery 1:170
in Sinai 1:125
from Yugoslavia 1:136
Coptic Church 3:142, 3:167, 3:168, 3:169,
3:170, *3:170*, 4:54, *4:55*
Córdoba
caliphate established in 4:41–2
caliphate in decline 4:43
Great Mosque of *4:38–9*, 4:43, *4:47*
Madinat al-Zahara, caliphate palace of *4:42*
Umayyad emirate in 4:41, **4:42**
Corinth *2:103*, *2:106*, 2:109
Acrocorinth fortress in *2:158*
Athenian economic threat to 2:119, 2:121
invention of triremes in **2:113**
League of 2:159
as Spartan ally 2:120
see also Sicily; Syracuse
Corn Laws 7:172, 8:118
repeal of 7:67–8, 7:69, 7:172–3
corruption
in China 10:154
in India *8:46*
in South Vietnam 10:36
in Soviet Union 10:32
Cortés, Hernán (1485–1547), Spanish
conquistador 6:139–40, *6:142*
Cos 2:157
Cosa, Juan de, Spanish cartographer *5:161*
cosmology 7:21
Cossack peoples 6:98, 6:100, 6:102, 6:106,
6:107
semi-autonomy of 6:103
cotton and cotton production 2:12–13,
6:173, *7:52*, *7:54*, 7:57, *7:157*, 7:158, 8:85
slavery and 7:158–60
Council of Europe 10:98
councils, ecclesiastical
Basle (1431–1449) 5:116
Chalcedon 3:166
Constance (1414–1418) 5:116–7
ecumenical 5:107, 5:113, 5:116
Ephesus *3:166*
Florence (1439) 4:118–19, 5:158
Nicaea 3:122–3, *3:123*, 3:141, 4:54
Pisa (1409) 5:116
Siena (1423–1424) 5:116
Troyes (1129) **5:155**
Worms (1048) 5:102
Counter-Reformation 6:48, 6:55–9, **6:55**, 6:63,
6:73–4, 6:87, 6:158, *7:10*, 7:24
Jesuits and 6:56–7
as missionary stimulus 6:171

Counter-Reformation (cont.)
in Poland 6:98
sale of indulgences ended by 6:56
see also Protestant Reformation; Protestantism
Courbet, Gustave (1819–1877), French artist
7:51
cranial development **1:25**
of hominids 1:24, **1:24**, 1:31, *1:31*, *1:34*,
1:37
of *Homo sapiens* *1:35*
of the Proconsul **1:16**
see also brain size
Crassus, Marcus Licinius (c.108–53 BCE), Roman
politician 3:42–3, *3:44*
Creoles 6:142–3, 8:24
Cresilis, Greek sculptor *2:156*
Cretaceous period **1:12**, **1:14**
Crete 8:119
agriculture of 1:144
conquest by Ottoman Turks 4:122
German capture of 9:72
Greek language of 1:140
loss by Venice 6:94
Minoan script of 1:140
Neolithic culture of 1:142–3
recovery by Byzantium 4:62
unification with Greece 9:35
wool of 1:144
see also Knossos; Minoan civilization
Crimea 6:116, 6:118–19
Crimean Tatars 6:118
Crimean War 7:129–30, *7:129*
Croatia 7:123, 7:125, 10:151
Croesus (d. c.546 BCE), king of Lydia 2:100,
2:109–10, 2:112, *2:112*
Cro-Magnon man *1:38*, **1:39**
Cromwell, Oliver (1599–1658), English soldier-
statesman 6:64–5, **6:65**, 6:88–9, 6:159–60
crusades 4:44, *4:103*, 5:103, 5:150–7
Albigensians 5:111
capture of Jerusalem and 5:151, **5:153**
Eighth (1270–1272) 5:154
First (1096–1099) 4:102, *5:6*, 5:107,
5:150–51, **5:153**, 5:154
Fourth (1202–1204) **4:74**, 4:75–6, *4:76*, 4:94,
5:153
massacres of prisoners and Jews and 5:151
military orders and 5:155–7, **5:155**
moral justification of 5:154
overseas imperialism and 5:153–4
religious fervour and 5:150–1
sack of Constantinople and 5:153–4
Second (1147–1149) 5:151
Seljuk Turks and 4:100, 4:102
Third (1189–1192) 4:103, *5:151*,
5:153
Ctesiphon
Parthian capital
conquest by Ardashir I 3:108
conquest by Trajan 3:43
Sassanid capital 4:31
Cuba 8:28, 8:30–31, 8:62, 10:68–71
infant mortality in 10:70
as member of COMECON **10:98**
missile crisis 10:12, 10:70–71, *10:71*,
10:78–9
request for arms by *10:72*
revolution in 10:68–9, 10:70–71
social reform in 10:70
Spanish settlement in 6:139
troops in Angola 10:61–2

Cuba (cont.)
United States and 10:69
Cuban missile crisis see Cuba
cultures (prehistoric)
Acheulian 1:27
Aurignacian 1:42
classified by implements 1:41
interaction between 1:72–3
Magdalenian 1:42, 1:49
Mousterian 1:36
Neolithic see Neolithic culture
Olduvan 1:27
Solutrean 1:42
Cuman peoples 4:16, 4:94
Curie, Marie (1867–1934) and Pierre
(1860–1906), French scientists 9:140
currency 1:138–9, 2:81
coinage see coinage
cowry shells 2:46
paper money 4:109
Curzon, George Nathaniel (1859–1925), Viceroy
of India 8:6
Cuzco 5:98, 5:99, 6:139
Cyclades 1:144, 1:154, 4:75
cylinder seals 1:80, 1:100
Cyprus 1:157, 1:173
annexation by Rome 3:27
conquest by Arabs 4:61
conquest by Ottoman Turks 4:122
lost by Venice 6:94
raiding by Arabs 4:25
recovery by Byzantium 4:62
Cyril, St (9th century CE)
Cyrillic alphabet 4:79–80, 4:91
Slavs and 4:79–80, 4:80, 4:93
Cyrus the Great (d. 529 BCE), king of Persia
1:178, 2:75, 2:76–8, 2:111
enlightened government of 2:77–8
king of Lydia, defeat by 2:111, 2:112
temple in Jerusalem and 2:77
tomb of 2:76, 2:81
Czechoslovakia 8:158
and EC 10:151
communist coup in 9:95, 9:95
communist government in 10:9, 10:149
Egypt, arms deal with 10:45
elections in 10:149
frontiers opened to East Germans 10:148
liberalizing movement in 10:96, 10:97
minorities in 8:160
Nazi occupation of 9:66–7, 9:66
Warsaw Pact invasion (Prague Spring) 10:96,
10:140, 10:140
Czechs, revolt against Habsburg rule 7:123,
7:124

D

Dacia, Roman province
abandonment of 3:112
conquest by Trajan 3:42, 3:44
gold mines of 3:69
Dada school of art 9:50, 9:51
Dhammapada 2:26
Dahomey, conquest by French 8:58
Dali, Salvador (1904–1989), Spanish artist 9:164
Dalmatia 4:140
Damascus
Amorite kingdom of 1:93

Damascus (cont.)
British capture of 9:39
Great Mosque of 4:29–30, 4:39, 4:113
surrender to Mongols 4:107
Umayyad caliphate 4:24, 4:28–9, 4:29, 4:31,
4:42
Dampier, William (1652–1715), English explorer
6:177
Dance of the Negro Slaves 6:24
Danegeld 4:155, 4:157
Danelaw 4:156, 4:158
Danes see Denmark; Norsemen (Vikings)
D'Annunzio, Gabriele (1863–1938), Italian
writer 8:170
Dante Alighieri (1265–1321), Italian poet 4:38,
5:122, 5:122, 5:171, 5:173
Danube River 3:42, 3:110–11, 3:125, 3:129,
3:132
Danzig (Gdansk) 9:67
Dardanelles campaign (Gallipoli) 8:148, 9:38,
9:38, 9:45
Darius I (c.558–486 BCE), king of Persia 1:178,
2:77, 2:78–9, 2:78, 2:111, 8:19
annexation of Thrace and Macedonia by
2:111, 2:112
failure against Scythians 2:112
Darius III, king of Persia (335–330 BCE)
Alexander the Great and 2:161–3, 2:163
Darkest England (Booth) 7:62
Darwin, Charles (1809–1882), British scientist
8:125–6, 8:125, 8:125, 9:50, 9:51, 9:144
Descent of Man, The 8:126
Origin of Species, The 8:125, 8:126
Dasgupta, Surendranath, Indian historian 2:23
Daumier, Honoré (1808–1878), French artist
7:136
David, Jacques-Louis (1748–1825), French artist
7:90, 7:103–4
David, king of Israel (c.1060–979 BCE) 1:168–9
Da Vinci, Leonardo (1452–1519) Italian artist
and inventor 7:6
Dayan, Moshe (1915–1981), Israeli minister of
defence 10:49
Dead Sea Scrolls (Qumran writings) 3:80, 3:80,
3:81
death-rates see infant mortality; mortality
Deccan 2:9, 2:20, 5:24, 5:28, 5:32, 5:34
Dravidian rule in 5:16
Decius, Gaius Nessius Quintus (201–251 CE),
Roman emperor
murder by Goths 3:118
persecution of Christians by 3:117
Declaration of Independence, American 7:72,
7:77, 7:77, 7:85, 7:161
Declaration of the Rights of Man and of the
Citizen 7:92, 7:94, 7:98–9
Declaration of the Rights of Women and Citizens
(Olympia de Gouges) 8:114
The Decline of the Carthaginian Empire (Turner)
7:41
deforestation see environmental concerns
Degas, Edgar (1834–1917), French artist 7:157
de Gaulle, Charles (1890–1970)
and Free French forces 9:70, 9:71
French president 10:47, 10:100–101, 10:100
de Klerk, F. W. (1936–), president of South
Africa 10:63
Delacroix, Eugène (1798–1863), French artist
7:118, 7:122
De legibus Angliae (Bracton) 4:175
De l'esprit des lois (Montesquieu) 6:36

Delhi 8:98
Babur and 5:26
capital of India
sacked 4:114
sultanate of 5:24–5
Timur Lang and 4:114, 5:24
Turkish sultans and 5:24
Delian League, the 2:118–20, 2:129, 2:131,
2:159
Delphi, site of oracle of Apollo 2:96, 2:97,
2:112, 2:137, 2:151
Athenian treasury at 2:119
decline of 2:173
theatre at 2:149
Demidov family, Russia 6:112
democracy, Athenian 2:105, 2:119,
2:122, 2:131–6, 2:131, 2:133, 2:134, 2:135,
2:157
aristocracy and 2:132
ostracism in 2:132
replacement by oligarchy 2:160
Socrates and 2:133, 2:136–7, 2:143
voting procedure in 2:131, 2:131, 2:132,
2:132–3
see also government and administration
Democracy in America (Tocqueville) 7:158,
7:159
demographic changes, world-wide 9:117–124
birth rates 9:117–18, 9:121–2, 9:122
differences in 9:119
economic growth and 9:123
emigration and immigration 9:121
in India and Pakistan 9:102–3
life expectancies 9:120
Malthusian theory of 9:118, 9:156
mortality rates 9:122
infant mortality 9:119, 9:120, 9:120
population density 9:121
population distribution 9:120, 9:121
population growth rates 1:73
pressure on resources 9:156–7
see also population; population growth
demographic patterns in the ancient world
in the Aegean 1:154, 2:92–3
in the Hellenistic world 2:167
over-population pressures 1:73
population growth rates 1:73
prehistoric 1:46, 1:54, 1:56, 1:58
Demosthenes (c.384–322 BCE), Athenian orator
2:157–60
Deng Xiaoping (1904–1997), Chinese communist
leader 10:110–11, 10:110–11, 10:154,
10:155
Denmark 4:138, 4:148, 4:157, 9:69
see also Norsemen
depression (economic)
in Germany post–1918 9:53
in Great Britain 9:98, 9:100
in Japan between wars 9:23
in Latin America 10:65
in United States, Great Depression 9:49,
9:54–5, 9:89
see also economic development
Derbent 4:128
Descartes, René (1596–1650), French
philosopher 6:71, 7:25–7
Description of Egypt, The 1:64
Devi, Hindu mother-goddess 5:20, 5:21
Devonport 6:163
dhamma or dharma 2:20, 2:24, 5:12–13, 5:18
diadochi, Alexander's "Successors" 2:164,
2:167

Dialogue on the Two Great Systems of the World
(Galileo) 7:23
diamonds 8:34, 8:37, 8:37
Diamond Sutra, earliest printed book 5:55
Díaz, Porfirio (1830–1915), president of Mexico
10:64, 10:64
Dickens, Charles (1812–1870), British writer
8:109
Diderot, Denis (1713–1784), French philosopher
7:30, 7:31, 7:31, 7:47
Didyma, oracle of Apollo 2:96
diet see food and diet
Diets
of Augsburg (1548) 6:49, 6:50
of Worms (1521) 6:49
Diocletian (Gaius Aurelius Valerius Diocletianus)
(245–316 CE), Roman emperor 3:14,
3:113–15, 3:114
Christians, persecution of 3:118
Dionysus, Greek god, festivals of 2:100,
2:148–9, 2:148
diplomacy
British imperial 6:160
commercial and colonial 6:20, 6:89,
6:130–31, 6:157–8, 6:160
professional 6:43, 6:78–9, 6:108
Venetian 6:78, 6:158
see also treaties and individual countries
The Discourse of Method (Descartes) 7:27
Discoveries of Captain Cook and de la Pérouse,
The 6:157
Discovery of the World, The (Marco Polo)
4:110
diseases
in Africa 5:85, 6:122, 6:127, 6:177
in China 10:27
effects of on native populations 6:140, 6:143,
6:145, 6:168, 6:170
epidemics 6:10, 6:14, 6:111, 9:103
in Europe 5:140, 5:148, 6:14, 7:45
bubonic plague 5:140–1, 5:140–41, 6:10,
6:14, 7:45
influenza epidemic 9:103
mental illness 9:165
smallpox 6:10, 6:143, 6:168
spread by colonizers 6:140, 6:143, 6:145,
6:168
syphilis 6:146
tropical 8:53, 8:63
in United States 10:84
vaccination 8:129
Disraeli, Benjamin (1804–1881), British prime
minister 8:141, 9:33
dithyramb, origin of Greek drama 2:148, 2:148
divination
by interpretation of omens 3:10
Oracle of Fortuna Primigenia 3:21
by reading of auguries 3:12
see also oracles
Divine Comedy (Dante) 5:122, 5:171
Djoser, king of Egypt (2630–2611 BCE) 1:105
DNA 1:46
A Doll's House (Ibsen) 8:115
dolmens 2:68, 2:70
see also megalithic monuments
Dome of the Rock, Jerusalem 4:39, 4:40
Domesday Book 5:124, 5:124, 5:147, 5:178
domestication of animals 1:53, 1:53, 1:54,
1:55
in China 2:34
in India 2:11, 2:20

Dominic, St (1170–1221), founder of Dominican order 5:111
Dominican order of friars (Dominicans) 5:109, 5:111–12
    St Thomas Aquinas and 5:168, **5:169**
    Savonarola and 5:117
    universities, formation of and 5:111
    see also Franciscan Order
Dominican Republic 8:28, 8:31
    American intervention in 10:71–2
Domitian (Titus Flavius Domitianus) (51–96 CE), Roman emperor 3:41
    residence on Palatine Hill **3:45**
Donation of Constantine 4:162
Donatists, Christian schismatics 3:121, 3:141, 5:86
    Augustine's attacks on 3:143–4, 3:148
Don Quixote (Miguel de Cervantes) 7:14
Dorians 1:153–4, 2:90
drainage and irrigation
    in Egypt 1:108, 1:118
    in Mesopotamia 1:77, 1:89–90
    well-sweeps 1:118
Drake, Francis (c.1545–1596), English navigator 6:144
drama see under Greek literature
drugs, pharmaceutical, imported into Europe 6:166
Dual Monarchy (Austro-Hungarian) 7:131
Dubcek, Alexander (1921–1992), Czech politician 10:140
Dumuzi, god of Sumer 1:77
Dupleix, Joseph (1697–1763), French governor in India 6:136
Dura-Europos 3:121
    synagogue of 3:73
    temple of Palmyran gods in 3:75
Durbars 8:6, 8:65, 8:98
Dutch, see the Netherlands
Dur Sharrukin 1:177
Dyck, Anthony van (1599–1641), Flemish artist 6:64
dynasticism 6:79–81, 6:87, 6:93–4

E

East Africa 6:122
    Italian 9:57
    Portuguese 8:57, 8:59
    Swahili speakers in 5:89
    see also Africa; British Empire; Olduvai Gorge; names of individual countries
East Bengal (Muslim) 8:97
    see also Bangladesh, Judia, Pakistan
East Berlin 10:77–8
    Berlin Wall 10:6, 10:78, 10:79, 10:147–8, 10:147, 10:149
    see also German Democratic Republic
East Germany see German Democratic Republic
East India Company (British) 5:31–2, 6:133, 6:135, 6:137, **6:138**, 6:166, 6:166, 6:176, 8:45, 8:46
    charter of 8:46
    dissolution of 8:51, **8:51**
    in Ormuz 4:127
East India Company (French) 5:35, 6:137, **6:138**

East India Company (Dutch) 6:131, 6:131–3, 6:166, 6:173, 8:103
Easter Island **6:177**
Eastern Mediterranean,
    classical culture of 2:86–8, 2:89, 2:124–5
    civilization of 2:84–5
    import of metals into 2:85
    languages of 2:87
    topography of 2:84–5
    see also Mediterranean
Eastern Question 7:122–3, 7:129–30, 7:144–5
Eastern Roman Empire see Byzantine Empire
Ebert, Friedrich (1871–1925), president of Weimar Republic 9:53
economic development 3:68–9, 3:70
    Adam Smith's theories of 7:28, 7:42, 8:16
    Africa, cash economy in 10:53
    agricultural base of 3:15, 3:69, 3:104–7
    capital investment and 7:47, 7:49, 7:54–5, 7:58, 7:151
    capitalism and 6:20–2
    Cold War and 10:15–16
    creation of wealth and 9:126–8, 9:132
    in Europe 8:107–8, 8:115
        collapse 8:177, 9:58, 9:91–2
        industrialization 6:24–6
        inter-war economic recovery 8:174–5
        northwestern Europe, importance of 6:19, 6:22
        state intervention 8:113, 8:178
        taxation 8:113
        unemployment 7:46, 7:63, 7:120, 7:123, 7:126, 7:126, 7:133, 8:108, 8:164, 8:178
    fiscal policies 3:46, 3:104–7, 3:114, 3:119, 3:165–6
    Free Trade 7:66–70, 7:69, 7:173
    gold discoveries and 7:133
    individualism and 7:66, 7:127
    inflation 3:107, 3:135, 6:26–7, 6:28, 6:31, 6:60, 6:68, 8:80, 8:84, 8:97, 8:170, 8:175, 10:103
    internationalization of capital markets 10:176
    laissez-faire theory of 7:65–6, 7:136, 7:147, 9:49
    Latin American economic crisis 10:74
    market economy, impact of 7:127, 7:167
    medieval recession 4:168–70
    money economy, restoration of 3:119
    national economies, world-wide growth of 9:125–8
    post-war world crisis 8:175–8
    socialism and 7:135–40
    state intervention and 7:65, 9:49, 9:56, 9:175–6
    steel production and 9:133
    tariff policies 8:61, 8:90, 8:101, 8:175, 8:177–8
    taxation 3:106, 3:114, 3:127–8, 3:133, 3:135
    trade 3:69, 3:70, 3:109–10, **3:109**, 3:128
    United Nations Economic and Social Council Organization (UNESCO) **9:85**
    wage and price freeze 3:114
    weaknesses of 3:104–7
    World Economic Conference 9:49
    world economy
        collapse of 8:177
        re-integration **9:88**, 9:177
    World War I and 8:121, 8:149, 8:156, 8:164, 8:167, 8:167
    see also depression and individual countries
Edessa, county of 4:102, 5:151

Edict of Milan 3:120–21
Edo (modern Tokyo)
    nobles, residence in 5:78, 5:81
    population of 8:80–81
Edomites 1:169
education 7:15, **7:32**
    clerical domination of 4:167, 5:166
    demand for 5:176
    of Egyptian scribes 1:108
    literacy and 7:14–15
    medieval scholasticism 5:168–9
    in New England 7:14
    public, neglect of 7:14, 7:173
    reform of 7:34
    Rousseau's influence on 7:38
    in Sumer 1:85
    universities as unifying Christian force in 5:166–7
    value of 7:12
    see also universities
Edward II (1284–1327), king of England 4:179
Edward III (1312–1377), king of England 5:125
Edward the Confessor, St (c.1003–1066), king of England 4:177
Egypt, Ancient 1:54, 1:58–61, 1:73, 1:93, 2:60
    Alexander the Great in **2:160**
    Alexandria 4:61
    arable land in **1:103**
    architecture in 1:108–10
    art in 1:64, 1:108, 1:115–16
        bas-relief 1:103
        Cretan influence on 1:146
        Mesopotamian influence on 1:100, 1:101, 1:103, 1:115
        naturalistic style of 1:115, 1:119–22, 1:123, 1:127
        New Kingdom revitalization of 1:126
        sculpture 1:108–9, 1:126
        wall paintings 1:120–1, 1:126
            in tombs 1:117, 1:119–20, 1:122–4
    Assyrians and 1:173, **1:173**, 2:75
    bureaucracy of 1:107–8
    Buddhist missionaries in 5:13
    calendar of 1:111–12
    chronology 1:104–5, **1:105**
    cities, growth of 1:69
    coinage of 1:39
    contraception in 1:118
    daily life in **1:122**
    decline of 1:128–9, 1:167, 2:74–5
    diseases of 1:114, 1:119
    dynasties of 1:104, **1:105**
    foreign relations in 1:124, 1:126, 1:126, 1:127
    Greek culture, influence of 2:73, 2:75
    Hamitic people in 1:102–3
    Hebrews in 1:129, 1:162
    historical periods of 1:103
        Old Kingdom 1:104, 1:106, 1:118, 1:124–5
        First Intermediate Period 1:104, **1:105**, 1:124, 1:125
        Middle Kingdom 1:104, 1:107, 1:114, 1:125–6
        Second Intermediate Period 1:104, **1:105**, 1:125
        New Kingdom 1:104, 1:106–7, 1:126–9, 1:146
        Ptolemaic period 2:164, 2:165, 3:38
    Hyksos incursions 1:125–6, 1:134, 1:146
    imperial expansion 1:126, 1:126
    influence beyond Nile valley 2:58

Egypt, Ancient (cont.)
    Julius Caesar and Cleopatra 3:34
    labour conscription in 1:120
    labour force of 1:108–9, 1:129
    limitations of 1:118, 1:129–31
    magic in 1:113, 1:118
    mathematics in 1:111
    medicine in 1:118–19
    metal working in 1:58, 1:118
    monarchy in 1:103, 1:105–7, **1:105**
        descent through female line 1:123
        divinity of kings 1:106–7
        foreign marriage policy 1:126–9
        pharaohs, role of 1:106–7
        rituals associated with 1:106
    mortality rates, infant, in 1:119
    mummification in 1:114, 1:119
    Nubia, conquest of 1:125, 1:125
    peasant society in 1:120
    Persia, independence from 2:156
    political organization in 1:102–3
    religion in **1:112**
        afterlife 1:107, 1:114, **1:122**
        Aton, cult of 1:115, 1:127, 1:127
        Book of the Dead 1:67, 1:118
        death and burial rituals 1:113–14, 1:113
        diversity of 1:115
        divinity of kings in 1:106–7, 1:125
        gods in 1:114, 1:123
        magic 1:113
        tombs 1:117, 1:119, 1:122, **1:122**, 1:123
        see also religion; temples
    rule by the Kushite kingdom 2:62, 2:74–5, 2:74
    scribes in 1:108–9
    sea peoples attack 1:127–9, 1:133, 1:161
    ships in 1:101, 1:102, 1:102, 1:137
    symbolism in 1:113
    technology in 1:109, 1:110–11, 1:118
    unification of 1:104
    see also pyramids
Egypt, medieval and modern
    Anglo-French settlement and 8:144
    annexation by Rome 3:38–9
    anti-American policy in 10:47
    Arab conquest of 5:87
    Arab League in 9:110
    Aswan High Dam 10:45, 10:45
    bankruptcy of 9:32
    as British protectorate 8:57, 8:57, 9:33
    Christianity in 3:123, 3:126, 3:166–7, 3:168
    constitution of 9:33
    Coptic Church in 3:142, 3:167, 3:169, 3:170, 4:54, 4:55
    European intervention in 9:31–3, 9:32
    Fatimid caliphate of 4:43, 4:43, 4:96, 4:97, 4:102
    independence of 6:97
    Islamic fundamentalism in 10:123
    Israel, peace with 10:121
    Mehemet Ali, pasha of 8:53, 9:30
    modernization of 9:30–31
    Monophysites 3:169
    Muslim conquest of 4:24, 4:25, **4:25**
    Napoleon's expedition to 8:52–3, 8:55
    nationalism in 9:31–3, 9:42,–3, 9:109
    Ottoman Turk conquest of 4:122, 6:95
    Persian invasion of 4:12
    population growth in 10:43

Egypt, medieval and modern (cont.)
  protectorate ended in 9:42
  religious disaffection in 4:26
  revolution (1882) 9:32, *9:32*
  Saddam Hussein, opposition to 10:135
  Saladin's seizure of power in 4:102
  Six Day war in 10:48–9
  Suez crisis and **10:43**, 10:45–6
  Syria, split with 10:121
  xenophobia in 9:32–3
  Yom Kippur war and 10:50, *10:50*
  see also Israel; Nasser; Palestinians; PLO; Suez
    Canal; Syria
Einhard (c.770–840 CE), Carolingian intellectual
  4:136, 4:143
Einstein, Albert (1879–1955), German-Swiss
  physicist 9:141, *9:141–3*
Eisenhower, Dwight David (1890–1969), United
  States president 9:83, 9:88, **10:12**, 10:14,
  10:47, 10:85, 10:89
Elam, kingdom of 1:91, 1:173, 2:76, *2:78*
  ruled by Achaemenids 1:176
Elamite people 1:78
  conquer Ur 1:92–3
El-Andalus (Islamic Spain) 4:41–3, **4:42**
Elba *1:99*, 3:11
  Bonaparte exiled to 7:111, *7:113*
electricity 9:129, 9:130
  as new energy source 8:107, 8:116, 8:129
  Faraday's studies in 8:126, *8:126*
  hydro-electric schemes 9:56, 9:133
  solar power and 9:133
electro-magnetism 9:140
elephants, used in warfare 2:18, 2:161, 3:19,
  3:28
Elijah (c. mid-9th century BCE), Hebrew prophet
  1:170
Elizabeth I (1533–1603), queen of England
  5:28, 5:31–2, 6:29, 6:54, 6:60, 6:62, 6:86,
  6:103, **6:107**, 6:158, *6:158*, 6:162
Elizabeth II (1926–), queen of Great Britain and
  Northern Ireland 10:154
Elizabeth Petrovna (1709–1762), empress of
  Russia *6:113*
Embarkation of the Doge of Venice, The 6:30
emigration, European, to Americas 6:18,
  6:150–51, 6:153
Emma, queen of Normandy *4:157*
Emporiae, Greek city 3:23
Enclosure Acts (England) 6:17, 7:49
encomienda system 6:142, 6:168
Encyclopédie (Diderot and d'Alembert) 7:20,
  7:30, 7:31, *7:31*, 7:47
energy 8:107, *8:116*, 9:133, *9:133*, 9:157
  hydro-electric schemes 9:56, 9:133
  input to agriculture of 9:128
Engels, Friedrich (1820–1895), German socialist
  7:61–2
engineering
  European 6:24–5, *6:25*
  Roman **3:52**
  see also technology
England
  agricultural progress in 6:17
  under Alfred 4:156–7
  Angevin inheritance of 5:124
  Calvinism in 6:51
  centralized government in 6:81
  Civil War of 6:63–4, *6:64*, 6:65–6
  class structure in 6:28–9, *6:29*, 6:30–33
  commercial developments in 6:20–2

England (cont.)
  Commonwealth 6:65–6, 6:159–60, 6:162
  Danish empire and 4:157
  defensive burghs in 4:156
  diplomacy, commercial and colonial, of 6:89
  foreign policy of 6:88–9
  France and 5:125–6
  Grand Alliance 6:91
  industrialization in 6:26
  monarchy in
    constitutional 6:69–70, 6:104
    legislative 6:69–70
    restoration of 6:66, *6:66*
  nobility 6:28–9
    powers surpassed by monarch
      6:41–2
  Norman administration of 5:124
  Norse raids on 4:154, 4:156
  papal authority, rejection of 5:114
  papal interdict and 5:113–14
  Parliament of *see* Parliament
  Peasants' Revolt in 5:141
  rebellions in 6:42–3
  Republic *see* England, Commonwealth
  Revolution *see* England, Civil War
  shire structure of 4:157
  slave trade and **6:147**, 6:160, 6:162,
    6:169–70
  social change in 6:30–1, 6:33–4
  South Sea "Bubble" 6:20
  standing army of 6:68
  taxation in 6:67
  trade 5:35, 6:22
    with India 5:31–2
    with Persia 4:127
  Tudor administrative measures in 6:42
  union with Ireland (1801) 7:177
  union with Scotland (1707) 6:91
  wool trade in 6:25–7
  see also British Empire; Church of England;
    Great Britain; India; wars and individual
    monarchs
English colonies 6:151–2, **6:155**
  Caribbean 6:168, 6:172
    Barbados 6:146–7
    St Christopher (St Kitts) 6:146
  North America 6:146, 6:151–53
    Maryland 6:150
    New York *6:149*
    Virginia 6:148–50
    Sierra Leone 6:170
  slave trade in **6:147**, 6:169–70
  see also British Empire and individual
    territories
English Muscovy Company *6:102*
English Revolution 6:66
Enki, Sumerian god 1:84
Enkidu **1:81**, 1:82–3
Enlightenment 7:26–38, **7:26**, 7:29, 7:70, 7:96,
  8:124
  anti-clericalism and 7:37
  Catholicism and *7:8*
  despotism, relations with 7:36–7
  earthly happiness, concept 7:30, 7:37
  God's role in universe 7:30
  intellectualism and 7:32
  liberalism, contribution to 7:37
  optimism and 7:27–8, 7:30
  Papacy, criticism of 7:37
  religious scepticism and 7:28–30, 7:37
Enlil, Sumerian god 1:84, *1:84*, 1:98

*Entry into the City of Lima of the Viceroy of
  Peru* *6:140*
Enver Pasha (Enver Bey) (1881–1922), Turkish
  politician and soldier 9:34–7
environmental concerns 9:153–8, 10:160,
  10:171–2
  chemical fertilizers 9:128
  cities and 9:156
  deforestation *9:131*, 9:153, *9:157*, **9:157**,
    9:158
  desertification 9:154
  global warming 9:157–8, *9:159*, 10:159,
    10:177
  human damage 10:113, 10:171, *10:171*,
    10:177
  ozone layer 10:159
  pollution 9:154, *9:154*, 9:156, *9:159*
  toxic emissions *9:154*
Ephesus, Council of *3:166*
Epicureanism 3:51
Epicurus (341–270 BCE), Greek philosopher
  2:173–4, *2:173*
Epigrams (Martial) *3:58*
Erasmus, Desiderius (c.1466–1536), Dutch
  humanist scholar 5:172, **5:172**, 5:178,
  6:45–6, *6:45*, **6:48**
  on Luther 6:49
Eratosthenes (276–194 BCE), Greek scientist
  2:170, 2:175
Eretria 2:112
Eridu 1:79
Erigena, Johannes Scotus (c.815–877 CE), Irish
  philosopher 5:168
Eritrea 8:57
Eskimos (Inuit) 4:154, 5:92, 8:38
Essay on the Elements of Philosophy
  (d'Alembert) *7:28*
Essay on Population (Malthus) 7:42
Essenes, Jewish sect *3:80*
Estonia **9:67**, 9:72
  independence from Soviet Union 10:146–7
Ethelred II, king of England (978–1016) *4:157*
Ethiopia 2:58–9, *5:84*, 5:89, 6:127
  animal breeding in 5:85
  Christianity in 5:85–6, *5:87*, 8:13
  conquest of Kush by 5:85
  Coptic Church in 4:54, *4:55*
  hominid sites 1:19, 1:21
  independence of 8:13, 8:53, **8:56**, 8:57, 10:55
  invasion by Italy **8:161**, 9:57–8, *9:57*
  liberation of 9:76
  life expectancy in 9:120
  Marxist-Socialist republic in *10:56*, 10:58
  Muslim emigration to 4:23
  revolution in *10:56*
Etruscans 2:109, 2:177, *3:8*, 3:9–11, *3:10*, *3:11*
  Latin cities revolt against 3:12
  lifestyle and beliefs of **3:10**
Euclid (323–283 BCE), Greek geometrician
  2:170, 4:34, 4:167, 5:170
Euphrates River **1:72**, 1:76–7, 2:176, 2:177
  as frontier of Roman Empire 3:42, 3:43
Euripides (c.484–407 BCE), Greek tragedian
  2:126, **2:148**, 2:149, 2:150
Europa, Greek heroine 1:148
Europe 3:112, **6:88**
  Africa and **8:55**, 8:59
  agriculture in 5:133–4, 6:15–18, 7:47,
    7:50–2, 7:53, *7:53*
    Common Agricultural Policy (CAP) 10:100
  Arab incursions into 4:25, **4:25**, 4:26

Europe (cont.)
  aristocracy *see* nobility
  banking services in *5:130*, 5:135, 5:139,
    5:139
  China and 6:167, 7:32
  chivalry in 5:143, *5:143*
  Christianity, effects of *3:72*, 5:102, 5:118–19,
    5:174
  cities in 8:108–109
  class structure in 5:142–7, 6:27–33, 6:99,
    6:103, 6:104–5, 6:109, 6:116, 6:142–3
  currency in 6:20, 10:106–107
  communist parties in 10:99
  Council of Europe 10:98
  culture
    Christianity and 5:174
    classical heritage of 5:168–70
    humanist movement and 5:172, 5:176
    Islam, debt to 5:170–1, *5:171*
    Renaissance and 5:172–4
    Rousseau and 7:38
    secular culture 7:8
  Customs Unions 10:98
  dietary changes in 6:166
  disease in *5:148*
    bubonic plague 5:140–1, *5:140–1*, **6:10**,
      6:14, 7:45
    see also diseases
  East–West socio-economic contrast 6:31,
    6:34–5
  Eastern Bloc 10:139–53
    agricultural yields in 10:140
    central planning in 10:140–41
    dissident groups in 10:141
    economic stagnation in 10:139–40
    land ownership in 10:140
    see also Balkans, Baltic States, individual
      countries
  eastern boundaries of 5:158–9
  economy *see* economic development
  emigration 7:43, *7:150*, 8:21–2, **8:107**
    to the Americas 6:18
  expansion of 6:123–4
  exports to colonies 6:153
  famine in 6:17–18
  female suffrage in *8:113*, 8:114–19
  feudalism *see* feudalism
  French Revolution, impact on 7:116–17
  geographical limits of 4:131, 4:134–5, **4:139**
  Germanic invasions and 3:150
  Habsburg dynasty and 5:129
  hegemony in 8:6, 8:8–9, 8:20, 8:53, 8:90
    end of 8:139, 8:163, 8:178
  Holy Roman Empire in 5:129
  influence of 3:176, 6:168–70
  imperialism in 8:42, **8:43**, 8:54
  India and 5:30–2
  industrialization of 5:136–9, 6:24–6, 8:9,
    8:107–109, 8:111
    see also industrialization
  interwar economy of,
    "Iron Curtain" in 9:81–2
  life expectancy in 9:147
  literacy in 7:11–15, 7:45, 7:62, 7:63
  map of **4:139**
  maritime exploration and 5:159–66
  mechanical and engineering skills in 6:24–5,
    6:25
  medicine in 4:132–6, 5:147
  merchant status in 5:143–4
  Middle Ages in 5:100–1, 5:168–9

Europe (cont.)
military 4:175, 8:13–14, *8:15*
monarchical power in 5:120, 5:131, 6:41–2
mortality rates in 5:140, 5:147, 7:44–6
nationalism in 5:121–2, 6:81, 6:93–4
natural resources of 8:107
Nazi occupation of 9:91–2, *9:91*
oil crisis, effect of 10:106
parliamentary development in 5:132
peace settlement (1918) 8:156–60
peasants 5:134, 5:141
political unity, moves towards 10:100–101, 10:106
population, rural *6:16*
population growth 4:170, 5:132–3, 5:140–2, *5:144*, **6:10**, 6:11–14, **6:11**, **6:13**, 6:27, 8:9, 8:22, 8:106–107, 8:75–6, 8:177
see also population growth
post-1945
domination of 9:81
state boundaries of 10:15
prehistoric 2:64–71
late cultural development of 2:64–5, 2:69–70
megalithic monuments of 2:67–9, **2:67**, *2:69–71*
metallurgy in 2:66–7, 2:70
North-South divide of 2:65
peoples of 2:66–7
resources of 2:64, 2:67
religion in *see* Christianity; Protestantism; Roman Catholic Church
Renaissance states in 6:42, *6:42*, 6:44, 6:59, 6:67
revolution in 7:116–17, 8:109–10
rural unrest in 8:109
serfdom in 6:34–5
ship design in 5:159–61
slavery and 6:23, 6:170
social change in 6:27–33
spheres of influence in 8:9–10
supranational organizations in 10:97–100
supremacy, end of 8:139, 8:163
taxation in *see* taxation
technological superiority 5:136–9, 6:123–6
trade and commerce
development of 6:19
commercial fairs in 5:136, *5:136*
exports to colonies 6:153
overseas trade 6:22–3, 6:123–4
revival of 5:134–6, *5:135*, **5:136**
slump in (1847) 7:123
transport in 5:140
Turkish threat 6:94
unemployment in 7:46, *7:63*, *7:120*, 7:123, 7:126, *7:126*, 7:133
universities in 5:111
urbanization and growth 5:134–5, 6:13–14, **6:13**, 6:19
values, spread of 8:8–13
witch-hunting in 7:8
women in 5:146–7
see also agriculture; economic developments; individual countries; papacy; popes; Roman Catholic Church and following entries
European civilization 8:10–11, 10:165–70
European Coal and Steel Community (forerunner of EEC) 10:98
European Community (EC) 9:176, 9:177, 10:100, 10:106–7, 10:151

European Community (EC) (cont.)
Maastricht Treaty 10:107, *10:107*
see also European Economic Community; European Union
European Defence Community 10:99
European Economic Community (EEC) 10:99, 10:103, 10: 106, *10:106*, 10:107
British entry into 10:101
de Gaulle's view of 10:100
expansion of 10:106
Japanese economy and 10:113
Spanish entry into *10:106*
see also European Community; European Union
European Economic Cooperation and Development Organization for (OECD) 10:97
European Free Trade Association (EFTA) 10:100
European Monetary System (EMS) 10:107
European Parliament *9:176*
European Union (EU) **10:99**, 10:108
see also European Community; European Economic Community
evolution 1:11–18, **1:12**, **1:14**, 1:35, 1:46
see also Darwin; science
Experiment on a Bird in an Air-pump (Wright) 7:21
exploration
of Americas 6:139–41, **6:141**
of Pacific and Australasia 6:156, 6:177–8, **6:177**
by Portuguese **6:128**
Extraction of the Stone of Madness, The (Hieronymus Bosch) 6:9
Ezekiel (7th century BCE), Hebrew prophet 3:73
Ezra (mid-5th century BCE), Hebrew prophet 3:75

F

factories 7:57, 7:175
assembly lines in *9:134*, 9:135–6, *9:135*
legislation of 7:173, 7:176
social pressures and 7:65
timekeeping in 7:64
see also industrialization
Factory Act (1801) 7:175
Faisal I (1885–1933), king of Iraq 9:40, **9:40**
Falkland Islands, invasion by Argentina 10:104–105, *10:104*
Fall of the Roman Republic (Plutarch) 3:31
famine 6:14, 6:17–18, 6:111, 9:81, 9:125
in Africa 10:58
in China 5:50–51
in Europe 5:140–41, 8:156
in France and Europe 7:123
in Germany 8:150
in India 8:93, *8:94*, 9:103
in Ireland 7:46, 7:123, 7:177
Malthusian consequence of rising population and 7:43, 7:177
in Pakistan 9:103
in Russia 7:46, 8:152, 8:167, *8:167*, 8:169, 9:129
in Somalia *9:117*, *9:120*
Far East *see* individual countries
Faraday, Michael (1791–1867), British scientist 8:126, *8:126*, *9:143*

farming
subsistence 4:170
see also agriculture; ploughs and ploughing
Faroe Islands, colonization by Norsemen 4:153
Farouk (1920–1965), king of Egypt *10:44*
Fars 2:76
Fascism 8:165, 8:170–174, 9:52, 9:65
in Italy and Germany **8:170**
violence and 8:171–2
Fascist Doctrines (Mussolini) **8:172**
fasting (*sawm*) 4:22
Fatima, daughter of prophet Muhammad *4:43*
Fatimid caliphate in Egypt 4:43, *4:43*, 4:96–7
Saladin and 4:102
see also Egypt
federalism 10:15
Federal Republic of Germany 10:11, 10:15
NATO and 10:15, **10:16**
re-militarization of 10:15
see also Germanic people; Germany
Feminist movement 8:113–4, **8:114**, 8:115–7, *8:117*
Ferdinand I (1503–1564), Holy Roman Emperor *6:80–1*, 6:82, 6:85
Ferdinand II (1452–1516), king of Castile and Aragon *6:80*
Ferdinand V (1452–1516), king of Castile and Aragon 5:128, *5:128*, *7:8*
Ferraguti, Arnaldo (1850–1924), Italian artist *7:50*
Fertile Crescent, the 1:53–4, **1:72**, 1:73–4, 1:76, 1:92, 1:132–3
Assyria and 1:173, **1:173–4**
cereal crops of 1:53–4, 1:77
Hittite hegemony in 1:159–61
Indo-European peoples and 1:133
map of **1:72**
nomadic intrusions in 1:162, 1:175–6
feudalism 4:170–77, *4:171*, **4:172**, 5:142–4, 6:28, 6:39, 7:49, 7:52, 7:127
abolition in France 7:51, 7:92, 7:93, 7:98–9
chain of obligation in 4:173–6
chivalry and 5:143, *5:143*
in Japan 8:82–3
knights and *4:175*
landowners and 4:170–72
military aristocracies and 4:175–6, 5:142–3
monarchies and 5:120–1, *5:121*
origins of **4:172**
seigneurial authority undermined in 6:42
slavery and 4:173
tournaments and *4:176*
vassalage and 4:172–3, **4:172**, *4:174*, 4:175–6
Final Solution 9:63, 9:79
financial services *7:65*
banking *5:130*, 5:135, 5:139, *5:139*, **6:13**, 6:20, *6:20*, 9:127–8, *9:128*
chartered companies 6:20–1
Great War and 8:156
growth linked to expanding trade 6:166
life insurance 6:21–2, 6:166
London and 8:15
pre-industrialization and 7:58
stock exchanges 6:20, *6:164*
Finland **8:165**, **9:67**
Finns 2:66
fire
earliest use of 1:27
social consequences of 1:28

fire (cont.)
use by Peking man 2:32
First World War (1914–1918) 8:55, *8:121*, 8:139, *8:140*, 8:145–52, **8:146**, 8:155–6, 8:140–144, 9:36–40
Arab revolt against Turkey 8:149
British blockade of Germany 8:150–151
casualties of 8:147–8, 8:150, 8:152, 8:156
cost of 8:156
Dardanelles campaign 8:148, 9:38, *9:38*, **9:45**
Eastern Front **8:146**, 8:148
French army mutiny 8:152
German territorial losses 8:158
infant mortality and 8:150
Japanese economy stimulated by 9:9–10
Mesopotamia and 8:149
Passchendaele, battle of 8:152
propaganda in *8:140*, 8:150–51
Somme, battle of 8:147
stalemate in 8:147
submarine warfare in 8:150–152
Treaty of Versailles 8:156–8
United States and 8:151–2, *8:152*, 9:39
Verdun, battle of 8:147, *9:6*
Western Front **8:146**
see also weapons
fishing industry 6:22–3
Flanders 4:146, 5:126, 5:135–6, 5:138
drainage in 6:16
independent tendencies of 6:59
Protestant cities in 6:59–60
see also Antwerp
Fleming, Alexander (1881–1955), Scottish bacteriologist *9:144*
Florence, Council of 4:118–19, 5:158
Florence, republican city-state 5:117, 5:130, 5:135, *5:135*, 5:139–40, *6:14*, 6:84
foederati 3:132, 3:134–5, 3:153
food and diet
in Africa 6:172–3
carbohydrate consumption 1:52
changes, caused by new imports 6:166
cooking 1:27
crops imported from Europe 6:172
in Egypt 1:108
in Europe 4:169, 5:134, 6:14, *6:18*, 6:27
improved technology and 8:116
in India 5:10, 5:36
in Japan 5:77
meat-eating 1:21, 1:28
olives 1:144
sources of 1:41
storage of **1:138**
taboos 2:17
see also cereal crops
food production *see* agriculture
food riots
in Germany 8:150
in Russia 8:152
Ford, Gerald (1913–), United States president *10:96*
visit to China 10:110
Ford, Henry (1863–1947), United States automobile manufacturer 9:134
Ford Model-T 9:134, *9:134*, **9:134**, *9:135*
Formosa (Taiwan) 5:63, **9:21**, 9:106
cession to Japan 8:74, **8:86**
as Dutch trading centre 6:132
see also China; Taiwan
Fort St George 5:35
fortification 1:133, 1:159

Fortune Teller, The (Caravaggio) 6:28
fossil hominids 1:19, *1:20*, *1:23*
    at Hadar *1:18*
    "Lucy" *1:18*
    at Olduvai *1:19*, 1:21, **1:21–2**
France **5:129**
    Académie des Sciences in 7:10
    agriculture in 6:66, 7:51
    Alsace and Lorraine
        reacquisition by Germany 8:158
        seizure by Germany 8:120, 8:143
    and American War of Independence 7:78,
        7:85, 7:87
    anti-Bolshevik feelings in 8:162
    aristocracy in 6:29, 6:54–5, 6:67, 6:71
        legal privileges of 7:88, 7:97
        end of 7:93, 7:98
    ascendancy of under Louis XIV 6:89–91
    Bastille, storming of the *7:91*, *7:93*
    Bourbon dynasty 6:55, 6:73, 6:80–81, 7:103,
        7:105, 7:111
        last king of 7:120
        restoration of 7:105, 7:111, 7:118
    Calvinism in 6:51
    Capetian dynasty of 4:146–7, 5:124–6, 6:38
    censorship in 7:15, 7:90, 7:93
    centralized administration of 7:175
    class structure in 6:28–30, 6:32
    colonies and empire of 7:104–10, *7:107*
        Africa, decolonization 10:52
        Algeria in 9:108–109
            rebellion in 10:45–6, 10:52, 10:100
            withdrawal from 10:100
        Anglo-French settlement in Africa 8:144
        colonial assimilation policy of 8:100
        Compagnie des Indes 6:137
        Dien Bien Phu, defeat at 10:34
        imperialist policies of 8:52–53, 8:100
        in India 6:133, 6:135–7
        in Indo-China 8:42–3, 8:59, 8:74, **8:91**,
            9:28, 9:107–108, 10:34
            opposition to French rule 8:100–103
            tariff policy of 8:101
        Lebanon, influence in 9:36, 9:38, 9:108
        Louisiana Purchase and 7:154, **7:156**,
            7:159–60, **7:161**
        in North Africa 8:52–3, 8:57
        in North America 6:149, 6:152, 7:78
        slave trade and 6:169
        Syria, influence in 9:36, 9:38, 9:108
        Vietnam and 9:23, *9:108*
        in Windward Isles 6:146
    communist party in 9:59, 9:60, 9:87
    constitution of 7:92–5, 7:97–8
    cultural primacy of 7:34–5, 7:92
    currency in 7:98
    domination of Europe 7:104–6
    Dutch, conflict with 6:90
    Enlightenment philosophers in 7:25–8, *7:27*,
        7:27, 7:28, *7:30*, 7:31–2, *7:31*, **7:33**
    Estates General 7:87, 7:88–92, *7:88*, *7:94*
    Falklands war and 10:104
    February Revolution (1848) 7:123–4
    feudalism in 6:28
        abolition of 7:50–1, 7:92, 7:93, 7:98
    Franco-Russian alliance *8:135*
    Free French (Fighting French) 9:70, *9:71*
    Gaullist policies of 10:100–101
    German conquest of 9:68, 9:69–70
    Germany, war against 9:68
    Habsburgs, conflicts with 6:66, 6:84–5, 6:87

France (cont.)
    Huguenots *6:54*, 6:66, 6:68, 6:71
    industrialization in 7:58–9
    intendants 6:66–7, 6:70, 6:151
    July Monarchy 7:120–1
    land redistribution in 7:51
    language 7:13, 7:34
    literacy in 7:13
    medieval constitution in 7:87–8
    metric system in 7:98
    military and economic inferiority of 8:136
    military mutinies in 8:152
    monarchy
        absolute 6:67–8, 6:70–2, 6:75–6, 6:104
        end of 7:94–5
        National Assembly of 7:90, 7:92–4, *7:92*
            achievements of 7:93
    nationalism in 6:81, 8:120
    NATO, withdrawal from 10:100
    Norse raids in 4:154
    nuclear weapons programme 10:100, 10:176
    Paris 4:146–7, 4:150
    parlements in 6:67, 6:71, 6:75
    peasants' revolt *(jacquerie)* in 5:141
    philosophes 7:32–3, 7:35–8
    political parties, development of 7:90
    political stability of 6:68, 6:71
    population growth in 6:14, 6:18
    see also population growth
    population in Neanderthal times 1:46
    reform and modernization obstructed in
        6:75–6
    regionalism in 6:68
    religious intolerance in 7:36
    religious orders of 7:14
    religious wars in 6:54–5, *6:54*, **6:55**
    Revolution *see* French Revolution
    St Bartholomew's Day Massacre *6:54*
    salons in 6:35–6, *6:35*
    satellite republics of 7:106, 7:108–10
    Second Empire 7:130, *7:130*, 7:132
    Second Republic 7:124, 7:130
    Spain, conflict with 6:90
    taxation in 6:66–7, 6:71, 6:76, 6:77, 7:87–9, 8:113
    trade and 6:23, 6:34
    Treaty of Versailles and 8:156
    UN Security Council and 9:85
    Versailles, Palace of 6:71, 6:89, *6:90*
    Vichy State in 9:70
    wars
        Austria 7:130–1
        Austria and Prussia (1792) 7:94
        with Great Britain 7:95, 7:105, 7:111
        in Morocco 8:52
        see also wars
    West Francia, roots in 4:146, 4:150
    see also French Revolution; Gaul; names of
        individual persons and countries
Franche-Comté 6:82, 6:90, 6:92
Francis I (1494–1547), king of France 6:83,
    6:83, 6:84, *7:10*
Francis I (1708–1765), Holy Roman Emperor
    6:77
Franciscan order of friars (Franciscans)
    5:109–10, **5:110**, 6:129, 6:143
    Inquisition and 5:115
    Poor Clares and **5:110**
    see also Dominican Order
Francis of Assissi, St (1182–1226), founder of
    Franciscan Order 5:109–10, *5:110*, **5:110**
    rule of poverty 5:109, **5:110**, 5:115

Franco, Francisco (1892–1975), Spanish dictator
    9:64, *9:65*, *10:141*
Franconia (East Francia) 4:147
Frankish Church, reformation of 4:135, 4:140,
    4:143, 4:162
Franklin, Benjamin (1706–1790), North
    American philosopher 7:74, 7:80
Franks 3:129, 3:152–6, 3:176, *4:134*
    Arabs, defeat of 4:25, *4:25*, 4:26, 4:135
    in Belgium 3:152, 3:153
    Clovis, king of 3:152, 3:153–4, 3:156, **3:157**,
        3:158, 4:68–9
    colonization of Germany by 4:135
    Constantinople and 4:75–6, *4:76*, 4:116
    East Francia 4:146, *4:146*
    feudal system originated by **4:172**
    as *foederati* 3:153
    Merovingian dynasty of 4:135
    papacy and 4:135
    Rome, invasion of 3:111
    Spain and 4:41–3
    West Francia 4:146–7, 4:150
        effect of Norse raids on 4:155
    see also Carolingian dynasty; Carolingian
        Empire; Charlemagne; Germanic peoples;
        Goths; Ostrogoths; Visigoths
Franz Ferdinand (1863–1914), Archduke of
    Austria 8:145, *8:145*
Franz Josef (1830–1916), emperor of Austria-
    Hungary *8:134*, *8:141*, *8:143*
Frederick I (Barbarossa) (c.1123–1190), Holy
    Roman Emperor 5:151
Frederick II (1194–1250), Holy Roman Emperor
    5:166, 5:170
Frederick II, king of Denmark (1559–1588) *7:22*
Frederick II "the Great" (1712–1786), king of
    Prussia 6:74, *6:75*, 6:116–18, *6:117*, 7:34,
    7:35, 7:131
Frederick III "the Wise" (1463–1525), Elector of
    Saxony *5:142*, 6:47
Frederick William I (1688–1740), king of Prussia
    6:116
Frederick William (1620–1688), "the Great
    Elector" of Brandenburg 6:116, *6:116*
Free Cities 7:106
Free Trade 7:65–70, 7:173, 8:16–17, 8:137,
    9:49, 10:15
freemasons 7:11, *7:11*
French empire *see* France
French Indo–China *see* France
French Revolution 6:92, 7:85–98, *7:85*,
    7:87–90, 7:99–101, *7:101*, 7:118, 8:24,
    8:28, 8:103, **8:114**, **8:164**
    Bastille, storming of *7:91*, *7:93*
    Church, effects on 7:94, 7:98–9
    Committee for Public Safety 7:94
    Commune of Paris 7:135
    Directory (1795–1799) 7:98, 7:102, 7:108
    Estates General 7:87, 7:88–92, *7:88*, *7:94*,
        7:98
    Jacobins 7:94, *7:96*
    National Assembly (1789–1791) *7:90*,
        7:92–4, *7:92*, 7:93, 7:98
    National Convention (1792–1796) 7:94–7,
        7:96
    National Guard 7:93
    sans-culottes 7:95, 7:98
    social and cultural divisions aroused by
    socialist ideas and 7:137
    Terror, the 7:96–7
    see also Bonaparte, Napoleon; France; Paris

frescoes *3:57*, *3:73*, *3:75*, *3:166–7*
    Boscoreale villa *3:51*, *3:56*, *3:105–6*
Freud, Sigmund (1856–1939), founder of
    psychoanalysis **9:50**, 9:51–2, *9:51*, 9:164
Freyr, Norse god **4:83**, *4:156*
Friedrich, Caspar-David (1774–1840), German
    Romantic artist 7:39
Frisia
    missionary work in 4:164
    Norse raids on 4:154
Frisians (Germanic peoples) 3:129
Frith, William Powell (1819–1909), British artist
    7:55
Frondes 6:67–8, *6:68*, 6:71
fuels 7:55, 7:59
Fujiwara clan, Japan 5:69, 5:72–3
    art and 5:76

G

Gaddafi, Muammar (1941–), Libyan
    revolutionary leader *10:123*, 10:132,
    10:138, *10:138*
Gaeta (city-state) 4:151
Gagarin, Yuri (1934–1968), Russian cosmonaut
    9:147, 9:148, 10:80
Gainsborough, Thomas (1727–1788), English
    artist 6:17
Gaius, Roman Emporer *see* Caligula
Galen (c.130–c.200), Greek physician 5:147,
    5:171
Galerius Valerius Maximianus, Gaius
    (c.250–311 CE), Roman emperor 3:118,
    3:124
Galilei, Galileo (1564–1642), Italian astronomer
    7:18, 7:23, *7:23*
Gallipoli 9:38, *9:38*
    see also First World War
Galvao, Antonio, Portuguese seafarer **8:63**
Gama, Vasco da (c.1460–1524), Portuguese
    navigator and explorer 5:161, 6:123,
    6:123, *6:127*, 6:129
gambling 1:142, *1:142*
Gandhara, Persian satrapy 5:8
Gandhi, Indira (1917–1984), Indian prime
    minister 10:117–18, *10:117*
Gandhi, Mohandas (Mahatma) (1869–1948),
    Indian social and political leader 9:98–9,
    9:99, 9:100, *9:101*, 9:102, *9:102–3*
    in South Africa 8:36
Gandhi, Rajiv (1944–1991), Indian prime
    minister *10:117*
Ganga, Hindu goddess **5:20**
Ganges River 2:9, 2:16, **5:20**
Ganges valley 2:13, 2:17–18, 2:20, 2:28,
    5:10
    cultural domination of 2:18
    Gupta Empire 5:17
    Turkish rulers of 5:24
Garibaldi, Giuseppe (1807–1882), Italian
    nationalist *7:132*, 8:97
Garuda, Hindu god *2:25*
gas 8:116, *8:116*
Gascony 4:146
GATT (General Agreement on Tariffs and Trade)
    9:127–8
Gauguin, Paul, French artist *8:60*
Gaul
    barbarian invasions of 3:111, 3:132–4, 3:152

Gaul (cont.)
defeat by Caesar 3:32, 3:42
as Roman province 3:27
Toulouse, Visigoth kingdom of 3:132–3, 3:156, **3:157**, 3:158
Tournai, Frankish kingdom at 3:152, 3:153–4
see also France
Gautama, Siddhartha see Buddha, the
Gebel Musa *1:167*
General Assembly see United Nations Organization
General Theory of Relativity (Einstein) *9:141*
genetic engineering see biological sciences
Geneva, theocratic state under Calvin 6:51
Genghis Khan see Chinghis Khan
Genoa **4:74, 4:77,** 4:116, 4:119
and Sardinia 5:108, 7:117
republican city-state 5:130–31, 5:135, 5:139, *6:83*, 6:84, 6:93
Geographica (Strabo) **5:9**
geography 7:17
Geography (Ptolemy) 5:163–4
geological timescale 1:10–11, **1:12**
George III (1740–1820), king of Great Britain and Ireland 7:72, 7:75, 7:84, 8:67
George IV (1762–1830), king of Great Britain and Ireland 6:38, 7:177
George V (1865–1936), king of Great Britain and Ireland and emperor of India 8:65, 8:98
George, Henry (1839–1897), American economist 8:77
George, St, patron saint of England 5:122
Georgia (Caucasus)
and Russia 7:144
internal divisions 10:152, *10:153*
Georgia (North America) 6:151, **6:155**
German Democratic Republic (GDR, East Germany) *10:8,* 10:9, 10:11, **10:16,** 10:140
collapse of *10:147,* 10:148–9
elections and 10:149
Poland and 10:15
as Soviet satellite state 9:88, 9:93
Soviet support for 10:78
see also Germany
German Federal Republic (West Germany) 9:123–4, 10:11, 10:148–9, 10:151
currency reform in 10:9–10
NATO and *10:11,* 10:15, **10:16,** 10:99
unemployment and *10:107*
see also Germany (post 1945)
The Germania (Tacitus) **3:132**
Germanic peoples 3:129–33, 3:46, **3:132,** 3:158, 4:93, 4:135, *4:135*
Angles 3:150
Burgundians 3:129, **3:152,** 3:153
Franks see Franks
Frisians 3:129
Jutes 3:150
legions defeated by 3:42
Lombards see Lombards
migrations of the **3:126,** 3:129, 3:132–3, 3:150–52, **3:160**
Ostrogoths see Ostrogoths
Saxons 3:129, 3:150, 4:135, 4:137–8, 4:147
Teutonic tribes 2:66
and Rome **3:33,** 3:110–12
Thuringians 3:129
Vandals see Vandals
Visigoths see Visigoths

Germanicus Julius Caesar (15 BCE–19 CE), Roman general *3:39*
Germany (pre-1871) 7:132
Bismark, unification under 7:131, **7:134**
Catholic and Lutheran states in 6:49–50
Confederation of (1815) 7:108, **7:116, 7:134**
East Francia, roots in 4:146
emigration and 7:46
Enlightenment in 7:33
expansion of **5:129,** 5:156
Frankfurt National Assembly 7:125, **7:134**
Franks, colonization by 4:135
Golden Bull and 5:129, 6:83
Habsburg dynastic role in 6:82, 6:87–8
Habsburg-Hohenzollern struggle in 6:118
Hanse, Baltic trade league and 5:136
Holy Roman Empire and 5:128–9, 6:82–3
industrial capacity of 6:25
law in 7:52
Luther and Protestantism 6:47
Napoleonic reorganization of 7:106–8
naval power of 8:120, 8:144
Ottonian Empire and 4:148
political fragmentation of 4:147
popular uprisings in 7:127
Protestant Reformation in 6:47
reunification of *10:147,* 10:149
revolution of 1848 and 7:124–5
Russian trade and 8:175–6
slavery in 8:12
social strains in 6:32
urban developments in 5:135
see also Europe; First World War; German Democratic Republic; German Federal Republic; Second World War; individual German states
Germany (1871–1918) ("Second Reich") 7:131, **7:134**
African colonialism 8:55, 8:57, 8:148–9
diplomacy and *8:133*
First World War and 8:145–8, **8:146,** *8:147,* 8:150–152, *8:150,* 8:156
military planning of 8:143, 8:145
submarine campaign of 8:150–151
foreign policies of 8:120, 8:134, 8:151–2
industrialization in 7:58–9
industrial superiority of 8:136–7
nationalism in 8:120
Alsace and Lorraine, seizure of 8:120, 8:143
Social Democratic Party in 8:111
Turkish interest of 8:143
Germany (1918–1939) 9.52
and Italy 9:58, 9:64, 9:66
Anschluss of Austria 9:66, 9:66
and Marxism 8:173
anti-semitism 9:41, 9:61–3, *9:63*
Guernica, bombing of *9:65*
colonies of 8:160
communists and 8:165–6, 9:60
containment in 9:53–7
Czechoslovakia, occupation of 9:66–7, *9:66,*
economic collapse in 8:173
famine in 8:150
Fascism in 8:170–174, **8:170**
Final Solution 9:63, 9:79, *9:79,* 9:109–10
German-Soviet Pact of Non-Aggression 9:67–8, *9:67,* **9:67, 9:69**
Memel 9:66
Munich agreements 9:67–8
nationalism in 8:864, 8:173, 9:53, 9:57, 9:61–2, 9:66, 9:69

Germany (1918–1939) (cont.)
National Socialist (Nazi) Party see Nazi Party
Nuremberg Laws *9:63*
Olympic Games in (1936) *9:61*
Poland, invasion of **9:67,** 9:68, **9:69**
rearmament of 9:66
Reichstag fire in 9:62
and Polish corridor 8:160
Rhineland, re-entry to 9:66
Sudetenland, seizure of 9:66, *9:66*
Versailles settlement, revision of 9:52–3
and Versailles Treaty 8:158
unemployment in 8:178
war reparations 8:158, 8:175, *8:176*
Weimar Republic of 8:163, 9:53, *9:53*
Germany (1939–1945)
cities in 9:78, *9:80*
Crete, capture of 9:72
concentration camps in 9:79, *9:79*
conquests
Denmark 9:69
France 9:68, 9:69–70
Low Countries 9:69–70
Norway 9:69, *9:70*
North Africa, defeat in 9:77
Russia ("Barbarossa"), invasion of 9:72–3
Stalingrad, siege of 9:77
United States, war with 9:73–4
see also Second World War
Germany (post-1945) 9:82, 9:92–3, *9:93*
Iron Curtain and 10:9, 10:15
see also German Democratic Republic; German Federal Republic
Geta, Lucius Septimius, brother of Caracalla *3:103*
Ghana
kingdom of 5:86–8
republic of 10:53, 10:55
see also Gold Coast
Ghazan (1271–1304), Mongol Il-khan 4:113, *4:113*
ghazis (petty princes) 4:119, 4:125
Ghaznavid dynasty in Iran 4:99
eviction of 4:100
invasion of India by 5:23
Ghent 5:135
Gibbon, Edward (1737–1794), English historian 5:116, 7:13
Gibraltar 4:25
Gilgamesh, Epic of *1:79,* 1:80–2, **1:81,** 1:97, 1:174
Gilgamesh, king of Uruk (3rd millennium BCE) *1:81,* **1:81**
Gillray, James (1757–1815), British artist *7:100*
Giotto (1266–1336), Italian artist *5:110*
Giza, pyramids at 1:110
glaciation
effects of 1:13–14
variation during Quaternary **1:13**
see also climate; Ice Ages
gladiatorial games and wild-beast shows 3:12, 3:58–9, **3:60,** *3:92, 3:94*
Gladstone, William Ewart (1809–1898), British Liberal prime minister *7:179*
global warming see environmental concerns
"Glorious Revolution", England 6:70
Gnosticism 3:94–6, 3:141
Goa
annexation by Union of India *6:129*
missionary activity in 6:171

Goa (cont.)
Portuguese in *6:129,* 6:132
Gogol, Nicolai Vasilyevich (1809–52), Russian writer 2:150
gold 2:64–5, 2:157, 8:37
in Africa 5:86–7, *5:88–9,* 5:90, 5:135, 5:161, 5:177
from the Americas 6:27, 6:82, 6:139, 6:141–2, 6:165
Aztecs and 5:96
Californian, discovery of 7:133,8:35, **7:161**
Gold Coast 6:162
see also Ghana
Golden Horde 4:107, 4:112
divisions within 5:157–8
Muscovy 5:157
Timur Lang and 4:114
gold standard, international 8:15, 8:175
abandonment of 8:177–8
Golovkin, Count (1660–1734), Russian State Chancellor *6:106*
González, Felipe (1942–), Spanish prime minister *10:106*
Good Hope, Cape of 5:161, 6:122, 6:132, *6:173*
Gorbachev, Mikhail Sergeyevich (1931–), Soviet leader 10:136–8, *10:137,* **10:137,** *10:138,* 10:144, 10:146–7, 10:149–51
Andrei Sakharov and *10:83*
China visit 10:155
disarmament proposal of **10:12**
failed *coup* of (1991) *10:152*
policies of 10:137, **10:137,** 10:143, 10:148
resignation of 10:153
Goths
in Crimea 3:164
Moesia and Greece, invasion by 3:111
see also Franks; Germanic peoples; Ostrogoths; Visigoths
government and administration
of Abbasid caliphate 4:33–4
in the Alexandrine Empire 2:162
archives 1:80, 1:96, *1:147,* 1:148
authoritarian 6:34–5, 6:175
Aztecs and 5:96
bakufu (Japan) and 5:78, 5:81–2
Bengal, partition of 8:96–7
of British army in India 8:91–3, *8:93*
of British India 8:47–9, 8:90–91, 8:93–4, 8:97–8
of Byzantine autocracy 4:49–51, 4:56
in ancient China 2:44–5, 5:44–7
Chou period 2:37
religious mandate 2:42–3
Shang period 2:37
in city-states 2:101–8, **4:77,** 4:151
African 5:86, 10:56
divine kingship and 4:8
East India Company, role of 8:45–7
in Eastern Europe 6:34–5
in England 6:81
Europe
castles, role of *5:120*
feudal system 4:170–76
parliaments 5:130–2, *5:131*
royal bureaucracies 5:120–1
France, départements of 7:93, 7:103, 7:105, 7:109
in France, revolutionary 7:92–5, 7:97–8
in French Indo-China 8:100–103
in Germany 9:62, 9:63, 10:151

government and administration (cont.)
  in Greece
    city-states 2:101–8
    democracies see democracy, Athenian
    military aristocracies in 2:96–8, 2:106
    in Mycenae 1:151–2
    oligarchies in 2:104, 2:106, 2:122, 2:133,
      2:160
    tyrants in 2:104, 2:104, 2:105–6
  in the Hellenistic world 2:167–9, 2:170–3
  in India 5:11, 10:117–18
  Indian National Congress 8:95–7, 8:96,
    8:96
  intendants, France 6:66–7, 6:151
  international cooperation 9:176–7
  in Italian republic 5:130–1
  in Japan
    bi-cameral Parliament 8:83
    democracy 10:114
    franchise expanded by 9:9
    militaristic government 9:75
    prefectorial system 8:83
    shogunate 5:72, 5:72–3, 5:75, 5:78–9
  Left and Right, concept of 7:92, 7:97, 7:100,
    7:119
  legislative sovereignty 6:40–1, 6:68–70,
    6:75–6
  liberal democracy 9:173
  Manchu dynasty and 5:62
  in Minoan Crete 1:148–50
  Moghul Empire and 5:28, 5:36
  Mongols and 4:107, 4:109
  in the Near East 1:173
  of New France (Canada) 6:151
  in North American colonies 6:152–3
  Parthians 2:176
  in the Persian Empire 2:77–9, 2:81
  in Renaissance States 6:42, 6:59, 6:67
  representative bodies 7:115, 7:118
    decline of 6:41
    in English colonies 6:152–3, 6:174–5
  in Roman Empire,
    Constantine reform 3:119
    decline 3:127–8, 3:135
    Diocletian, reorganization under 3:113–14,
      governors, provincial 3:24–5
    imperial bureaucracy 3:39–40, 3:46–7,
      3:101–103, 3:113
    Justinian reform 3:164–6
      3:118
  Roman republic 3:12–17, 3:24–5
  Russian reforms 6:108–9
  Sassanid system 4:9–10
  of the Seleucid dynasty 2:167, 2:173, 2:167,
    2:169
  Seljuk Turks and 4:99, 4:101
  Spanish American colonies, viceroys in 6:140,
    6:141
  state power, growth of 6:76, 7:115–16,
    7:133–4, 9:170–171, 9:174–6
  T'ang dynasty and 5:43–4
  Tsarist Russia
    under Napoleon 7:103–6
    under Nicholas I 7:141, 7:143
  of Umayyad caliphate 4:30–31
  in United Kingdom, social legislation 7:173
  United States constitutionalism 7:81–5
  welfare state 9:175
  see also political systems
Goya, Francisco de (1746–1828), Spanish artist
  7:9, 7:50, 7:109

Gracchus, Gaius (153–121 BCE), brother of
  Tiberius Gracchus 3:29
Gracchus, Tiberius (163–133 BCE), Roman
  agrarian reformer 3:29–30
Granada, Muslim capital of Spain 4:42, 5:151
Grand Alliance against Louis XIV 6:91, 6:116
gravity 7:24
Great Altar of Zeus and Athene 2:146
Great Britain 6:72, 6:93, 6:120, 7:170
  Aden, withdrawal from 10:119
  Africa, decolonization in 10:52
  agricultural revolution in 7:48–50
    capital investments in 7:47, 7:49
    capitalist market economy and 7:49
  Anglo-French settlement 8:144
  Anglo-Japanese alliance 8:88, 8:144
  Boers, relations with 8:33–7
  colonial administration reforms of 7:74
  Colonial Development and Welfare Fund of
    10:53
  Corn Laws in 7:67–8, 7:69, 7:172–3
  diplomatic representation of 8:74
  economic growth in 6:33–4, 7:173,
    7:175–6, 8:15–16
  economy of 10:101, 10:103, 10:105
  EEC, entry to 10:100
  electoral reform in 7:171–2
  emigration from 7:170, 8:21–2
  Enclosure Acts 7:49
  Enlightenment philosophers in 7:26–8, 7:33
  European policies of 8:144–5
  formation of 6:91
  Free Trade in 7:66–70, 7:69, 7:173
  German competition with 8:17
  German industrial superiority and 8:137
  government, local reform in 7:173, 7:175
  Great Exhibition in (1851) 7:59, 7:173
  Home Rule of 10:101
  Hong Kong and 10:39, 10:41, 10:112
  House of Lords in 8:113
  IMF loan to 10:103
  imperial interest of 8:31–2, 8:44
  India, supremacy in 6:133–7, 6:136, 6:138
  industrial growth in 7:57–60
  industrial society, first 7:58, 7:137, 7:170
  inflation in 10:103
  Irish problem and 7:177–8, 7:177, 7:179,
    8:119–20, 8:137
  iron output of 7:59
  middle classes in 7:176
  North American colonies see North American
    colonies
  Nuclear Non-Proliferation Treaty and
    10:175–6
  overseas commerce of 7:58
  parliamentary flexibility of 7:175–6
  parliamentary reform in 7:170, 7:172
  parliamentary sovereignty 7:75, 7:77
  peasant class, disappearance in 7:49
  political parties in 7:170–73
  population growth in see population growth
  post-1945 radical politics in 8:173˙
  Quadruple Alliance (with Russia, Austria,
    Prussia) 7:117
  Royal Society 7:10, 7:20
  Sinn Fein cease fire agreement 10:101
  social services in 10:101, 10:103, 10:105
  Suez crisis and 10:43, 10:45–6
  support for Malaysia by 10:24–5, 10:39
  territorial acquisitions of 8:43–4
  trade union movement in 8:111

Great Britain (cont.)
  Treaty of Versailles and 8:156
  Ulster and 10:102
  unemployment in 10:105
  United States, investments in 7:151
  United States, similarities to 7:150–2
  urbanization of 7:60, 7:60
  war with France 7:95, 7:105, 7:111
  see also Acts of Parliament; agriculture;
    England; Europe; Ireland; London; Scotland;
    United States of America
Great Britain (pre-1939)
  Asian policies of 9:14, 9:23
  Chinese concessions surrendered by 9:20
  Dominion status 9:98
  Egypt, intervention in 9:32–3
  Egypt proclaimed protectorate 9:33
  Europe, policing of 9:56–7
  financial collapse in 9:59
  Free Trade abandoned in 9:49
  Germany and 9:57
  Government of India Act by 9:100–101
  Imperial Conference and 9:98
  Indian policy of 9:23, 9:98–102
  Japan, alliance with 9:8, 9:18
  Middle East and 9:108–10
  Munich agreements and 9:67
  as oil-exporting nation 10:103
  "open door" policy of 9:8
  Persian oil supplies defended by 9:37–38
  Polish guarantee offered 9:67
  rearmament of 9:57, 9:66–7
  imperialism, retreat from 9:42, 9:94, 9:95,
    9:97–103
  Russia, negotiations with 9:67, 9:67
  Russia and Prussia, coalition with 7:107
  Suez Canal, protection of 9:32, 9:33, 9:37,
    9:41–2
  welfare state in 9:59–60, 9:175
  Zionist policy of 9:39, 9:39
  see also Germany; Hitler; Russia
Great Britain (1939–1945)
  destruction of French fleet by
    Dominions 9:70, 9:82, 9:98
  Germany, blockade of 9:69
  Iran occupied by 9:76
  North Africa, war in 9:75–7, 9:83
  Royal Air Force 9:71, 9:80
  and Second World War 9:68, 9:82–3, 9:70
  Syria, invasion of 9:108
  see also Churchill; Germany (1939–1945);
    Italy; Russia; United States of America
Great Britain (after 1945) 9:94
  communist guerillas and 9:86, 9:92, 9:94
  decolonization and 9:95, 9:97–103
  Greece, withdrawal from 9:95
  Indian independence and 9:94, 9:98–103
  Security Council and 9:85
Great Schism see papacy
Great War see First World War
Greater Antilles, Spanish settlement of 6:145
Greece 8:119
  Bulgaria, invasion by 8:161
  communist guerilas in 9:92
    British intervention against 9:86, 9:94
  EC, entry into 10:106
  in First World War 8:147
  Germany and 9:72
  independence of 7:122
  language of 1:140
  literacy in 1:140

Greece (cont.)
  literature of 1:155, 1:155
  metals, first use of 1:142
  Minoan Crete and 1:145–6
  Mycenaean civilization of 1:151–2
  Ottoman Turks, conquest by 4:120
  Russian post-1945 threat to 9:88
  transport in 1:136
  Turkey, interest in 9:43
  Turks, revolt against 7:123
  United States aid and 9:95
Greek art 2:94, 2:99–100, 2:151–5, 3:13,
    3:26
  decline of 2:136, 2:151
  Egyptian influence on 2:99, 2:102, 2:152
  sculpture 2:90–91, 2:99, 2:104–5, 2:107,
    2:120, 2:127, 2:135, 2:146, 2:152–3,
    2:154
    eastern influence on 2:174, 2:175
    influences on 2:99, 2:99, 2:102,
    Great Altar of Zeus 2:146, 2:168
    Laocoön 2:179
    memorials 2:101–2, 2:104, 2:155
      2:152–3
    naturalism and 2:153
    theatrical figurines 2:99, 2:151
Greek civilization 2:91, 2:123–9
  agriculture in 2:125
  aristocracies in 2:96–8, 2:106
    land-owning 2:96, 2:128
  citizenship in 2:102–4, 2:107, 2:126, 2:128
  classical 2:124–5
  coinage of 2:103
  colonization and 2:93, 2:100, 2:105, 2:108–9
  divorce in 2:126–7
  economic foundations of 2:125
  education in 2:127
  in Europe 2:92–3
  freemen in 2:97–8, 2:107, 2:126
  Hellenistic world and 2:156–79, 2:90–91,
    2:93–4
  helots in 2:107–8, 2:118
  homosexuality in 2:127–8
  Iliad and Odyssey, importance of 2:95–6
  marriage in 2:127
  men, status in 2:126
  metics 2:98, 2:126, 2:146
  Minoan and Mycenaean contributions to
    2:91
  political development in 2:101–8, 2:118–23
  population pressure on 2:100
  rational thought, development of 2:136–9
  slavery in 2:97–9, 2:99, 2:125–6
  social institutions in 2:126–8
  superstition in 2:136–7, 2:141, 2:142
  trade in 2:98, 2:128
  women in
    denial of education to 2:127, 2:127
    subordinate status of 2:125, 2:126–7,
      2:126
  see also civilization; Greek culture; Greek
    literature; Greek mythology; Greek people
Greek culture
  and Alexander the Great 2:163–4
  in Asia Minor 2:89
  Egypt, influence on 2:73, 2:75
  Hellenistic kingdoms 2:166, 2:167
  influences on 2:99, 2:166
  language in 2:90–91
  Persian architecture, influence on 2:75,
    2:79–80

Greek culture (cont.)
 Rome, influence on *3:13*, 3:26–7, 3:48–51, **3:50**
 legacy of 2:153–4
 legal code of *2:87*
 philosophy of 2:124
 pottery in **2:108**
 see also Greek art; Greek literature
Greek fire *4:56*, 4:57, 4:61, 4:84
Greek literature
 history of 2:146–8
 poetry and drama 2:124, *2:124*, *2:146*, 2:148–51, **2:148**
  comedy **2:148**, 2:150–1, *2:151*
  tragedy 2:148–50, **2:148**
 theatrical developments in 2:88, 2:124–5, 2:148–9, **2:148**
Greek mythology *2:146*, 2:149
Greek people 1:156, 2:90–117, 2:134–5
 hoplites 2:100–1, *2:101*, 2:102, *2:106*, *2:117*, 2:126
 language of 2:87, 2:90–1, 2:93–4
 population size of 2:123–4
 see also Athens; Sparta
Greek religion
 astrology and 2:173
 decline of in Hellenistic period 2:173
 humanizing tendencies of 2:94–5
 oracles in 2:96, *2:97*, 2:112, *2:137*, 2:161
 oriental cults in 2:173, 2:175
 pantheon of 2:94, **2:94**
 superstition in 2:136–7, 2:141, 2:173
Greek science 2:139–43
 abstract thought and 2:139
 astronomy 2:142–3
 atomic theory 2:141
 elements, theory of 2:141–2
 experiment in 2:143
 Hellenistic period 2:170
 mathematics 2:141–2, 2:170
 medicine **2:142**, 2:143
 mysticism, numerical in 2:141–2
 nature of the universe in 2:140–1
 superstition in 2:141
 see also medicine; philosophy
Greek warfare
 Eurymedon, battle of **2:111**
 fleet, role in **2:113**, 2:115
 mercenaries, use in 2:72, 2:81, 2:93, 2:99, 2:173
 military techniques of 2:100–101, *2:101*
 Persian wars 2:82, 2:111–16, 2:122–3, **2:129**
greenhouse effect see global warming
Greenland, colonization by Norsemen 4:154
Gregory I (the Great), St (540–604 CE), pope *3:173*, 3:174–6, *3:174–5*, *4:71*, *4:91*, 4:160, *4:161*
Gregory VII (Hildebrand) (c.1023–1085), pope **4:165**, 5:104, *5:104–5*
 clash with Henry IV 5:105–7
Gregory IX (1170–1241), pope **5:110**
Gregory XI (1329–1378), pope 5:115
Gregory XIII (1502–1585), pope *6:125*
Gregory, St (538–594 CE), bishop of Tours 3:154
Grey Friars see Franciscan order
Gross Domestic Product (GDP) 9:126, **9:127**
Guadeloupe, French colony 6:147
Guam, captured by Japanese *9:74*
Guatemala 5:93, 10:68, 10:70

Gudea, king of Lagash (21st century BCE) *1:93*
Guernica (Picasso) 9:65
Guevara, Ernesto "Che" (1928–1967), Latin American revolutionary 10:72
Guide for the Perplexed (Maimonides) 4:37
Gujarat 2:13, 2:20
gunpowder see weapons
Gupta Empire 5:17–20
Gutenberg Bible 5:175, *5:175*
Gutenberg, Johannes (c.1400–1468), German printer 5:175
Gutian people 1:91, 1:93
Guy de Lusignan, king of Jerusalem (1186–1192) *4:102*
Güyük Khan, successor of Chinghis Khan (1246–1248) **4:105**

H

Habsburg dynasty 6:78, 6:80, *6:81*, 6:83, 7:108, 7:117, 8:155, 8:159
 Bourbons and 8:23
 conflict with Prussia 6:116, 6:118
 Dual Monarchy of 8:135
 France, wars against and 6:84–5, 6:87
 Holy Roman Emperors 5:129, 6:74
Habsburg empire 6:73–5, 6:81–5
 Austro-Hungarian (Dual) monarchy 7:131
 Catholicism predominant in 6:74
 educational reform in 7:34
 fiscal and administrative reform in 6:75
 Hungary regained by 6:96
 revolutions of (1848) *7:123*, 7:124–6
 secularization in 6:75
 territorial losses of 7:130–1
 see also Austria
Hadrian I, pope 4:136
Hadrian (Publius Aelius Hadrianus) (76–138 CE), Roman emperor *2:172*, 3:41, *3:43*, *3:53*, 3:68, 3:90
Hadrian's Wall *3:42*, *3:43*, 3:125, 3:151
Hagia Triada, Crete *1:151*
Haile Selassie (1891–1975), emperor of Ethiopia (1930–1974) *10:56*, 10:57, *10:57*
Haiti 8:28
 American protectorate over 8:31
hajj, pilgrimage to Mecca **4:22**
Halicarnassus 2:86, 2:146
Hamdanid dynasty 4:96–7
Hamitic peoples 1:74, 1:102, 2:59
Hammurabi, king of Babylon (c.1792–1750 BCE) 1:93–4, 1:98
 code of laws of 1:93, 1:94–5
Han dynasty, China 2:31, *2:34*, *2:43*, 5:40–1
 civil service examinations and 5:44
 coinage, monopoly on 5:44
 extent of empire of 5:41
 peasant rebellions and 5:48
 see also Later Han dynasty
hand-axes 1:23, 1:26, *1:26*
Hannibal (247–182 BCE), Carthaginian general 3:19–20, 3:28
Hanoi 5:59, 9:107
Hanseatic League 4:88, 5:144, **5:145**
 in Germany 5:136
 merchants expelled from Pskov and Novgorod by 5:158
Hanuman, Hindu god **2:20**
Harappa, city **2:8**, 2:12

Harappan culture *2:11*, 2:12, *2:12*, 2:20
 bathing in *2:11*, 2:12
 city planning in *2:11*, 2:12, *2:15*
 decline of 2:13–14
 figurines in *2:10*, *2:12*, *2:14*, *2:29*
 seals 2:13, *2:13*, 2:21, 2:23
 Shiva worship in 2:21–3
Hardwar, Hindu sacred city *5:20*
Hargreaves, James (d.1778), inventor of spinning Jenny *7:54*
Harold II (c.1020–1066), king of England *4:177*
Haroun-al-Raschid (c.766–809 CE), Abbasid caliph 4:34, **4:35**, 4:41, 4:43, *4:140*, 5:51
Harvey, William (1578–1657), English physician 7:19
Hastings, Warren (1732–1818), governor-general of India 8:46
Hathor, Egyptian goddess *1:100*, *1:106*
Hatshepsut, queen of Egypt (c.1490–1470 BCE) 1:126
 mortuary temple of *1:116*, *1:126*
Hattusas, Hittite capital **1:160**
 Lion Gates of *1:162*
Hawaii 8:61–2
Hay Making in July (Brueghel the Elder) *6:15*
Hebrews, Semitic people
 Babylon, exiled in 1:172
 Canaanite culture and religion, destruction of 1:167
 in Egypt 1:129
  exodus from 1:166, *1:167*
 God, concept of 1:162
 iron, use of 1:168
 monotheism 1:163–6, 1:170–1
 in Canaan 1:163–4, 1:166–7, 1:170
 origins 1:162–3
 prophets 1:68, 1:168, 1:170–71, 1:178, 3:73, 3:75
 rulers of **1:165**
 see also Israel; Jews; Judaism
Hegira (Muhammad's flight to Yathrib) 4:23
Heisenberg, Werner (1901–1976), German physicist 9:142
Hellenes see Greek people
Hellenistic civilization
 Byzantium influenced by 4:56
 Persian damage of 4:60
 Turkish annihilation of 4:121
Hellenistic world, the 2:156–79
 academic life of 2:169–70
 cities of 2:167–9
 Greek culture in **2:166**, 2:167–9
 irrationality in 2:173
 kingdoms of 2:164–7, **2:165**, **2:166**, *2:167*
 literature in *2:167*
 Macedonian Empire 2:156–64
 oriental cults in 2:173, 2:175
 predecessors of 2:167
 science in 2:170
 Stoic school of philosophy in *2:171*, 2:174–5
Helsinki agreement (1975) 10:130, 10:141
Helst, Bartholomeus van der (1613–1670), artist *6:159*
Henry I (the Fowler) (c.876–936 CE), king of Saxony 4:147, 4:149
Henry II (1133–1189), king of England *5:107*
Henry II (973–1024), king of the Saxons, Holy Roman Emperor *4:147*, 4:149–50
Henry III (1551–1589), king of France *6:31*
Henry IV (1050–1106), Holy Roman Emperor *5:104*, 5:105–7

Henry IV (1367–1413), king of England *5:104*
Henry IV (1553–1610), king of France 6:55, 6:80, 7:9
Henry VII (1457–1509), king of England 5:131, 6:81
Henry VIII (1491–1547), king of England 5:121, *6:52–3*
 and Catholicism, break with 6:52, 6:53
 dissolution of the monasteries by 6:53–4
 imperial throne, candidacy for 6:83
 and Luther, refutation of 6:53
 navy shipbuilding and 6:162
Henry the Navigator (1394–1460), prince of Portugal *5:160*, 5:161, **6:128**
Hera, Greek goddess **2:94**, *2:95*
Heracles, Greek hero 1:153, 2:156
Heraclius (c.576–641 CE), Roman emperor in East 4:12–13, *4:13*, 4:17, 4:60–61, *4:70*, 4:79
 Monophysitism debate and 4:54–5
Hercules see Heracles
heresies 3:141, 3:166–7, *3:166*, 5:112, 5:116, 6:44–5, 6:50–51, 6:53–4, *6:58*, 6:60
 Albigensian *5:111*
 persecution of heretics 5:111, 5:117, *5:117*, *5:125*
 of Wyclif and Hus 5:117
Hermes, busts of *2:136*
Herodium *3:79*
Herodotus (c.484–c.424 BCE), Greek historian 1:112, 1:177, 2:58–9, 2:78, 2:86, **2:86**, *2:106*, **2:114**, 2:146–7
Herod Agrippa I (10 BCE–44 CE), Jewish king of Palestine 3:90
Herod the Great (74–4 BCE), king of Judaea *3:79*
 Temple rebuilding begun by *3:78*
Hero of Alexandria (2nd century CE), Greek engineer 2:170
Herrero tribe 8:57
Herschel, William (1738–1822), British astronomer *7:19*
Herzl, Theodor (1816–1904), founder of Zionist movement *9:36*
Hesiod (c.700 BCE), Greek poet *2:146*, 2:148
Hideyoshi (1536–1598), Japanese general and dictator 5:77, 5:79
hieroglyphs see writing, hieroglyphic
Hildebrand see Gregory VII, pope
Himalayas **2:8**
Hindenburg, Paul Ludwig Hans von (1847–1934), Field Marshal and president of Germany 8:147, 9:62
Hinduism 2:20–25, 2:27–8, 8:94–5, *8:97*, *8:98*, **8:99**, *10:17*, 10:18, 10:22
 bhakti movement and *5:19*
 Brahmanical tradition and 5:10, 5:18, 5:21
 child marriage and 5:21
 development of 5:13–14, *5:19*, 5:22, 5:30
 dharma and 5:13, 5:18
 in Indonesia 10:24
 Islamic influences on 5:30
 and Muslims see Hindu-Muslim conflicts
 mysticism in **2:23**
 pantheon of 2:21, 2:23, **2:23**
 prohibition by Aurungzebe of 5:34
 religious tolerance and **8:95**
 social practices of 8:93
 suttee and 5:21

Hindu Kush
  crossing by Aryans 2:14
  crossing by Persians 2:76
Hindu-Muslim conflicts 6:138, **6:138**, **8:96**,
    8:97, 8:98–101, *9:100*, 9:102, 9:168,
    10:116, 10:117
Hindu nationalism 8:94–6
  anti-partition riots and terrorism and 8:97
Hippocrates of Cos (c.460–c.357 BCE), Greek
    physician **2:142**, 2:143, 5:168, 5:171
Hirohito (1901–1989), emperor of Japan 10:37,
    10:38
Hiroshima *see* atomic bomb
Hispaniola, Spanish settlement 6:139, 6:*145*
historians, role of 10:159–60, 10:170–171,
    10:177–8
Histories (Herodotus) 2:146
Histories, The (Tacitus) 3:41
historiography 6:8–11
  Greek 2:146–8
  see also individual historians
History of the Conquest of the World, The
    (Ala-al-Din) 4:*111*
History of the Franks (Gregory) 3:154
History of the Kings of Britain, The
    (Geoffrey of Monmouth) 5:123
History of memorable things that happened in
    the East Indies (Jarric) **5:31**
History of the Peloponnesian War, The
    (Thucydides) **2:122**, 2:123, **2:133**
Hitler, Adolf (1889–1945), German dictator
    9:60–61, 9:60, 9:66, 9:176
  Chancellor of Republic 9:61
  eastern strategies of 9:66, 9:72, 9:74
  and Franco 9:64, 9:*65*
  Holocaust 9:61–3, 9:*63*, 9:79, 9:*79*, 9:109–10
  Mein Kampf **9:60**, 9:61
  racial theories of 9:61, 9:72
  rise to power of 9:60–63
  Russia, invasion of 9:72–3
  and Slavs 9:72
  suicide of 9:78
  and United States 9:73–4
Hittites, the 1:*160–61*
  Amorites, neighbours of 1:93
  in Anatolia 1:74, 1:159
  Babylon and 1:94, 1:98, 1:159
  cuneiform script adopted by 1:98
  decline of 1:129, 1:160–61, 1:172
  empire of **1:160**, **2:72**
  iron and 1:135, 1:159–60
  Mitanni and 1:127
  mother goddess and 1:*61*
  Mycenae and 1:152
  Qadesh, battle of 1:*129*, **1:160**
Ho Chi Minh (1892–1969), president of North
    Vietnam 9:107–108, 9:*107*
Hobbes, Thomas (1588–1679), English
    philosopher 6:68–9, 6:*69*
Hohenstaufen dynasty **4:149**
Hohenzollern monarchy 6:73–4, 6:116–18,
    7:131
Holbein the Younger, Hans (1497–1543), artist
    6:*21*, 6:*43*, 6:*45*, 6:*52*
Holocaust 9:61–3, 9:*63*, 9:79, 9:*79*, 9:109–10
Holy Alliance (Russia, Austria, Prussia) 7:118,
    7:123, 7:129
Holy League 6:96
Holy Roman Empire **4:77**, 4:150, 5:128–9,
    6:38–9, 6:83
  abolition of 7:108

Holy Roman Empire (cont.)
  Habsburg family, domination of 5:129
  Ottonian Empire, roots in 4:148
  see also Charlemagne; Ottonian dynasty;
    Ottonian empire
Homer, Greek author of the *Iliad* and *Odyssey*
    1:140, 1:*153*, 1:155, **1:155**, 2:16, 2:90,
    2:95–6, **2:95**, 2:96–9, 2:104, 2:135, 2:148
  sculptures related to 2:*94*, 2:*96*, 2:*120*, 2:*167*
hominids **1:17**, 1:18–19, **1:20**, 1:34, 1:39
  archaeological sites relating to
    Ambrona 1:29
    Atapuerca 1:30–1
    Dmanisi **1:22**
    Koobi Fora **1:22**
    Lan-t'ien 1:23
    Nariokotome **1:22**
    Olduvai Gorge 1:21
    Princevent 1:48
    Shanidar Cave 1:37
    Skhul Cave 1:38
    Terra Amata 1:25
    Torralba 1:29
  Australopithecus sp: **1:11**, 1:*18*, 1:19–20,
    1:20, 1:23, **1:24**, 1:28
  brain size of 1:19, 1:23–4, 1:34, 1:36
  dating methods **1:32**
  diffusion of 1:22–3
  evolution of 1:11
  fossils at Olduvai 1:*19*, 1:21, **1:21**, 1:22
  Homo sp: *see* individual species
  infancy in 1:24–5
  life expectancy in 1:30
  "Lucy" 1:*18*
  oestrus and 1:24–5
  physiological changes in 1:23–5, **1:26**
  Proconsul (*Dryopithecus*) **1:16**
  stone artifacts of 1:39
  tools of 1:18, 1:20–3
  Homo erectus 1:23–4, 1:28, 1:32, 1:34–5
    building abilities of 1:*25*
    characteristics of 1:32
    cranial development of **1:24**, 1:*34–5*
    culture and tradition of 1:30
    dispersion beyond Africa of **1:22**, 1:*23*
    Dmanisi, Georgia **1:22**
    environment and 1:26
    fire and 1:27, 1:*28*, 1:31
    hunting and 1:28–30, 1:*29*, 1:31
    Olduvai Gorge **1:21**
    tools of **1:27**
  Homo habilis **1:11**, 1:*19*, 1:20, **1:20–21**, 1:22,
    1:24
    tools of **1:27**
  Homo sapiens **1:11**, 1:23, 1:34, 1:*38*, 1:45,
    1:60–62, 1:64
    adaptability of 1:52, 1:56, 1:61
    cranial development of **1:24–5**, 1:*34–5*
    diffusion of **1:39**, **1:40**
    DNA analysis of **1:46**
    ethnic, racial and cultural differentiation of
      1:36–7, 1:46–8, 1:73
    as hunter-gatherers 1:46, 1:48, 1:52, 1:57–8
    Neolithic culture of 1:50–4
    origins of 1:32, **1:35**
    physiological changes of 1:52
    warfare and 1:57–8
  Homo sapiens neanderthalis see Neanderthals
  Homo sapiens sapiens 1:36, 1:38–9
    in Europe 1:40
    origins of **1:35**, 1:38

Homo sapiens sapiens (cont.)
    tools and weapons of 1:41
Honduras 6:162, 10:67
Hong Kong 10:39
  China, return to *10:41*, 10:112
  economic growth of 10:112–13, **10:113**
  Great Britain, cession to 8:16
  Japanese, capture by 9:*74*
Honorius, Flavius (384–423 CE), Western Roman
    emperor 3:*134*
Honorius, pope (625–638 CE) 4:54–5
hoplites 2:100–101, 2:*101*, 2:102, 2:*106*, 2:131,
    2:157
  arms and armour of 2:100, 2:*101*, 2:*117*,
    2:126
  Spartan aristocracy and 2:106
horses 2:14, 2:58, 2:*65*, 2:77, 2:*101*
  and Achaean peoples 1:150–51
  in agriculture 5:137, 9:128
  in Americas 5:92, 6:173–4
  in Ethiopia 5:85
  riding of 1:54
  in Sahara 5:85
  technology and 8:129
  in warfare 1:134–5
Horthy, Miklos (1868–1957), Hungarian head of
    state 8:*174*
Horus, Egyptian god 1:*104*, 1:106, **1:112**,
    1:114
Hospitallers 5:*153*, **5:155**
Hottentot people, South Africa 6:168
House of Contracts, Seville 6:*156*
Hsi River 2:32
Hsiung-Nu *see* Huns
Hsün-tzu (3rd century BCE), Chinese philosopher
    2:50
Hudson, Henry (d:1611), English explorer
    6:149
Hudson's Bay Company 6:160
Hugh of Payns, founder of Templars **5:155**
Hugo, Abbot of Cluny 5:104
Hugo, Victor (1802–1885), French novelist
    7:65
Huguenots, French Calvinists
    persecution under Louis XIV 6:71
    privileges of 6:66
    St Bartholomew's Day Massacre 6:*54*
    Florida, settlement in 6:158
    and monarchy 6:68
Hulugu, Mongol khan 4:112
human experience, growing unity of
    10:160–164, 10:169
Human Genome Project 9:145
humanism 6:44–6
  Erasmus of Rotterdam 6:*45*
  Huldreich Zwingli 6:*50*
humanity, origins of 1:10–32, 1:34–8, 1:52
  see also hominids; individual *Homo* sp:
human rights 10:61, 10:165–6, **10:165**
Hume, David (1711–1776), Scottish philosopher
    7:33
Hunas (Huns) *see* Huns
Hundred Years' War (1337–1453) 5:125, 5:*127*
  chronology of **5:126**
Hung Hsiu-ch'uan, leader of Taiping rebellion
    8:71
  court in Nanking 8:71
  death of 8:73
Hungary 5:129, **5:129**
  agrarian society in 6:31
  Calvinism in 6:51

Hungary (cont.)
  EC application 10:151
  Bolshevik government in 8:165, 8:*174*
  communism and 9:96, 10:9, 10:46, *10:77*,
    10:78, 10:149
  defeat by Ottoman Turks 4:122
  Dual monarchy 7:131
  elections in 10:149
  frontiers opened to East Germans
    10:148
  Habsburg rule, revolution against 7:123–5,
    7:130
  Magyar nationalism in 8:135
  Mongols, defeat by 4:106
  Slav nationalism in 8:119, 8:155
  Soviet invasion of
  Treaty of Versailles and 8:158
  Turks, occupation by 6:*93*, 6:94
  see also Austria
Huns, Asian nomads (Hsiung-Nu) 4:15–16,
    4:*15*, **4:17**, 4:78–9, 5:23, 5:41
  Attila and Leo the Great 3:174
  China, threat to 4:15
  Goths and **3:126**, 3:132
  Sassanid Empire, invasion of 4:16
  Visigoth army, defeat by 3:134, 3:152
  westward movements of **4:9**, 4:15–6
hunter-gatherers 2:8–9
  in North America 5:92
  San people as 5:85
hunting 1:21, 1:27, 1:31, 1:41, 1:46
  aquatic animals 1:41
  and aristocracy 1:57–8
  in art 1:42, 1:*43*, 1:*134*, **1:173**
  big-game 1:28–31, 1:*140*
  and farming 1:53
Hus, John (c.1373–1415), Church reformer
    5:117, 5:*117*
Hussein, Saddam (1937–), president of Iraq
    10:121, 10:135
  Ba'athist régime, leader of 10:133
  Gulf War and 10:134–5, *10:134–5*
  Iran, war with 10:133, *10:133*
  Kuwait invasion and *10:133*, 10:134–5
Hussein ibn Ali (c. 1854–1931), sherif of Mecca
    9:36, 9:38, **9:40**
  displacement of 9:41
  as king 9:39–40
  sons of 9:40, **9:40**, 9:41
Huxley, Thomas (1825–1895), English scientist
    8:131
Hyksos, Semitic people,
  in Egypt 1:125–6, 1:*125*, 1:126,
    1:134
  Joseph, at the time of 1:163
  and Minoans 1:146

I

Ibn-Sina (Avicenna) 4:38
Ibsen, Henrik Johan (1828–1906), Norwegian
    dramatist 2:150, 8:115
Ice Ages 1:12–14, **1:13**, 1:34, 1:37
  Upper Palaeolithic 1:39–41, 1:45, 1:50, 1:52,
    1:56
  see also climate; glaciation
Iceland
  colonization by Norsemen 4:153–4
  Norse legacy of 4:158

Ivan IV the Terrible (1530–1584), Tsar of Russia
     5:158, 6:100–2, *6:100–101*, 6:103–4
Ivan VI (1740–1764), tsar of Russia 6:114
Izanagi and Izanama, Japanese myth *5:69*

J

Jackson, Andrew (1767–1845), United States
     president 7:159
Jackson, Thomas Jonathan "Stonewall"
     (1824–1863), American Confederate general
     7:153
Jacob, Hebrew patriarch 1:163–4
Jacobin club, French revolutionary association
     7:120
Jacobite Church (Syria) 4:54, 4:114
jade 2:34, *2:37*, *2:40*, 2:54, 2:63
     burial suit of Prince Tou Wan *2:43*
     disks *2:52*
Jagiellon dynasty in Eastern Europe 6:94, 6:98
Jahan (1592–1666), Moghul emperor *see* Shah
     Jahan
Jahangir (1569–1627), Moghul emperor 5:27,
     5:32
Jainism 2:25, 5:11–12
     Varanasi and **5:20**
Jakarta (Batavia) *6:131*, 6:132–3
Jamaica 6:160, 6:162, 6:173
James I and VI (1566–1625), king of Scotland,
     Great Britain and Ireland 6:63, 6:86, 6:133
     charter to colonizing Virginia company 6:149
James II and VII (1633–1701), king of England
     and Scotland 6:69, 6:160
James (later St), apostle and brother of Jesus
     3:85
James, Henry (1843–1916), American writer
     8:109
James, son of Zebedee (later St) (d.44), apostle of
     Jesus 4:159
Jamestown, Virginia, English settlement 6:149
James Stuart "the Pretender" (1688–1766) 6:91
Janissaries 4:120, *4:121*
Januarius, Saint 7:8–9
Japan 5:68–82, 9:8–10, 9:14, 9:16, 9:23–5,
     9:27–9, 10:36–9, 10:112–16
     agrarian revolts in 8:85
     Ainu peoples of 1:59, 5:69, 5:73–4
     and Great Britain 9:8, 9:18
     American occupation of 10:36–7
     American trade embargo on 9:74–5
     anti-western feelings in 9:23
     'Asia for the Asians' 8:76, 8:87, 8:101, 9:29,
          10:37
     automobile industry in 9:134, 10:113,
          10:115, *10:115*
     autonomy retained 8:53
     and China 5:69–70, 5:74–5
          attacks on **9:12**, **9:24**, 9:25, 9:27–8, *9:27*,
               9:104
          domination of 9:14, 9:23
     'China Incident' 9:27, *9:29*
     Chinese oil and 9:74
     Chinese revolutionaries and 8:76–7, 8:87
     civil service in 5:73
     class divisions in 5:76, 5:78–9
     class system abolished in 8:83
     constitution of 10:37
     cotton-spinning in 8:85
     court art in 5:76

Japan (cont.)
     culture of **8:88**
          art at the imperial palace *5:76*
          cultural contamination 8:20
          expansion in growing economy 5:82
          militaristic element of 5:77–9
          subservience to China of 5:74
          see also art
     eastern Asia and 10:18, 10:26
     economy of,
          agriculture and 5:80, 8:84–5
          coinage debased by shogunate 8:80
          depression in 9:23
          growth of 9:8, 9:9–10, 10:112–113
               during Tokugawa shogunate 5:80–2
          inflation 8:80, 8:84
          Korean war, boost by 10:39
          peasant base 5:77, 8:80, 8:84–5
          reform failure 8:80
          taxation 8:80, 8:85
          urban prosperity and 5:80–82
     education in 8:81, 8:83
     EEC market penetration and 10:113
     electronics industry in *9:140*
     emperor of 5:72–3, 10:37, *10:38*
     feudalism 8:79–80, 8:84
          abolition of 8:82–3
     foreign policies since World War II 10:39,
          10:114–16
     foreign relations
          Europeans, contact with 6:122, 6:130,
               6:132, 6:176, *8:12*, 8:13
          in First World War 8:146
          Korea **8:86**, 8:87–8
          Manchuria, invasion of **8:86**, **8:161**
          military policy 8:86–7, **8:86**
          trade treaties 8:81, *8:81*, 8:84
          Treaty of Versailles and 8:156
          war with China **8:86**, 8:87
          war with Russia 8:88–9, 8:96, 8:138
          Western contact re-opened 8:81
          Westernization 8:83–4, *8:85*
     Fujiwara clan in 5:69, 5:72–3, 5:76
     Heian period 5:72
     imperial court, transference of 8:82
     imperialism of 9:9, *9:24*, **9:24**, 9:25, 9:43,
          9:80
     industrialization in 8:15, 8:20, 8:149
     Inner Mongolia and 9:14, 9:25
     international commerce in 10:114
     isolation of 5:79–80, 5:82
     Kamakura, capital city of 5:72
     Kamakura period 5:72, 5:74–7, *5:76*
     Korea and 10:115
     Korea, threat to 5:60
     Kwantung expeditionary force in **9:24**
     land reform of 10:38
     militaristic government of 9:75
     military advisers to *8:20*, 8:84
     military rule in 5:73–4
     Minamoto clan and *5:73*, 5:74, *5:76*
     monarchy in 5:72–3, 10:37, *10:38*
     Mongol invasions of 5:59, 5:74, 5:75–7
     mythology of *5:69*
     nationalism in 8:82, 8:86, 9:23, **9:24**
     nuclear weapons and 10:115
     Okinawa and 10:115
     over-fishing in 10:114–15
     parliament of *8:84*
     peace treaties and 10:38–9
     Pearl Harbor attack by 9:74, *9:74*, 9:75

Japan (cont.)
     pirates and *5:75*
     population growth in 5:69, 5:77, 5:80,
          10:113
     pottery of 1:59
     reform in 8:75
     religions in
          Buddhism 5:70, **5:71**, 5:72, 5:77
          Christianity 5:77, *5:78*, 5:79
          Shintoism 5:71–2, *5:71*, 8:85
     rice cultivation in 8:84–5
     samurai warriors 5:77–9, *5:79*, 5:80, 5:82,
          8:79, 8:81, 8:83–6
     Satsuma rebellion in (1877) 8:85–6
     Second World War **8:86**, 9:74, 9:75
          atomic bombs and 9:78, **9:78**, 9:88–9, *9:89*
          attacks on British and American territories
               9:74,
          United States, defeat by 9:83
          kamikaze tactics in 9:75
          post-1945 recovery of 10:37–9
          prisoners of war, brutality toward *9:98*
          surrender of 9:78, 9:79
     shipbuilding industry in 10:113
     shrines in
          Miyajima (Shinto) *5:71*
          Todaiji (Buddhist) *5:70*
     society in 5:78–9, 10:114
          clan influence 5:72, 5:73
          clan structure 5:68–9, *5:71*, 5:78
          class structure 5:78–9
          feudalistic ideals 5:77
          Shinto, focus on 5:71–2
     sovereignty restored in 10:39
     suffrage in 9:9
     technical receptivity of 8:81
     territorial aggression of 9:9, 9:23, **9:24**, 9:25,
          9:27–9
     Tokugawa shogunate 5:77–8, 5:80–2, 8:79,
          8:84
     trade in
          concessions made to Western powers 8:82
          trade treaties 8:81–2, 8:87
     Twenty-One Demands of 9:14
     urbanization of 9:8, 10:113–14, *10:114*
     Western acceptance of 8:87–8
     see also China; Meiji Restoration; Taiwan
Jaurès, Jean (1859–1914), founder of French
     Socialist Party *8:112*
Java 5:59, **8:91**, *8:104*
     British, occupation of 8:103
Jaxartes River 4:14
Jefferson, Thomas (1743–1826), United States
     president 7:161
Jehu, king of Israel (842–814 BCE) *1:169*
Jenner, Edward (1749–1823), English physician
     7:45
Jeremiah (626–586 BCE), Hebrew prophet 1:171
Jericho, prehistoric settlement in 1:56, *1:57*,
     1:66
Jerome, St (c.340–420 CE), Christian churchman
     3:148, *3:174*
Jerusalem 3:78, **3:78**, 5:163, *10:42*
     annexation by Israel 10:49, 10:127
     Antonia fortress *3:78*
     Ark of the Covenant *1:166*
     and Babylon, conquest by 3:73
     Babylonians, destruction by **1:168**, *1:171*,
          1:172, 1:176
     and Britain, capture by 9:39, *9:39*
     capital of Israel 1:168, 9:111

Jerusalem (cont.)
     capital of kingdom of Judah **1:168**, 1:172
     Christ's entry into 3:81–2, *3:83*
     crusader kingdom of 4:102
     Dome of the Rock 4:39, *4:40*
     and early Hebrews 1:167
     First Crusade and 5:151, **5:153**
     Hadrian and 3:90
     Holy Sepulchre *5:6*
     and Muslims, capture by 4:25
     Persians, sack by 4:12
     Romans, sack by (70) 3:88
     Saladin, recapture by 4:103
     see also Hebrews; Israel; Jews; Solomon's
          Temple
Jesuits (Society of Jesus) 5:28, 5:61, 5:63, 5:77,
     6:56–7, *6:57*, 6:126, 6:167, 8:66
     dissolution of 6:73, 7:10, 7:37
     see also Loyola, St Ignatius
Jesus of Nazareth 3:68, 3:72, 3:84–5, *3:100*,
     3:117, *3:138*
     baptism of 3:81, *3:81*, *3:122*
     crucifixion of 3:82
     disciples of (Apostles) 3:82–3, *3:84*, 3:85,
          3:85, *3:122*
     entry into Jerusalem of 3:81–2, *3:83*
     Jewish reactions to teachings of 3:82–5
     life of 3:80–82
     resurrection of 3:82, 3:85, **3:87**, *3:89*, **3:91**,
          3:96
     teachings of 3:82–3, **3:82**
jewellery *1:152*, *2:64*, *3:124*, *3:132*, *3:154*,
     3:156, *3:176*
     Gemma augustae *3:39*
The Jewish State (Herzl) *9:36*
Jews,
     and Christian emperors, persecution by
          3:137, 3:166
     covenant with God 3:73, **3:76**
     diaspora (dispersion) **3:76**, 3:90, 3:95
     divisions between 3:79–80
     Exile of 3:73–5
     Final Solution 9:63, 9:79
     Hellenization of 3:75–6
     Holocaust 9:61–3, *9:63*, 9:79, *9:79*, 9:109–10
          Final Solution *9:63*, 9:79
     Judean War against Rome (66–74 CE) 3:68,
          3:78, 3:89
     Justinian, civic status under 3:166
     legal status of 3:90, 3:166
     Maccabaean revolt and (168–164 BCE) 3:75,
          3:75
     Messiah, prophesied by the 3:80, 3:82–3,
          3:85
     nationalism, spiritual under Rome 3:47–8,
          3:68, **3:76**, 3:80, 3:89–90
     nationalism, territorial and 9:36
     Nazi persecution of 9:41, 9:79, *9:79*,
          9:109–110
     Palestine, immigration to 9:36, 9:41, 9:110,
          9:110
     as Persian allies 3:168
     Portuguese, harassment by 6:19
     and Roman populace 3:77
     Roman rule and 3:77–80
     Russia, migration from **8:107**
     Spanish domains, expulsion from 6:58
     theocratic view of history of 3:73, 3:77
     see also anti-semitism; Hebrews; Israel;
          Judaism
Jhelum River *2:8*

Jiang Qing, widow of Mao Tse-tung *10:110*

jihad (defence of the faith) **4:22**

Jinnah, Muhammad Ali (1876–1948), governor general of Pakistan 10:21

Joan of Arc, St (1412–1431) 5:125, *5:125*

Johannesburg 8:35

John (1167–1216), king of England 5:114

John II Comnenus (1088–1143), Byzantine emperor *4:73*

John II Kalojan, king of Bulgaria (1197–1207) *4:118*

John III (Sobieski) (1624–1696), king of Poland 6:96, 6:98–100, *6:99*
  relief of Vienna, liberation of Hungary 6:96, *6:99*

John III (1502–1557), king of Portugal *5:78*

John VI Cantacuzenus (d:1383), Byzantine emperor *4:115*

John VIII, Byzantine emperor (1425–1448) 4:118

John XXIII, pope (1410–1425) 5:116

John Paul II (1920–), pope 9:169

Johnson, Dr. Samuel (1709–1784), English man of letters 1:8

Johnson, Lyndon Baines (1908–1973), United States president
  civil rights legislation of 10:87–8
  domestic policies of 10:88–9
  Latin America and 10:71–2, 10:86
  re-election, refusal to stand for 10:91
  Vietnam War and 10:89–91
  see also Kennedy, John Fitzgerald; United States of America; Vietnam

John the Baptist (1st century BCE), prophet 3:81, *3:81, 3:122, 3:146*

John the Constant (1468–1532), Elector of Ernestine Saxony *5:142*

Jones, John Paul (1747–1792), United States naval officer *7:80*

Jordan 10:44–6
  British military assistance in 10:46
  PLO, support for 10:48
  Saddam Hussein, support for 10:135
  Six Day war, defeat of 10:48

Joseph, Hebrew patriarch 1:163

Joseph II (1741–1790), Holy Roman Emperor 6:75, *6:77,* 6:118, *7:36, 7:37*

Josephus, Flavius (37–c.100), Jewish historian 3:89

journalism 7:14–15

Jovellanos, Gaspar de (1744–1811) **7:32**

Joyce, James (1882–1941), Irish writer 9:50

Juan Carlos (1938–), king of Spain *10:141*
  and China, visit to *10:154*

Juárez, Benito (1806–1872), president of Mexico 8:27, 8:28

Judaea 3:76, 3:79–80, 3:88
  Titus, conquest by 3:69
  Jewish rebellion in 3:89
  Simon bar Kochba and 3:90

Judah, Hebrew kingdom of **1:168,** 1:172, 3:74, 3:75
  independence of 3:76
  punishment of 3:73
  exile of tribes by Babylonians **1:168,** *1:171,* 1:172, *1:176*

Judaism 1:171, 3:76–7
  and Christianity 3:73
  beliefs of **3:76**
  and Exile 3:74

Judaism (cont.)
  Law of Moses (Mosaic Law) 3:73–5, **3:76,** 3:83, 3:89
    Christianity and 3:87, **3:91**
  orthodoxy 3:101
  Pharisaic reformation of 3:76
  proselytism of 3:76–7, 3:137
  synagogues, development of 3:74
  Zoroastrian influence upon 2:81
  see also Hebrews; Jews

Julian calendar 3:35

Julian "the Apostate" (Flavius Claudius Julianus) (332–363 CE), Roman emperor 3:135–6, *3:135*

Jurassic period **1:14**

Justinian I (c.482–565 CE), Roman emperor in East 3:157, 3:160–69, *3:161–2,* 4:48, *4:50–51,* **4:51,** *4:53,* 4:57
  administrative reforms of 3:165–6
  Athens Academy closed by 3:166
  building programme of *3:159, 3:162,* 3:163, **3:163,** *3:164, 3:165*
  and Ravenna, capture of *3:159*
  Codex Constitutionum of **3:54**
  ecclesiastical supremacy and 3:166, 3:168, 3:174
  empire of **3:160**
  and Churches, unification of 3:168–9

Justin Martyr (c.100–c.163), Christian churchman 3:117

Jutes, Germanic peoples 3:150

K

Kaaba *4:18, 4:19,* 4:21

Kabul, conquest by Arabs 4:25

Kabul valley 5:16

Kafka, Franz (1883–1924), Czech writer 9:50

Kalidasa (4th century CE), Indian poet 5:18, **5:18**

Kalka-Simla Railway *8:18*

Kama Sutra, Indian literature (Gupta period) 5:18

Kamchatka, Russians in 5:66

Kandahar 5:11

K'ang-hsi (1654–1722), Manchu emperor *5:61, 5:62–6, 8:66*

K'ang Te (Pu-Yi) (1906–1967), puppet emperor of Manchukuo *9:10, 9:25*

Kanishka (3rd century CE), Kushan ruler 5:21

Kant, Immanuel (1724–1804), German philosopher 7:26, **7:26,** 7:33

Kashgaria 5:41

Kashmir 2:20, 8:46, 10:20, 10:117

Kassite people 1:133–4
  ziggurats *1:83*

Katanga, attempted secession of 10:55

Kazan, Tatars driven out of 6:101, *6:101*

Kemal Atatürk *see* Mustafa Kemal

Kennedy, John Fitzgerald (1917–1963), United States president 9:148–9, 9:151, *10:12,* **10:12,** 10:88
  Alliance for Progress 10:71–2
  Bay of Pigs operation and 10:70
  civil rights legislation of 10:87–8
  Cuban missile crisis and 10:70–71, *10:71,* 10:78–9
  election and 10:85–6
  Khrushchev and *10:70,* 10:71

Kennedy, John Fitzgerald (cont.)
  South Vietnam, intervention in 10:36, 10:89
  see also Johnson, Lyndon Baines; United States of America; Vietnam

Kenya 8:57, 8:59
  independence 10:55

Kenyatta, Jomo (c.1889–1978), president of Kenya 10:55

Kepler, Johannes (1571–1630), German astronomer 7:18, 7:22–3

Keynes, John Maynard (1883–1946), British economist 8:156

Khadijah, wife of prophet Muhammad *4:21*

Khai Dai, emperor of Annam (1932–1945) *8:105*

Khalifa *see* Abd Allah

Khan, Reza (1878–1944), shah of Persia 9:45–6, *9:47*

Khazars, Central Asian tribe 4:16–7, 4:26, 4:78, 4:81
  decline of 4:84
  and Islam 4:85, 4:98
  and Judaism 4:60, *4:60*
  St Cyril and 4:80

Khorsabad, Assyrian palace 1:174

Khrushchev, Nikita (1894–1971), Soviet premier *8:169,* **10:12,** *10:76,* 10:80
  agricultural expansion and *10:81*
  and China 10:31, *10:31*
  and Cuba 10:70
  Cuban missile crisis and 10:70–71, *10:71,* 10:79
  Kennedy, discussions with *10:12,* 10:70, 10:71
  removal from office 10:80
  and Stalin 10:76, 10:80–81
  see also Soviet Union

Khurasan, conquest by Arabs 4:25, 4:97

Khusrau I, Sassanid king of Persia (531–579 CE) **4:9,** *4:10, 4:12,* 4:140, *4:140*

Khusrau II, Sassanid king of Persia (590–628 CE) *4:10, 4:12,* 4:13

Khuzistan 2:76

Khyber Pass 2:9

Kiev 4:81, 4:83, 6:103
  and Lithuania, duchy of 5:157
  Mongol capture of 4:94, **4:105,** 4:106, 4:108, 5:157

Kiev Rus 4:83, *4:85,* 4:88
  Byzantium and 4:83–4, 4:88
  Chinghis Khan, defeat by 4:94, **4:105,** 4:106
  Cyrillic alphabet in 4:88
  decline of 4:89–91, 4:94
  expansion of 4:93
  map of **4:89**
  Norsemen, absorption of 4:158
  Orthodox Christianity, adoption of 4:87–8
  rule of succession in 4:83, 4:88
  society of 4:87–8, 4:91

King, Martin Luther (1929–1968), United States civil-rights leader *10:87,* **10:87**

Kipling, Rudyard (1865–1936), British writer **8:54,** 8:55
  The White Man's Burden (Kipling) **8:54,** 8:55

Kissinger, Henry (1923–), United States diplomat *10:93*

Kitchener, Horatio Herbert (1850–1916) *8:15*

Kition, Phoenician trading station 1:157

Klerk, FW *see* de Klerk

Knights of St John of Jerusalem, military order 5:155

Knights Templar, military order 5:155, *5:155*

Knossos 1:144, 1:158
  collapse of 1:150–51
  Minoan palace 1:143, *1:143,* 1:145–6, *1:146,* **1:147,** *1:150*

Kochba, Simon bar (2nd century CE), Jewish messianic claimant 3:90

Kohl, Helmut (1930–), German chancellor *10:107,* 10:109, *10:149*

Kongo, kingdom of 5:89

Koran 4:20–21, **4:21,** 4:22, **4:44,** 5:170
  Muhammad's recital of 4:20–21
  see also Arabs; Islam; Shi'ites; Sunnites

Korea 10:16, 10:39
  division of 10:12–13
  eastern Asia 10:18
  independence of 8:74
  Japan
    annexation by (1910) 8:89
    expulsion from 5:60, 5:74
    Japanese territory in 5:68
    occupation by **8:86**
    threat by (1876) 8:87
  Later Han dynasty, invasion by 5:41
  Manchus, conquest by 5:63
  see also North Korea; South Korea

Korean War **10:12,** 10:13–14, **10:13**
  armistice 10:13
  casualties of 10:91

Kornilov, Lavr (1870–1918), Russian general *8:155*

Krak des Chevaliers, crusader castle, Syria 5:153

Kremer, Gerhard *see* Mercator

Krishna, Hindu god (avatar of Vishnu) 5:13

Kruger, Paul (1825–1904), president of Transvaal Republic 8:34, 8:35

Krum, Bulgarian king (803–814 CE) 4:79, *4:79*

kshatriyas (warrior caste) 2:16, 5:19

Kubilai Khan (c.1216–1294), Mongol emperor of China 4:107, 4:110, **4:110,** 5:58, *5:58–9,* **5:59,** 5:74
  death of 4:113
  Peking palace of 4:108

Kufa 4:31–2, *4:33*

Kumba Mela festival 5:20

Kun, Béla (1885–1938), Hungarian communist leader 8:174

Kuomintang (KMT; Chinese National People's Party) 9:11, *9:12,* **9:12,** 9:14, *9:15,* 9:25–6, **9:26,** 9:104–106
  American support for 10:28
  and CCP 9:19–22, **9:21,** 9:26–7, 9:104–106
  defeat of 9:105–106
  divisions of, internal 9:22
  Nanking, capital of 9:25
  nationalist movement of 9:12, **9:12,** 9:25
  and Russia 9:25, 9:93
  in Taiwan 10:26, 10:28

Kurdistan, conquest by Ottoman Turks 4:122

Kurds 9:41

Kurile islands 10:37, 10:115

Kush, African kingdom of 1:125, 2:60–62, 5:84, 5:86
  and Ethiopians, conquest by 5:85
  Egypt and 2:62

Kushana peoples, in India 5:15

Kusharas 5:41
Kuwait 9:36
   Iraq invasion of **10:43**
   oil boom in 10:48

L

labour
   agricultural wage-labour 6:17
   skilled craftsmen 6:25
   slaves 6:24, *6:24*, 6:142, *6:145*, 6:173
   in Spanish colonies 6:142–3, 6:145, 6:143, 6:145
   see also slavery; serfs; Industrial Revolution; industrialization
La Brea fossil site *1:33*
Lafayette, Marie Joseph du Motier, Marquis de (1757–1834) *7:93*
Lagos *8:13*
Lahore 5:25
Lake Chad **2:59**
Lake Rudolf, Kenya 1:19
Landa, Diego de, Bishop of Yucatán **5:94**
landowners
   English 6:29, 6:33
      and common land 6:26–7
      rent increases by 6:26
   Polish 6:99
   Russian 6:110–12, 6:115
Langland, William (c.1332–c.1440), English poet 5:122
languages **1:26**, 1:28, 1:74, 3:126, 4:31, 4:102
   Arabic 4:31, 4:34, 4:38, **4:42**, 10:44
      Koran, influence of 4:20
   Aramaic 1:173, 2:79
   Bantu group 5:88–9
   Charlemagne's mastery of 4:143
   Chinese 2:44, **2:45**, 2:50
   Classical 2:87–8
   development of 1:31
   dialects 1:153, 2:103
   English 8:47, 10:169
   European 8:20
   French as international language 7:13, 7:34, 7:92
   Greek 2:87, 2:90–1, 2:93–4, 2:103, 2:151, 2:167, 3:48, 3:77, 4:31, 4:52, 4:56, 6:46
      in Crete 1:140
      Doric dialect 1:153
   Harappan culture and 2:13
   Hebrew **4:42**
   Hindi 8:95
   Indo-European 1:74, 1:98
   Latin 2:87, 3:48, **3:50**, 3:156, 3:160, **4:137**, 5:177
      decline of 4:52
      in European universities 5:168
      written 4:109
   in Latin American colonies 6:143
   Mediterranean 2:85
   Norse influences on Irish 4:153
   Persian 4:31, 8:46, 8:47
   Romance (Catalan, Provençal) **4:42**, 4:153
   Russian 10:83
   Sanskrit 2:23, 5:12, 5:18, 8:47, 8:94
   Sino-Tibetan 2:45
   in Soviet republics 10:147
   Sumerian 1:78, 1:80, 1:82

languages (cont.)
   Swahili 5:89
   transcription systems **2:45**
   translations
      Arabic to Latin 4:38, 5:170
      Arabic and Persian to Turkish 4:100
      Chinese to Manchu 5:63–4
      Greek to Latin 5:168
      Arabic 4:34, 4:38
      Urdu 5:30
   vernaculars 5:122, 5:131, 5:174
Languedoc 5:111
Lan-t'ien Ape-Man (*Homo erectus*) *1:23*
Lao Tzu (c.604–531 BCE), Chinese philosopher **2:50**, *2:51*
Laos 8:100, 9:107, 10:34
   see also Indo-China
La Plata, Spanish vice royalty 8:23
   war of independence and 8:24
Las Casas, Bartolomé de (1474–1566), 'Apostle of the Indians' 6:143, 6:144, 8:45
Lascaux Cave, Dordogne *1:49*
The Last Farewell to England (Ford Madox Brown) *7:150*
Last Judgement, The (Stephan Lochner) 5:118
Later Han dynasty, China 5:41
   Buddhism, arrival of *5:47*
   conquests 5:41–2
   culture of 5:42
   decline of 5:42, 5:70
   see also Han dynasty
Latin America 8:23–31, **10:67**
   Alliance for Progress and 10:71–3
   American economic aid for 10:68
   American investments in 10:65
   anti-Americanism in 10:69, 10:71–3
   anti-clericalism in 8:28
   economic problems in 10:65, 10:73–4
   First World War and 10:64–5
   industrialization in 10:65–6, 10:73
   instability between wars 10:64–5
   military régimes in 10:73
   oil crisis impact in 10:74
   population growth in 8:28, 9:121–2, 9:123, 10:73
   racial tensions in 8:27, 8:29–30
   republican states, development of 8:24
   resources of 8:28–9
   and Second World War 10:65
   social divisions in 10:73, *10:75*
   Spanish imperial development of 8:23
   wealth in 8:28–30
   see also individual countries; individual states
Latin people 3:12
   see also Romans, the
Latvia 9:72
   independence of 10:147
Laurium silver mines 2:125, 2:130
Lavoisier, Antoine Laurent (1743–1794), French chemist and biologist **7:20**, *7:44*
law and legal institutions 1:141, 6:40–1
   Assyrian, standardization 1:173
   blood feuds 3:158
   Chinese "Legalists" 2:47
   democracy and 2:131–2
   Germanic codifications 3:158
   Gortys, laws of *2:87*
   Greek city–states 2:103, 2:106
   Hammurabi, code of 1:93–5, **1:95**
   Hittite 1:159

law and legal institutions (cont.)
   judicial review, United States Supreme Court 7:84
   jury service 2:132
   legal privilege and 7:88, 7:93, 7:97
   Mosaic Law 3:73–5, **3:76**, 3:83, 3:89
   Napoleonic legal codes 7:109, *7:119*
   Roman 3:27, 3:51, **3:54**
      codification by Justinian *3:162*, 3:164
   Romano-Visigoth code **3:157**
   slaves, legal rights of 1:95
   in Sumer 1:86–7, 1:95
   training *6:40*
   women, legal rights in Sumer 1:86–7, 1:95, 1:123
Lawrence (of Arabia), Thomas Edward (1888–1935), British soldier *8:149*, *9:40*, **9:40**
League of Corinth 2:159
League of German Princes 6:118
League of Nations 8:160–1, **8:161**, 8:163, 9:46, 9:84
   and Italy 9:58
   Japanese aggression and 9:25, 9:27
   Japanese seat on Council 9:14
   Middle East mandates 9:40
   United States and 9:55
Leakey, Louis (1903–1972), British paleontologist *1:19*
Lebanon
   Arab League in 9:110
   cedar from 1:83
   civil war in **10:43**
   collapse of 10:131
   French cultural influence in 9:36
   French mandate in 9:108
   government attitude to West 10:46
   independence of 9:108
   and Israel, invasion by **9:111**, 10:121
   Phoenicians in 1:156
   and PLO 10:131
   and Sumerians 1:91
   United States military assistance for 10:46
   see also Levant
Le Duc Tho (1911–1990), North Vietnamese diplomat *10:93*
legalism 5:44
Leibniz, Gottfried (1646–1716), German mathematician 7:27
leisure, in pre-historic times 1:28, 1:30
Le Nain, Antoine (c.1588–1648), artist *6:11*
Le Nain, Louis (c.1593–1648), artist *6:11*
Le Nain, Matthieu (c.1607–1677), artist *6:11*
Lenin, Vladimir Ilyich (1870–1924), Bolshevik leader 8:152, *8:153*, *8:164*, **8:164**, 8:165, **8:166**, 8:167–8, 10:14
Left-Wing Communism: A Childhood Illness (Lenin) **8:166**
Leo I the Great (c.390–461 CE), pope 3:174, 4:16
Leo III, Byzantine emperor (717–741 CE) 4:62, 4:64
Leo III, pope (795–816 CE) 4:136, 4:138–9, *4:142*, 4:162
Leo IV, Byzantine emperor (775–780 CE) 4:65, 4:66
Leo V, Byzantine emperor (813–820 CE) 4:65
Leo IX (1002–1054), pope *5:102*, 5:103–4
León 4:158, *4:158*
   conquest of by Al-Mansur 4:159
Leonardo da Vinci (1452–1519), Italian artist and inventor 5:137, *5:137*

Leonidas (d.480 BCE), king of Sparta **2:114**, 2:115
Lepcis Magna, Africa *3:104*
Les Misérables (Victor Hugo) 7:65
Lesseps, Ferdinand de (1805–1894), French diplomat **8:19**, 8:63
Levant 1:133, 4:44, 4:75, 4:103, 4:112, 10:134
   coast of the 1:54, 1:126–7
   communal monasticism in the 3:170
   French influence 9:37
   French interests 8:52, 8:53
   Greek trading posts 2:93
   Muslim reconquest of the 4:103
   Mycenaean trading post 1:152
   Ottoman rule in the 9:36
   see also Lebanon; Syria
Leviathan (Hobbes) 6:69, **6:69**
liberalism 7:37, 7:100, 7:118, 7:127
   British politics and 7:175
   in China 9:16–7, 9:19
   democracy and 7:115–16
   federalism and 7:84
   in Germany 7:124–5, 7:131–3
   industrialism and 7:66–8
   Interwar years and 9:49, 9:51–2
   nationalism and 7:115, 7:117, 9:173
   in Russia 7:140–1
   socialism and 7:136
   see also conservatism
Liberia
   autonomy of **8:56**, 8:57
   independence of 10:55
Liberty Leading the People (Delacroix) *7:118*
Libya
   dictatorship of 10:132
   Egyptian delta, raid on 1:161
   independence of 10:47
   Islamic republic of 10:123, *10:123*
   Italian, capture of 8:57
   and Gorbachev 10:153
   military *coup* in *10:123*
   oil boom in 10:48
   terrorism in 10:138
life expectancy 6:12–13, **6:12**, 7:44–5
   in ancient Egypt **1:122**
   of hominids 1:30
   of Upper Palaeolithic people 1:52
   see also infant mortality
Life of Akbar, The 5:27, 5:29
Lincoln, Abraham (1809–65), United States president 7:163–6, **7:164**, *7:165–6*
   emancipation of slaves and 7:165–6
   see also American Civil War; slavery
Lincoln Cathedral *5:112*
Lindisfarne monastery, raids on by Norsemen 4:154, *4:155*
lingam, emblem of Shiva 2:21
Li Po, poet (T'ang dynasty) *5:51*
Lisbon 6:22, 6:130, *6:148*
   slave trade and 6:23
Lister, Joseph (1827–1912), British surgeon 8:126, 8:129
Li Ta-chao, Chinese Marxist 9:17
literacy 2:81, 7:11–15, 7:45, 7:62–3, 9:162, *9:162*
   in Africa 10:53
   Aztecs and 5:96
   in barbarian kingdoms 3:158
   in China 2:36–7, 10:112, *10:112*
   clerical monopoly of 4:167

literacy (cont.)
  demand for 5:176
  in the eastern Mediterranean 2:86
  in England and Netherlands 7:13
  Etruscans and 3:11
  in Europe 8:118, 8:124, *8:136*
  in France 7:13
  Incas and 5:98
  in India 2:13, 2:29, 5:11, 10:19
  Islamic 4:35
  in Japan 8:82
  and press 7:14–15
  printing and 6:48, 7:13–14
  propaganda and 8:150
  religious scepticism spread by 8:124
  in the Roman army 3:48
  in the Soviet Union 10:82
  spread of 1:140–2
  in Sumer 1:80
  see also education
literature
  19th-century **8:109**
  Arabic 4:31, 4:35–7, 4:100
  Ashurbanipal, library of 1:174
  Carolingian 4:142
  eastern Mediterranean 2:86
  European 5:122, 5:174
  Greek see Greek literature
  Gupta period 5:18
  Hindu epics 5:13
  Indian 2:15–16, 2:18, **2:20, 2:23**
  Manchu dynasty and 5:63–4
  in Mesopotamia 1:174
  Norse Sagas 4:154, **4:156**, 4:158
  Russian 4:88
  in Sumer 1:80–2, 1:83
Lithuania **9:67**, 9:72
  independence from the Soviet Union
    10:146
  see also Polish-Lithuanian kingdom
Lithuania, duchy of 5:157, 5:158
  Ivan III's invasion of 5:158
Livy (Titus Livius) (59 BCE–17 CE), Roman
    historian 3:51, 3:62
Lloyd George, David (1863–1945), British
    statesman 8:162
Locke, John (1632–1704), English philosopher
    6:167, 7:26–7, 7:33, 7:85
Lombards 3:129, 3:156, *3:161*, 3:163, 3:175,
    4:61, *4:150*
  Catholicism adopted by 4:150
  Charlemagne and 4:150
  and Ravenna, conquest of 4:161
  Pepin the Short, defeat by 4:135
  Gregory the Great's opposition to 3:176
London 5:135, *5:139*, 8:15–16
  cholera epidemics in 7:45
  coffee-houses in 6:20, 6:35, 6:133
  commercial development in 6:20, *6:32*
  corn exports from 6:16
  Crystal Palace 7:174
  Great Exhibition (1851) in 7:173, *7:174*
  growth of 7:60
  Houses of Parliament in *7:173*, 7:177
  as international port 6:16, 6:166
  living conditions in 7:61
  plague in 6:14
  population growth in 6:14
  Stock Exchange 6:20, *6:164*, 8:16
  see also Great Britain
Long Island, Dutch settlement 6:149

Long March, of Chinese communist army
    9:26–7, **9:26**
Lorraine 6:92
Lothair I (795–855 CE), Holy Roman Emperor
    4:145, *4:145*
Lothair II (825–869 CE), king of Lotharingia
    4:164
Lothal 2:12, 2:13
Lotharingia 4:145–7, 4:162
lotteries and tontines 6:20
Louis I the Pious (778–840 CE), Holy Roman
    Emperor **4:137**, *4:145*
  Norse raiders and 4:155
Louis II, king of Poland (1516–1527) *6:93*
Louis II the German (805–876 CE), king of East
    Francia 4:145–6
Louis IX (1215–1270), king of France *5:154*
Louis XI (1423–1483), king of France *5:177*
Louis XIII (1601–1643), king of France 6:67
Louis XIV "the Sun King" (1638–1715), king of
    France 5:63, 6:41, 6:68, 6:70–2, *6:72*,
    6:87, 6:89–92, *6:90*, 6:160, 7:34, 7:87
  absolute monarch 6:71–2, 6:104
  death of 6:75
  foreign policy of 6:89
  navy and 6:164
  War of Spanish Succession and 6:91
Louis XV (1710–1774), king of France 7:9
Louis XVI (1754–1793), king of France *7:31*,
    7:86, 7:87, 7:120
  execution of 7:95, 7:96
  public views of 7:90, *7:91*, 7:93–4
Louis XVII (1785–1795), nominal king of France
    7:118
Louis XVIII (1755–1824), king of France
    7:118–9
Louisiana 8:24
Louisiana Purchase (1803) 7:154, **7:156**,
    7:159–60, **7:161**
Louis Philippe (1773–1850), king of France
    7:120–1, *7:121*, 7:123
Low Countries, the
  agriculture in 6:16
  industrialization in 6:25–6
  Germany, occupation of (1940) 9:69–70
  and Jews, influx of 6:19
  see also Belgium; Netherlands
Lowell, Percival (1855–1916), American
    astronomer **10:173**
Loyang, capital of Later Han dynasty 5:41
Loyola, St Ignatius (1491–1556), founder of
    Jesuits 6:56, *6:57*
Lubbe, Marinus van der, alleged Reichstag
    arsonist 9:62
Lübeck, chief city of Hanseatic League 5:145
Lucca, republican city-state 6:84, 6:93
Lucknow, siege of 8:50
Lucretius 1:39
"Lucy", female hominid, Ethiopia *1:18*
Ludendorff, Erich von (1865–1937), German
    general *8:147*
Luther, Martin (1483–1546), Protestant reformer
    6:46–50, 6:46, **6:46**
  Diet of Worms 6:49
  Henry VIII's refutation of 6:53
  as Hussite 6:47
Luxor, temple of *1:65*
Luzon, capture by Japanese 9:74
Lycurgus (9th century BCE), Spartan legislator
    2:106
Lydia, kingdom of 2:100, 2:109–11

Lydia, kingdom of (cont.)
  Persian defeat of **2:111**, 2:112
Lyell, Charles (1797–1875), Scottish geologist
    8:124–5
  Principles of Geology 8:124

M

Macao 10:112
  Portuguese trading centre 5:61, 6:129, 6:132,
    8:74
MacArthur, Douglas (1880–1964), United States
    general 10:37
Macartney, Lord George (1737–1806), British
    ambassador to China 8:67, 8:68
Macauley, Thomas Babington (1800–1859),
    English historian 6:6
Macedon 3:21, 3:26
  Antigonid dynasty 2:165
  Athens and Thebes, defeat of 2:159
  expansion under Philip II 2:156–9
  gold mines of Mount Pangaeum 2:157
  military techniques in 2:157
  as Roman province 3:22
  as Spartan ally 2:120
  warrior aristocracy of 2:156
Macedonia 5:13
  independence from Yugoslavia 10:151
Macedonian dynasty, Byzantium 4:63, **4:69**
Macedonian Empire
  Celtic invasion of 2:165
  creation by Alexander 2:160–4
  government of 2:162
Machiavelli, Niccolo (1469–1527), Italian
    politician 6:39, **6:39**
Machu Picchu, Inca city 5:99
Madeira **6:128**, 6:173
  Portuguese settlement of 5:161
Madras 5:35
Magadha, Indian kingdom 2:18, 5:8
  Chandragupta and 5:10
Magdalenian culture *1:42*, *1:49*
Magellan, Ferdinand (c.1480–1521), Portuguese
    navigator 5:162, 5:163
Magna Graecia 2:109, *2:115*, 2:140
Magyar tribes 4:84, 4:93–4, 4:130, 4:132,
    4:134, 4:147–8
Mahabharata, Indian epic 2:18, **2:20**, *2:22*,
    5:13
Mahavira (c.599–527 BCE), founder of Jainism
    5:12, **5:20**
Mahayana Buddhism 5:21, *5:22–3*, 5:48
  spread of 5:22
Mahmud, Afghan ruler of Persia (1722–1725)
    4:128
Mahrattas, Hindu opposition to Moghuls
    5:34–5
Maimonides, Moses (1135–1204), philosopher
    4:37
Maitland, Frederick William (1850–1906),
    English constitutional historian 7:84–5
maize 5:36, 5:77, 5:92, 5:99
Major, John (1943–), British prime minister
    10:105
  Exchange Rate Mechanism and 10:107
Malabar 5:31, *5:36*
Malacca Strait 6:132–3
Le Malade Imaginaire (Molière) *7:13*
Malaya 6:173

Malaya (cont.)
  British interest in 8:44, 8:59, **8:91**, 8:100
  capture by Japanese 9:76
  see also Malaysia
Malaysia 10:17, *10:26*
  economic growth in 10:113
  Indonesian attack on 10:24–5, 10:39
  Islamic society in 10:119
  see also Borneo; Malaya; Sarawak
Malcolm X (1926–1965), United States black
    nationalist leader **10:87**
Mali, African kingdom, 5:135, *5:86*, 5:87–8,
    5:88, 10:53
Malta, British acquisition of 8:43
Malthus, Thomas R (1766–1834), English
    economist **6:12**, 7:42–4, *7:42*, 7:46–7,
    8:107, 8:126, 9:118
Malthusian problems
  in China 9:20
  world-wide concerns and 9:156–7
Mamelukes, Turkish mercenaries *4:98*, 4:103,
    4:107
  Ayyubid dynasty in Egypt and 4:103
  Mongol advance and 4:103, 4:112–13
  Timur Lang, defeat of 4:114
mammals
  anthropoids **1:17**
  evolution of 1:12–18, **1:12**, **1:14**
  hominids see hominids
  monkeys and apes 1:15–18, *1:16*
  primates 1:14, 1:16, **1:17**, 1:18
  prosimians 1:14–15
Manchu (Ch'ing) dynasty, (1644–1912) **8:70**
  China and 5:61–2
  culture of 5:64
  decline and fall of 8:66, **8:78**, 8:79, 8:89
  K'ang-hsi, empire and 5:61–6
  popular resentment against 8:68, 8:75, 8:77
  reforms 8:78
  Russia and 5:63, 5:66
  territorial expansion under 5:63
  see also China; Manchuria
Manchuria 5:41, 5:61, 9:14, **9:24**, 9:88, 10:26,
    10:28
  as Japanese puppet state (Manchukuo) 9:10,
    9:23, 9:25, *9:25*
  Japanese seizure of **8:86**, **8:161**
  Mukden incident 9:25
  Russian invasion of 9:105–6
  Soviet occupation of 10:30
  war between Russia and Japan 8:89
Mandela, Nelson (1918–), president of South
    Africa 10:63–4, *10:63*
Manhattan, Dutch settlement 6:149
Manhattan Project **9:78**, 9:138–9
Mani (Manichaeus) (c.216–c.276), founder of
    Manichaeism *4:11*
Manichaeism, Christian heresy 3:141, 4:11
  in Africa 3:143
  Albigensians and 5:111
Mansa Musa, emperor of Mali (1312–1337)
    5:86, *5:88*
Mao Tse-tung (1893–1976), Chinese
    revolutionary statesman *10:27*, 10:29
  and CCP 10:31
  communism, conversion of peasants to 9:20–21
  Cultural Revolution and 10:32–4, *10:33*,
    10:110–11, *10:111*, 10:112
  death of 10:110, *10:110*
  Great Leap Forward and **10:30**, 10:31
  Little Red Book of 10:34, *10:34*

Mao Tse-tung (cont.)
  Long March 9:26–7, **9:26**, 9:105–106
  Peking University 9:17
  political ideology of 10:30–34
Maori people, New Zealand 8:32, *8:38*, 8:39
  exploitation by settlers 8:38
Mappamundi (Fra Mauro) *5:163*
maps
  Aegean 2:92
  Africa and Asia, decolonization in 10:54
  Africa in 1880 8:55
  Africa in 1914 8:56
  Africa in the early modern era 6:128
  agriculture, development of 1:55
  Alexander's march to the east 2:161
  Allied Invasion of Normandy, the 9:77
  American Civil War (1861–1865) dates of
    states' admission to Union 7:164
  the Americas, colonization and exploration of
    1:40, 6:41
  the Americas, pre-imperialist 5:92
  Arabia in the 7th century 4:20
  Asia, major religions in the early 20th century
    8:99
  Assyrian Empire, the 1:174
  Athens, the Acropolis 2:129
  Australia, early colonization of 1:41
  British American colonies' economic resources
    in 18th century 6:155
  British Atlantic trade in the 1770s:
    the slave-trade triangle 6:147
  British Empire and Protected Territories
    (1815–1914) 8:9
  British India 8:51
  British power, growth in India 6:138
  Byzantine Empire, The 4:61
  calorie intake, worldwide, daily (1992) 9:125
  Charlemagne's Europe 4:139
  China (1918–1949) 9:26
  China, physical 2:31
  Chinghis Khan, The Mongol Empire of 4:106
  Christendom in the 11th century 4:173
  Christendom before the Islamic Conquest
    4:160
  Christian missionary activity in the European
    colonies 6:172
  civilization, early sites of **1:66**, 1:72
  crusades, the 5:152
  Egypt, location of arable land 1:103
  energy resources, world 9:132
  Europe during the Second World War
    (1939–1945) 9:69
  Europe in 1815 7:116
  Europe in the Middle Ages 5:119
  Europe, political situation during 12th and
    13th centuries 4:77
  Europe post-1945: economic and military blocs
    (1949–1989) 10:98
  Europe, Treaty of Westphalia (1648) 6:88
  European trade in the 13th century 5:136
  European trading stations and possessions in
    Africa and Asia c.1650 6:126
  European Union, expansion of (1957–1995)
    10:99
  Fertile Crescent, the 1:72
  First World War 1914–1918 8:146
  German eastward expansion 5:129
  Germanic peoples, migrations of 3:126
  Germany and Central Europe, post-1945
    10:16
  Gross Domestic Product, world-wide **9:127**

maps (cont.)
  Hanseatic League, The 5:145
  Hellenism and the city of Pergamum 2:166
  Hellenistic world, soon after 200 BCE 2:165
  Hinduism and the Ganges river 5:20
  Hittite Empire, the 1:160
  hominid distribution 1:20
  Homo erectus, dispersion of 1:22
  Homo sapiens, spread of 1:39
  Indus valley, the 2:8
  Islam beyond the Arabic world until 1800 CE
    4:45
  Islam, the early spread of 4:25
  Islamic Iberia 4:43
  Israel 1948–67 and 1982–93 9:111
  Israel, the twelve tribes 1:168
  Italy, southern 509–272 BCE 3:9
  Japanese expansion (1895–1942) 8:86
  Jerusalem 3:78
  Judaism in the ancient world 3:69
  Justinian's empire 527–565 CE 3:160
  Kiev Rus 4:89
  Korean War 10:13
  Latin America, post-1945 10:67
  Manchu China (1644–1912) 8:70
  medieval Empire, The 4:149
  medieval universities 5:168
  Mediterranean, in 600 BCE 2:178
  Megalithic Europe 2:67
  Migration from Europe in the 19th century
    8:107
  Miletus 2:138
  Moghul India 5:30
  Muslim India 5:10
  Napoleonic Europe and the collapse of the
    French Empire 7:107
  Neanderthal remains 1:36
  Near and Middle East, post-Ottoman 10:43
  Ottoman decline and the emergence of modern
    Turkey (1683–1923) 8:119
  Ottoman expansion in the 14th and 15th
    centuries 4:122
  Ottoman retreat, the beginning in Europe
    6:97
  Palaeolithic Venuses 1:45
  Palatine Hill, imperial residences on 3:45
  Peloponnesian War, the 2:121
  Persian Empire and the Archaemenids 2:111
  population density 9:121
  Punic Wars 3:20
  Near East, early civilizations in 2:72
  Reformation and Counter-Reformation Europe
    6:55
  Roman Empire
    expansion of 3:35
    two parts 3:125
  Roman roads 3:55
  Russia during the First World War 8:165
  Russian expansion 1500–1800 6:107
  Sahara, climatic changes in 2:58
  St Paul, journeys of 3:88
  Sassanid Empire
    in 4th century CE 3:109
    at the time of Khusrau I 4:9
  Seven Wonders of the ancient world 2:174
  South America, post-colonial 8:26
  Southeast Asia, imperial expansion in
    (1850–1914) 8:91
  South and East Asia, population pressure and
    post-1945 recovery in 10:35
  Soviet Union and its successors 10:146

maps (cont.)
  United States and the slavery issue 7:161
  United States, emergence and
    consolidation 7:156
  United States, the winning of the Far West
    7:168
  Venice as a Mediterranean power 4:74
  Western world in 1000 CE 4:133
  World according to Herodotus 2:86
Marco Polo (1254–1324), Venetian merchant
    traveller *4:108*, 4:109, **4:110**, *4:111*, 4:112,
    5:57–9, *5:59*, 6:128
Marconi, Guglielmo (1874–1937), Italian
    scientist 9:137
Marcus Aurelius Antoninus (121–180 CE),
    Roman emperor 3:33, 3:41, *3:41*
Marduk, Babylonian god 1:97–8, 1:164,
    1:176–7, 2:76–7
  statue abducted by Elamites 1:98–9
  supreme status of 1:176–7
Mari
  Babylonian city 1:94, *1:96*
  Hammurabi sack of *1:96*
  palace of *1:92*, 1:96
  Sumerian religious centre *1:84*, 1:85–6, *1:87*
Maria Theresia (1717–1780), archduchess of
    Austria and empress 6:75, 6:77, 6:118,
    7:34, *7:34*
  as opponent of Frederick the Great 6:117
Marie Antoinette (1755–1793), queen of France
    and wife of Louis XIV 6:77
Marius, Gaius (155–186 BCE), Roman general
    and consul 3:29–30, **3:31**, 3:146
Mark Antony (83–30 BCE), Roman general,
    Cleopatra and 3:38, *3:38*
  Parthians' defeat of 3:43
Marlow, William (1740–1813), artist *6:32*
marriage 3:156, 6:12–13
  of Akbar and Rajput princess 5:28
  of Alexander the Great 2:162–3
  of children 5:21
  civil 7:8, 7:10
  diplomatic 5:28
  in India 2:17
  in Sparta 2:107
marriage and family
  Chinese Cultural Revolution and 10:32–3
  in Egypt 1:123
  in Hindu society 8:93
  in Sumer 1:86–7
Mars exploration *10:173*, **10:173**
Marshall, George Catlett (1880–1959), United
    States Secretary of State 9:94, **9:94**, 9:95
Marshall Plan (European Reconstruction
    Program) **9:94**, 9:95–6, 9:126, 10:9, 10:97,
    10:98
  Soviet rejection of 10:9, 10:12
Martel, Charles (c.689–741 CE), Frankish warrior
    4:135, 4:159
Martial (Marcus Valerius Martialis)
    (c.40–c.104 CE), Roman writer 3:58
Martin V (1368–1431), pope 5:116
Martinique, French colony 6:147
martyrdom, Christian 3:85, 3:90–91, *3:92*,
    3:94, 6:53–4
Marx, Karl Heinrich (1818–1883), German
    socialist philosopher 7:138–9, *7:138*,
    7:139, 8:20–21, 8:131, **8:131**, **8:164**
  Paris Commune, views on 7:139–40
Marxism 7:138–40, 8:155, 8:165
  in Africa *10:56*, 10:58, 10:60

Marxism (cont.)
  anarchists and 8:111
  Bolsheviks and 8:112
  in China 9:17–20, 10:30–31, 10:44,
    10:111
  in Cuba 10:69, *10:69*, 10:70
  European socialism, dominance in 8:111–12
  intellectual satisfaction of 9:52
  rural revolution and 9:20–21
  in Russia 9:59
  theory of 9:20
  workers' movements, development of 7:139
  see also communism
Mary I (Tudor) (1516–1558), queen of England
    6:53–4, *6:53*, 6:59, 6:86
Mary I (Stuart) (1542–1587), queen of Scotland
    6:62
Mary II (Stuart) (1662–1694), queen of England,
    Scotland and Ireland 6:69–70, 6:90
Maryland 6:150, **6:155**
Masada 3:89
Massachusetts 6:150, 7:75, 7:77
Massawa 6:129
mass production 8:127, *8:130*, 9:134, *9:134*,
    9:135, *9:135*
mathematics 7:19, 7:23, 7:25, 7:27
  Arabic 4:37–8
  Arabic sources of 5:170–1
  Babylonian 1:97
  decimal system 5:18
  Egyptian 1:111
  Maya calendar and 5:94
  Sumerian 1:87–8
Matilda (1046–1115), Countess of Tuscany
    5:104
Maurice (582–602 CE), Byzantine emperor 4:12
Mauritius 8:43
Maurya Empire 5:9–11, 5:14
mausoleums
  of Constantina (Rome) *3:120*, *3:171*
  of Ravenna *3:138*, *3:156*
Maximian (Marcus Aurelius Valerius
    Maximianus) (c.240–310 CE), Roman co-
    emperor 3:113
Maximilian (1832–1867), emperor of Mexico
    8:27
Maximilian I (1459–1519), Holy Roman
    Emperor 5:129, *5:142*, 6:78, 6:81
Maximilian II (1527–1576), Holy Roman
    Emperor 6:103
Maximinus, Gaius Julius Verus, Roman emperor
    (235–238 CE) 3:103
Maxwell, James Clerk (1831–1879), British
    physicist 9:140, *9:143*
Maya civilization 1:59, 5:93–5
  calendars of 5:94, *5:95*
  codices of *5:94*, 5:94
  decline of 5:94–5
  Spaniards and 5:95
  see also Aztec civilization; Inca civilization
Mazzini, Giuseppe (1805–1872), Italian
    nationalist 7:118, 7:124–5, 7:133, 8:94,
    8:97
Mecca, holy city of Islam *4:18*, 4:19–20, *4:19*,
    4:23, *4:40*
  Kaaba *4:18*, *4:19*, 4:21
  pilgrimage (*hajj*) to 4:19, **4:22**, 4:23, 4:96,
    4:126
  trade in 4:20, **4:20**
Medes 1:175–6, 1:178
  Assyrians overthrown by 2:75

Medes (cont.)
  Cyrus's defeat of 2:76
Medici family 6:39, 6:84
medicine 6:10, **6:10**, 8:53
  anaesthetics 8:129–30
  antiseptics in surgery 8:126, 8:129
  Arab influence on 5:171, *5:171*
  aspirin 8:127
  bacteriology 8:130
  in First World War 8:149
  and infant mortality 7:45
  premature births and *8:106*
  vaccinations 7:45, 8:129
  see also Greek science
Medina, City of the Prophet 4:23, *4:23*, *4:40*,
    4:96, *4:126*
  Arab siege of 9:39, **9:40**
  mosque of *4:47*
Mediterranean 8:18
  commercial activity in area 5:131
  see also Eastern Mediterranean
megalithic monuments 2:67–9, **2:67**,
    2:69–71
  age of 2:68–9, *2:70*
  distribution of **2:67**, 2:68
Megasthenes (4th century BCE), Greek
    ambassador and writer 5:9, **5:9**, 5:10–11
Mehemet Ali (1769–1849), pasha of Egypt
    8:53, 9:30
Mehmet I, sultan of Turkey (1413–1421)
    4:119
  religious tolerance of 4:123
Mehmet II "the Conqueror" (1429–1481), sultan
    of Turkey *6:94*
  Constantinople, capture of *4:48*, 4:120–21
Meiji Restoration, Japan *8:12*, 8:82–7
  agrarian revolts and 8:85
  class system abolished by 8:83–4
  emperor cult in 8:85
  feudalism abolished by 8:82–3
  foreign policy in 8:87–9
  nationalism and 8:86
  westernization of Japan by 8:83
  see also Japan
Mein Kampf (Hitler) **9:60**, 9:61
Meir, Golda (1898–1978), Israeli prime minister
    10:50
Memel, seizure by Germany 9:66
Memphis, capital of Old Kingdom, Egypt
    1:105–6, 1:109, 1:120, 1:125
Menander (c.342–291 BCE), Greek comic
    dramatist **2:148**
Mencius (Meng-tzu) (4th century BCE), Chinese
    philosopher **2:50**, 2:51–2
Mendel, Gregor (1822–1884), Austrian biologist
    9:144
Menes (32nd century BCE), king of Egypt 1:104,
    1:106, 1:124
menhirs 2:69
  see also megalithic monuments
Mentuhotep II, king of Egypt (2061–2010 BCE)
    1:70
Mercator, Gerhardus (Gerhard Kremer)
    (1512–1594), Flemish cartographer 5:164
Mercator's projection 5:164
mercenaries
  Greek 2:72, 2:81, 2:93, 2:99, 2:111, 2:156,
    2:173
  Indian 2:72
  Macedonian 2:173
merchant marine *6:148*, 6:162–4

merchants, status in society of 5:143–4
Meroë, Kushite capital 2:62, 5:84
Merovingian dynasty **3:152**, 3:153–4, 4:135
  Childeric I, king *3:129*
  coinage of 4:169
  Paris as capital of **3:152**, 3:154
  see also Franks
Merton, Walter de (d. 1277), bishop of Rochester
    and Lord Chancellor 5:166
Merv (city) 4:14
Merv oasis, conquest by Ardashir I 4:8
Mesoamerican civilizations 5:92–7
  agriculture in 2:63
  Aztecs *5:93*, 5:95–7, 5:96
  building skills of 5:92
  ceremonial sites of 5:92–3
  cities in 1:69
  early civilization in 1:68
  Maya 1:59, 5:93–5, **5:94**, *5:95*
  Olmecs 2:62, 2:63–4, 5:92–3
Mesolithic era 1:40, *1:50*, 1:51
Mesopotamia 1:73, 1:76, 1:93–4, *1:94*, 2:12,
    2:72, 3:108–9, 4:8, 4:13, 4:62, 4:102
  Arabs in 4:17
  architecture in 1:79
  Black Sheep Turks and 4:114
  business methods in 1:138
  carts, first use of in 1:136
  city growth in 1:69
  early civilization in 1:68, 1:76–8
  Fertile Crescent, the 1:54
  Hammurabi, unification of 1:93
  history of 1:89–92
  Islamic conquest of *4:24*
  literacy, spread of 1:140
  money, invention of 1:138
  Ottoman rule of 9:36
  Parthian kingdom of 2:176
  Semite and Caucasian interaction in 1:74
  Timur Lang's conquest of 4:114
Messenia 2:107, 2:123
metallurgy 1:135, **1:135**, *5:85*, 5:137–8,
    6:24–6, 6:125–6, 7:55, 7:59
  in the Bronze Age 1:58–9, *1:58–9*
  in China 2:36, 2:37, 2:44–5, 2:54
  Etruscan *3:8*, 3:11
  in Europe 1:135–6, 2:66–7, 2:70
  in the Hellenistic world 2:170
  in the kingdom of Kush 2:62
  Neolithic beginnings of 1:53
  spread of 2:81
  see also iron
Methodius, St (9th century CE), mission to the
    Slavs of 4:79–80, *4:80*, 4:93
metics 2:98, 2:126, 2:146
metric system *see* weights and measures
Metternich-Winneburg, Clemens von
    (1773–1859), Austrian statesman 7:124
Mexico 8:27, 8:29
  Aztec civilization in 5:95–7, 6:139–40
  cultivation of maize in 2:63
  Diaz, overthrow of 10:64
  "feudal" lordship under Spanish rule 6:142
  independence, war of 8:24, *8:24*
  Lake Texcoco 5:96
  Maximilian, emperor 8:27
  oil companies in 10:65
  Olmec culture in 2:62, 2:63–4, *2:63*
  population growth in 6:14
  population reduced by disease 6:168
  revolution in (1910–11) *10:64*

Mexico (cont.)
  social divisions in 8:28
  Tenochtitlán 5:96
  Teotihuacán **5:93**
  United States and 7:156, *7:156*
  Vera Cruz, occupation of 8:31
Mexico City 8:30
Michael II, Byzantine emperor (820–829 CE) 4:63
Michael Romanov (1596–1645), tsar of Russia
    6:103
microscopes 7:19
Middle East *see* Near East and individual
    countries
Mieszko I, king of Poland (960–992 CE) 4:91–2
migration 8:21–3, *8:21*, 8:22–3, **8:107**
mihrab (niche in wall indicating direction of
    Mecca) 4:39, *4:47*, *4:124*
Milan, duchy of 5:130, *6:83*, 6:84
Mildenhall Treasure *3:24*
Miletus 2:139–40, **2:160**
  philosophy in 2:139–41
  theatre in *2:138*
  woollen goods in 2:125
militarism
  Akkadia 1:90
  Japan 5:77, 5:78–9, 8:87–9, 9:75
military orders
  Knights Hospitallers *5:153*
  Knights of St John of Jerusalem 5:155
  Knights of the Teutonic Order (Teutonic
    Knights) *5:156*, 6:116
  Order of Calatrava 5:155
  Order of the Knights of the Temple (Templars)
    5:155, **5:155**
  Order of Santiago 5:6, *5:155*
military power, as expression of statehood
    1:141
military techniques 1:133–5
  archery 4:14–15
  Assyrian 1:132, 1:175
  bombing 9:78, 9:80–81, *9:80*
  in China 2:46
  elephants and 2:18, 2:161, 3:19, *3:28*
  Greek fire 4:56, 4:57, 4:61, 4:84
  of Greek hoplites 2:100–1, *2:101*
  heavy cavalry *4:172*, 4:175–6
  Hittite 1:159
  Indo-European advances in 1:133–4
  Macedonian phalanx 2:157, **2:159**
  of Mongol army 4:105, 4:108
  Parthian cavalry 3:42
  of Parthian mounted archers 2:176
  Roman infantry 3:18
  siege-warfare 2:157
  single combat 2:100
  stirrups, introduction of *1:134*, 1:135, 4:16,
    4:175
  see also weapons
Mill, John Stuart (1806–1873), British
    philosopher 8:77, 8:94
millennial beliefs 4:132, *4:132*
Minamoto clan, Japan 5:73, 5:74, *5:76*
mineral resources, in Europe 2:64, 2:67
Ming dynasty 2:30, 5:50, 5:60, **8:70**
  European traders and 5:61, *5:67*
  foundation of 5:60
  Portuguese influence on 5:61
mining 6:25, 6:112, 6:141–2, *6:165*
  use of slaves 2:125
Minoan civilization in Crete
  agricultural yields improved in 1:144

Minoan civilization in Crete (cont.)
  art of the 1:143–7, *1:145*, *1:148*, *1:151*,
    1:159
  city growth in 1:69
  destruction of 1:144
  development of 1:68
  government of 1:148–50
  lifestyle in 1:147–8
  palaces of 1:143, *1:143*, 1:144, 1:146–7,
    1:148–50
  religion in 1:148, *1:151*
  sea power of 1:145–6
  town planning in 1:146
  trade and piracy in 1:145
  see also Knossos; Minos; Minotaur
Minos, legendary king of Crete 1:143–4, 1:148
Minotaur, legendary monster 1:143, 1:148
Minuit, Peter (c.1580–1638), Dutch colonial
    governor *6:160*
Miocene era **1:11**, **1:12**
Mir Jafar (c.1691–1765), Bengal general 6:136
Miró, Joan (1893–1983), Spanish artist *9:50*
missionary activities
  Buddhist 5:13
  see also Christian missionary activity
Mitanni people 1:127–8, *1:172*
Mithraism 3:65, 3:66, *3:67*, **3:68**, 3:93, *3:121*
Mithras, Persian god 4:8
Mithridates I (171–138 BCE), king of Parthia
    2:174–5, 2:176
Mithridates II (c.124–87 BCE), king of Parthia
    2:176–7
Mithridates VI (132–63 BCE), king of Pontus
    3:27, *3:31*
Mitsuhito, emperor of Japan (1868–1912) *8:12*
Mitterrand, François (1916–1996), president of
    France *10:109*
modernization 9:115–16, 9:160, *9:163*, 9:171,
    9:174
  in China 9:171
  in Egypt 9:30–31
  in Ottoman Empire 9:33, **9:34**, 9:35
  in Russia 9:171
  in Turkey 9:35, 9:44
Moghul Empire in India 5:25–36
  collapse of 6:135, **6:138**, 8:50
  decline of 5:35
  European trading posts established in 5:31–2,
    5:35
  Hindu opposition in 5:34–5
  religious tolerance in 5:28, 5:32
  tombs of emperors in 5:32, *5:34*, *5:37*
Mohenjo-Daro, Harappan city **1:70**, *1:73*, *2:10*,
    2:11, 2:12–14, *2:15*, 2:21
  dancing girl figurines *2:12*, *2:14*, *2:29*, 2:29
  map of **2:8**
Moldavia **7:129**
Molière (Jean-Baptiste Poquelin), (1622–1673),
    French playwright *7:13*
Molotov, Vyacheslav Mikhailovich (1890–1986),
    Soviet foreign minister 9:67, 10:76
Moluccas (Spice Islands) 6:129, 6:131–2
  Japanese threat to *9:74*
Momper, Joost de, artist *6:33*
monarchy in the ancient world
  and bureaucracy 1:141
  Egyptian *see* Egyptian monarchy
  Hebrew 1:168–70
  Sumerian 1:85, 1:89
monasteries
  Chora *4:91*, *4:116*

monasteries (cont.)
Cluny 4:164–7, **4:165**
Grand Lavra **4:69**
Lindisfarne 4:154, *4:155*
Moldovita *4:17*
Mount Athos **4:69**
Patleina *4:81*
Santo Domingo de Silos *4:169*
monasticism
Christian 3:170–73, **3:172**
Cistercian Order 5:103
Cluniac order 4:164–7, **4:165**, *4:168*, 5:103
in England 4:157
medieval reform of 4:164
Orthodox tradition of 4:53
Indian 2:25, 2:27
money
invention of 1:138–9, **1:138**
see also coinage; currency; money economies
Money Changer and his Wife, The
(Marinus van Reymerswaele) *6:20*
money economies 6:16, *6:19*, 6:20–3, *6:20–21*
in China 5:55–6
in Europe 5:134, 5:141, 5:143
in Eastern Europe 6:35
in Japan 5:80
see also inflation; money
Möngke Khan, successor of Chinghis Khan
(1251–1259) 4:105–6
Mongol China 5:57–60
gentry in 5:60
Japan and *5:74*, 5:75–7
Kubilai Khan, emperor of 5:58, *5:58*, *5:74*
Mongol-Chinese relations in 5:58
religious tolerance in 5:59–60
territorial expansion of 5:59
see also China; Mongols
Mongol Empire 4:104, **4:105**, 4:106, 4:107–8
decline of 4:113–14
extent under Chinghis Khan **4:105**
khanates of **4:105–106**, 4:107
Persian Il-khans in 4:112
Mongolia 4:15–16, 4:104, 5:41–2, 10:30, **10:98**
Mongoloid peoples 1:46, 2:62–3
Mongols 4:6, 4:104–14, *4:107*, 5:50
Abbasid caliphate and 4:44
army discipline of **4:105**
Chin state, defeat of 4:104, **4:105**
China, invasion of 5:57–8
Chinese assimilation of 5:58
Chinese hostility to 5:58
Europe and 4:106
first empire of 5:43
Islam and 4:45, 4:106–7, 4:112–13, *4:113*
Kiev, capture of 5:157
Kiev, conquest of 4:94, **4:105**
Mamelukes and 4:107
money and 4:109
Peking, attack on 5:61
religion of 4:110
religious tolerance of 4:105, 4:108, 4:112
Russia, tribute from 5:157
Sung dynasty and 5:51, 5:59
supremacy, assumption of 4:110–11
Timur Lang and 4:114, 5:24
warfare and 4:108, *4:111*
see also Chinghis (Genghis) Khan
monkeys and apes 1:15–16, *1:16*, **1:17**
Monophysitism, Christian heresy 3:166, 3:168,
3:169, 4:54–5, *4:55*
Monothelitism 4:54–5

Monroe, James (1758–1831), United States
president *7:155*
Monroe doctrine 7:155–6, 8:30, 8:61
corollary to 8:31, 8:63
and imperialism 8:44
Latin America, intervention in 8:30
monsoon, in India 2:10, 2:15
Montenegro 8:119
Montesquieu, Charles Louis de Secondat
(1689–1755), French philosopher
6:36, 7:32, *7:33*
monuments, Roman **3:52**
Ara Pacis Augustae *3:40*
archway, Glanum *3:23*
funerary *3:29*, *3:156*
to Gelio Publicola, censor *3:24*
to Marcus Aurelius *3:41*
to Mark Antony *3:21*
Trajan's column *3:44*
triumphal arch, Arausio *3:34*
moon-landing program *see* Apollo, space
exploration
More, Sir Thomas (1478–1535), English
statesman *6:45*, **8:164**
Morocco 8:52, 8:55, 8:57, 8:144
emirate of 4:41
French interest in 9:37
independence of 10:45
Islamic fundamentalism in 10:123
mortality rates **6:12**, 9:122
in the Caribbean 6:168, 10:70
in Europe 5:140, 5:147, 7:44–6
infant 1:119, 7:45, 8:150, *9:119*, 9:120,
9:120, 10:70
on slave ships 6:24
mosaics *3:138*, *3:140*, *3:171*
Byzantine 3:161–2, **3:163**
Roman *3:16*, *3:60*, *3:92*, *3:138*, *3:140*
depicting Christ *3:72*, *3:81*, *3:85*, *3:122*,
3:171
depicting St Ambrose *3:141*
depicting St Paul *3:86*, *3:116*
in North Africa *3:49–50*, *3:128*
Moscow 4:89, *6:101*, *6:102*, 6:105, 6:114
Tatar burning of 6:101
see also Russia
Moses (c.13th/14th century BCE), Hebrew
patriarch 1:129, 1:166, *1:167*, *3:74*, **3:76**
moslems *see* muslims
mosques
al-Azhar (Cairo) *4:97*
Ala-al-Din (Konya) *4:101*
Dome of the Rock (Jerusalem) *4:39*, *4:40*
Friday Mosque (Isfahan) *4:99*
Great Mosque (Córdoba) *4:38–9*, 4:43, *4:47*
Great Mosque (Damascus) *4:29–30*, 4:39
Great Mosque (Mecca) 19
at Kufa (Iraq) *4:32*, *4:33*
Lutfullah (Isfahan) *4:126*
Sulaimaniye (Istanbul) *4:123*
Mosul 4:102
motor car economy 9:133–6, **9:134**
motorized transport 8:107, 8:127, 8:129, *8:130*
in First World War 8:149
spread of 8:18
Mo-Tzu (5th century BCE), Chinese philosopher
2:51
Mountbatten, Louis, 1st Earl Mountbatten of
Burma (1900–1979), Viceroy of India *9:102*
Mount Olympus 2:96
Mousterian culture *1:36*

Mozambique
guerilla base in 10:60–61
independence of 10:52, *10:52*, 10:60
Mr and Mrs Andrews (Gainsborough) *6:17*
Mu-Awiyah, first Umayyad caliph (661–680 CE)
4:28, *4:29*
Muhammad, prophet of Islam (c.570–632 CE)
4:18–24, *4:23*
ascent to Heaven of 4:39
birth of 4:18, *4:18*
death of 4:24, **4:25**
flight to Yathrib 4:23
marriage of 4:20, *4:21*
in Mecca 4:19
succession of 4:24, *4:24*
Muhammad VI, sultan of Turkey *9:44*
Mukden, Manchurian capital 5:62
mummies *see* burial rituals, in Egypt
Mumtaz Mahal, wife of Shah Jahan 5:32, *5:37*
Münster, Congress of *6:86*
Murasaki, Lady (978–c.1015), Japanese writer
5:76
Muscovy 4:94, 4:158, 6:100, 6:104
Ivan III and 5:158
princes of 5:157
Russian development from 6:34
territorial expansion 5:158
Museum of Alexandria, founded by Ptolemy I
2:170
Muslim League 8:99
Muslims
Islamic expansion 3:160, 3:164
population pressures on 4:26
in Spain 3:157
see also Islam
Musset, Alfred de (1810–1857), French poet
7:120
Mussolini, Benito (1883–1945), Italian fascist
leader *8:170*, **8:170**, 8:171–2, **8:172**, *8:173*,
9:57, 9:58, 9:64, *9:66*, 9:78, 9:82
Mustafa I, sultan of Turkey (1617–1618) *4:124*
Mustafa II (1664–1703), sultan of Turkey *6:96*
Mustafa Kemal (Atatürk) (1880–1938), Turkish
leader 9:43, *9:45*, **9:45**
Armenia and 9:43
modernization and secularization 9:44, *9:47*
Muwatallis, king of the Hittites *1:129*, **1:160**
Myanmar *see* Burma
Mycenae 1:151
civilization 1:151–2
collapse 1:152–3
and the Hittites 1:152
tombs *1:140*, *1:155*
Mycerinus (Menkaure), king of Egypt
(2532–2510 BCE) **1:105**, *1:106*, *1:110*
Myron, Greek sculptor *2:91*
mysticism
Chinese **2:50**, 2:51–2, *5:47*, 5:48, 5:59
Christian 5:112, 5:117
Greek 2:96
Hindu **2:23**
numerical 2:141–2
Pythagorean 2:173

N

Nadir Kali (1688–1747), shah of Persia 4:128
Nagasaki 5:77, 5:80, *8:88*, **9:78**, 9:88–9
as Dutch trading post 8:81

Nagy, Imre (1895–1958), Hungarian prime
minister *10:77*
Namibia 10:62
Nanking 9:22
Chu Yan-chang's seizure of 5:60
Japanese capture of 9:29
Kuomintang, capital of 9:25
Manchu troops' recapture of 8:73
Taiping army's capture of 8:71, **8:72**
Napata, Kushite capital 2:62
Napier, John (1550–1617), Scottish
mathematician 7:25
Naples 4:118, 4:151, *6:83*, 6:84
revolution against Spain 6:67
university 5:166, *5:169*
Napoleon I (Bonaparte) (1769–1821), First
Consul and emperor of France 7:97, *7:102*,
7:104, *7:106*, *7:113*, 8:24
abdication of 7:111
civil liberties and 7:103
Egypt, expedition to 8:52
French Empire and 7:104–9, **7:107**
monarchy reinstituted by 7:103, *7:103*
nationalism 7:110–11
papal Concordat and 7:103–4, *7:105*
Revolutionary principles, consolidation
7:103–4, 7:106, 7:109–10, 7:111
rise to power 7:98, 7:102–3
Russia, invasion of 7:105, **7:107**
Waterloo, battle of 7:111, *7:111*
see also France; French Revolution
Napoleon III (1808–1873), emperor of France
7:130, *7:130–31*, *7:132*
Napoleonic Wars *see* Wars, Napoleonic
Naram Sin, Akkadian king (2254–2218 BCE)
1:90
Narmer, king of Egypt (c.30th century BCE),
palette of *1:100*, *1:101*, *1:104*
Nash, Joseph (1802–1878), English artist *7:173*
Nasser, Gamal Abdel (1918–1970), president of
Egypt **8:19**, *9:42*, *10:22*, 10:44–6, *10:44*,
10:49
Algerian rebellion, support for 10:45
Suez Canal, nationalization of 10:45
see also Egypt
Natal, Boer republic made British colony 8:34
National Liberation Front (NLF), Algeria *10:47*
National Socialist German Workers Party *see*
Nazi Party
nationalism 7:38, 7:118, *7:123*, 7:124–6,
9:97–8, 9:171–3, *9:174*
in Africa 10:52–3
Islamic Africa 9:30
African Americans and **10:87**
in Algeria 9:108–109, 10:45
Anglo-French warfare and *5:124–5*
anti-Marxist régimes and 8:173
Arab 9:38, 9:40–43
in Burma 8:104
in Chechnya *9:171*
in China 9:12, **9:12**, 9:23, 9:25
colonial territories 8:6, 8:32, 8:58
communism and 10:77
in Cuba 10:69
Eastern Question and 7:123, 7:128–9
in Egypt 9:31–3, 9:42–3, 10:45
in Europe 5:121–2, 10:97
extremism of 9:23, **9:24**, 9:52
in France 8:120
French Revolution and Napoleon, stimulation
of *7:109*, 7:110–11, 7:114–15

nationalism (cont.)
in Germany 7:124–5, *7:125*, 8:120, 8:164, 8:173, 9:53, 9:57, 9:61–2, 9:66, 9:69
in India 8:94–9, 9:98–9, 10:18–19
in Indonesia 8:103
in Iraq 9:108
in Ireland 7:178, 8:119–20, 10:101–103
Islamic fundamentalism and 10:122
in Italy 8:171
in Japan 8:82, 8:86, 9:23, **9:24**
Jewish 9:36
in Latin America 10:65, 10:68, 10:72–3
liberal democracy and 9:173
Magyars, among 8:135
Napoleon III and 7:130
in Ottoman empire 9:33–6, 9:43
in Palestine **9:110**
pan-Arabian 9:31
PLO and 10:49
political organization, as basis for 10:169
revolutionary 8:141
in Russia 9:173
Slavs and 8:119, 8:155
in South Korea 10:115
space race and 9:147–9, 9:152
the state and 9:171–2
in Turkish Europe 8:118–20
in Ulster 10:102
in the United States 7:153, 8:139
in Vietnam 8:101, 10:93
in Yugoslavia *9:172*, 9:173
Native Americans 5:92, **7:168**, *7:169–70*
abuse by colonists 6:168
early colonial relations with 6:152
Plains Indians 8:38
Pontiac's rebellion 7:74
rights of 6:153
territorial losses of **7:156**
War of Independence and 7:79
NATO (North Atlantic Treaty Organization) *10:11*, **10:11**, 10:96–7, **10:98**
France and 10:100
West Germany and 10:5, **10:16**, 10:99
Nattier, Jean-Marc (1685–1766), artist *6:74*
Naucratis, Greek trading post 2:75, 2:99
naval bases
Aden 8:43–4, 10:119
British 8:43–4
Hong Kong 9:19
Pearl Harbour 8:62, 9:74, *9:74*, 9:75
Port Arthur 8:88, *8:89*
Samoa 8:61
shipyards *6:163*
naval power and tactics
Athenian 2:112, **2:113**, 2:120–22, 2:130–31
Battle of the Atlantic and 9:70, 9:76–8
at the battle of Salamis 2:115, 2:116
British 8:14, 8:24, 9:57
French warships destroyed (1940) 9:70
Royal Navy defeat of French 7:105
supremacy of 8:44, 8:120, 8:148–9
Crete 1:145–6
German 8:120, 8:144
in Japan 10:37, *10:37*
Japanese fleet, crippling of 9:76, 9:81, 9:88
limitations of 9:18
Napoleonic Europe, blockade of 7:107
oil-powered ships 9:42, 9:135
Persian 2:111–12, 2:114
of Solomon 1:169
in Soviet Union 10:119

naval power and tactics (cont.)
submarine warfare 9:76, 9:78
United States fleet, attack on Pearl Harbor *9:74*, *9:75*
warships **2:113**
Navarre, kingdom of **4:43**, 4:158
navigation 5:159–60, 5:170
Navigation Act (1651) **6:155**, 6:159–60, 6:163
Naxos 2:118–19
Nazi Party (Nazis)
anti-communism of 9:63
anti-semitism of 9:41, 9:61, 9:62–3, *9:63*, 9:79, *9:79*, 9:109–110
democratic institutions and 9:63
economic collapse and 9:61–3
emergence in Germany 9:58
founding of 9:61
Holocaust 9:61–3, *9:63*, 9:79, *9:79*, 9:109–10
radio propaganda of 9:63, 9:176
see also Germany, Second World War
Neanderthals (*Homo sapiens neanderthalis*) **1:11**, *1:28*, 1:35–8, *1:37*, **1:37**, *1:38*, **1:39**, 2:32
afterlife, concept 1:37, 1:44
artifacts of 1:36
burials of 1:36–8, 1:44
cannibalism and 1:38
Mousterian flint tools of 1:36
population size of 1:46
remains, distribution of 1:35–6, **1:36**
warfare and 1:38
Near East, ancient
agriculture in the 1:53, 1:67
Assyrian influences in the 1:173
Caucasian stock in the 1:73–4
cultural diversity in the 1:56
developmental zone 1:53–4, 1:59, 1:67–70, 1:72–4
early civilizations of the 1:159–78
ethnic classifications in the 1:36–7
Flood, traditional stories of the 1:81
iron in the 1:160
literacy, spread in the 1:140
papyrus, invention of 1:117–18
religious developments in the 1:163–4
trade *see* trade
see also individual countries
Nebuchadnezzar II, king of Babylon (604–562 BCE) *1:168*, *1:171*, 1:176–8, 2:75
Necho II, king of Egypt (610 BCE–595 BCE) **8:19**
Necker, Jacques (1732–1804), French director-general of finance 7:87
Nefertiti, wife of Akhnaton *1:127*
Negroid peoples 2:58–60, 2:62
Nehru, Pandit Jawahralal (1889–1964), Indian prime minister *9:101*, *10:19*, 10:20–21, **10:22**, 10:29, 10:117
Neo-Fascism **8:170**
Neolithic culture 1:50–54, 1:56–62
agriculture in 1:52–8
archaeological sites
Çatal Hüyük *1:60–61*
Cueva de los Murciélagos *1:56*
Jericho *1:57*
Langweiler *1:62*
in the Aegean islands 1:142
and basket-making 1:56
canoes in 1:137
in Crete 1:142
in Egypt 1:102–3
food surplus in 1:56

Neolithic culture (cont.)
pottery in **1:55**, *1:56*, *1:62*, 1:67–7
tools in 1:51, *1:52*, *1:54*
in Yangshao *1:61*
Neolithic era 1:40, 1:51
in China 2:32, *2:34*, 2:54
Mesopotamia, farming settlements in 1:76–7
neo-Platonism 3:51
Nero Claudius Caesar (37–68 CE), Roman emperor 3:40
persecution of Christians by 3:87, 3:90, *3:91*
Nershinsk, Treaty of 5:63
Nerva (Marcus Cocceius Nerva) (c.35–98 CE), Roman emperor 3:41
Nestorians, Christian heretics 3:166, *3:166*, 3:168, 4:12, *4:55*, 4:114
Mongols and 4:105–6, 4:112
Netherlands 6:34, 6:82, 6:91, 6:92
Anglo-Dutch wars 6:88–9, 6:159–60, 6:163
Belgium, unification with *7:116*, 7:117
Calvinism in 6:51, 6:60–61
commercial imperialism of 6:22, 6:130–3, 6:159
diplomacy of, commercial and colonial 6:89
Dutch East India Company 8:103
Ethical Policy of 8:103
in Indonesia and Java 8:103, 9:106–7
industrialization in 6:26
inflation in 6:60
journalism in 7:15
literacy in 7:13
nobility in 6:60
in North America 6:147, 6:149
shipping and 6:22, 6:163, 6:166
slave trade and 6:147, 6:169
society, open structure of 6:32
socio-economic progress in 6:33–4
Spain, revolt from 6:59–61, 6:85–6, 6:158
Spanish provinces of 6:59
Thirty Years' War 6:87
United Provinces *see* United Provinces
see also Low Countries
Neustria 3:154
Frankish conquest of **3:152**
Nevsky, Alexander (1220–1263), Grand Duke of Novgorod 5:157
New Amsterdam (New York), Dutch settlement 6:147, *6:160*
English seizure of 6:159, *6:160*
New England 6:148, 6:150–52, **6:155**
Calvinistic Protestantism in 6:150
education in 7:14
independence movement in 7:75–6
New France 6:148, 6:151
New Granada, Spanish viceroyalty in 8:23
war of independence in 8:24
New Guinea, attempted annexation by Queensland 8:64
New Hebrides **6:177**
New Orleans *7:153*, 7:154, *7:154–5*, *7:157*
New Spain *see* Mexico
newspapers 7:14
pro-abolition campaign in 7:162
see also journalism
New Sweden 6:148
New Testament, the
Acts of the Apostles *3:83*, 3:87, **3:88**, 3:90
Erasmus, Greek translation by 6:46
Gospel record of Jesus 3:80–82, **3:91**
Luther, Latin translation by 6:49
see also Bible; Old Testament

Newton, Sir Isaac (1642–1727), British mathematician and philosopher *7:19*, 7:23–4, *7:24*, 7:25, 7:33, 7:38, 9:51–2
New York, British colony 6:149
New Youth, revolutionary journal 9:12, 9:17
New Zealand **6:177**, 6:178, 8:32
food production and distribution 7:52–3
and Japan 10:39, 10:114
Maoris in 8:38
wool, meat and dairy, production of 8:37
Nicaea, Council of 3:122–3, *3:123*, 3:141, 4:54
Nicaragua 10:67
American intervention in 8:31
Nicephorus I, Byzantine emperor (802–811 CE) *4:79*
Nicholas I, pope (858–867 CE) 4:162–4, *4:164*
Nicholas I (1796–1855), tsar of Russia **7:129**, 7:140–3, *7:140*
death of 7:145
policies of 7:143–4
serfdom and 7:146
Nicholas II (1868–1918), tsar of Russia, abdication of 8:152
Nietzsche, Friederich (1844–1900), philosopher **9:50**
Nigeria
civil war in 10:56
kingdom of 5:88–9
Nightingale, Florence (1820–1910), British hospital reformer 7:128
Nile River 1:100–101, *1:101*, 1:131
annual flooding of 1:101, **1:103**, 1:112, 1:120
cosmic rhythm of 1:113
pharoahs' control of 1:106
transport on *1:101–102*
Nimrud, Babylonian city 1:94, *1:156*
Nineveh, Babylonian city *1:90*, 1:94, *1:134*, 1:173, 1:174
bas-reliefs of *1:134*, *1:136*
Medes, sack of 1:176
Nippur, Sumerian city *1:84*, *1:86*
nirvana **2:23**, 2:27
Nixon, Richard M. (1913–1994), United States president (1969–1974) 10:91, *10:129*
China, visit of 10:93
resignation of 10:94, *10:96*
Soviet Union, visit of 10:93
Vietnam, withdrawal from 10:91
Njörd, Norse god **4:83**
Nkrumah, Kwame (1909–1972), Ghanaian prime minister (1957–1966) *10:55*
nobility
English 6:28–9, 6:41–2
French 6:29, 6:54–5, 6:69, 6:71
legal privileges among 6:30–1
in Netherlands 6:60
rebellions of 6:42–3
religious support for waning 6:30–1
in Russia *6:103*, 6:104–5, 6:109, 6:115
nomadic peoples
Alans 3:132–3
Arabs 4:19–20
culture of 4:14, *4:14–15*
Euro-Asiatic 4:13, **4:17**
Huns (Hsiung-Nu) **4:9**, 4:15–16, *4:15–16*, **4:17**, 4:78–9
in India 5:15
Mongols 4:94, 4:103–14
Oghuz Turks 4:99–100
Pechenegs 4:16, 4:72–3, 4:84–5, 4:89–91

nomadic peoples (cont.)
Scythians 4:14–15, *4:14*
Tatars 4:104
Tuaregs 2:58, *5:86*
Normandy
duchy of 4:158
acquisition by France 5:124
and Rollo 4:146
Normans
Bayeux Tapestry *4:177*
and Byzantine Empire 4:72
England, conquest of **4:172**, *4:177*, 5:123
in Mediterranean 4:72, 4:74–5
Sicily and southern Italy, conquest of 5:151
Norsemen (Varangians) 4:81–4, **4:89**, 4:153
Norsemen (Vikings) 4:81–4, *4:82*, 4:130, 4:134, 4:158
Byzantium, conflict with 4:80–82
colonization by 4:153–4, 4:156
England, settlement in 4:156
at Kiev 4:81
longboats of *4:82*, 4:153
mythology of **4:83**
navigational skills of 5:160
Newfoundland settlement of 4:154
North America and 5:91
at Novgorod 4:81
piracy and plunder by *4:153*, 4:154–5, *4:154*, 4:156
Slavs subjugated by 4:81
trade of 4:153–4
West Francia and 4:146
North Africa 8:52–3
see also individual countries
North America
British Empire and 6:161–2
colonial resources **6:155**
emigration from Europe to 6:18, 6:151, 6:153
English inheritance of 6:154
European settlement in 6:148–51
Florida, Spanish settlement of 6:148
fur-trading in 6:148, 6:150, 6:160
native population in 6:168, 6:172, 8:38
population growth in **6:155**
slave trade and 6:23, 6:169
society, open structure of 6:32
Spain's claim to 6:149
see also Native Americans; North American colonies; United States of America; individual states
North American colonies 6:161–2, 7:78–80
Boston Massacre (1770) 7:75
Boston Tea Party (1773) 7:75
British rule in **7:72**, 7:73–7
Continental Congress and (1774) 7:75, 7:77
Declaration of Independence and **7:72**, 7:77, **7:77**, 7:85, 7:161
emigration from 7:80
independence and **7:72**, 7:73–8
politicians in 7:74–6
resources **6:155**
Stamp Act and (1765) **7:72**, 7:74–5, *7:74*
taxation in **7:72**, 7:74–5
see also American Revolution; United States of America
North Atlantic Treaty Organization *see* NATO
North Carolina **6:155**
North Korea 10:13
North Vietnam
South Vietnam and 10:93–4

North Vietnam (cont.)
United States and 10:90–91
see also Vietnam
Northern Ireland 10:101–103
religious violence in 9:168, *9:169*
Norway 9:69, *9:70*
see also Norsemen
Novgorod 4:81, 4:83, 4:88–9, **4:89**, 5:157, 6:102
Nubia 1:125, *1:126*, *1:139*, 1:161, 2:60
and Egyptian army mercenaries *1:124*
Egyptian conquest of 1:125, *1:125*
nuclear physics 9:138, 9:140–142
nuclear power 9:133, 9:137
Chernobyl disaster 9:154–6, *9:156*
nuclear weapons 10:13, 10:79–80, 10:95, 10:121, 10:128–9, 10:130, 10:139
arms limitation agreements 10:93, 10:129, **10:137**, 10:138–9, *10:138*, 10:175–6
disarmament conferences *10:79*
Japan and *10:38*, 10:115
Mutually Assured Destruction (MAD) 10:128–9
proliferation of **10:13**, 10:14, 10:31, 10:50, *10:79*, 10:100, 10:171, 10:175–6
testing, restrictions on 10:80
see also atomic bomb
nursing profession 7:128
Nut, Egyptian god **1:112**

O

Octavian *see* Augustus
Odin, Norse god 4:82, **4:83**, *4:156*
Odoacer (d.493), German chieftain 3:134, *3:147*, 3:160
Odysseus 2:135
Odyssey (Homer) 1:155, **1:155**, 2:95–6, **2:95**
oestrus, loss of in developing female hominids 1:24–5
Oghuz Turks 4:99–100
see also Seljuk Turks; Turkish peoples
Ogoday Khan, son of Chinghis Khan (1229–1241) **4:105**, 4:106
oil *8:17*, 8:29, 8:107, 9:108, 9:116, 9:133, 9:134, 10:42, 10:47–8, 10:50
Anglo-Persian Oil concessions 9:46
energy crisis (1973) 10:50, 10:58, 10:160
Latin American companies 10:65
North Sea fields 10:103
pipeline from Iraq to Haifa 9:41
politics and 9:38, 9:46
in Sahara 10:45
in ships as fuel 9:42, 9:135
Okinawa, return to Japan 10:115
Old Stone Age 1:40, 1:46, 1:48
see also Upper Palaeolithic
Old Testament, the, sacred writings of Jews 3:74, **3:76**, 3:77, *3:83*, **3:91**
books of
Daniel 1:177–8
Genesis 1:166
Isaiah 1:178
Joshua 1:167
historic evidence of 1:162, 1:166, 1:169, 1:173
see also Bible, the; New Testament, the; Pentateuch
Olduvai Gorge, Tanzania *1:19*, 1:21, **1:21**, **1:22**, 1:28

Olduvan culture **1:27**
Oleg (10th century CE), prince of Russia 4:83–4
Olga (d.968 CE), ruler of Kiev 4:84
Oligocene period **1:17**
Oljeyetu, Mongol Il-khan (1302–1317) *4:113*
Olmec culture in Mesoamerica 2:62, 2:63–4, *2:63*, 5:92–3
gods adopted by Aztecs 2:63
writing in 2:63–4
Olympian games 2:90, *2:91*
Olympian gods **2:94**
Olympic Games (1936) 9:61
Olympus, Mount 2:96
Omdurman, Sudan 8:15
battle of 8:14
On the Admission of Women to the Right to Sovereignty (Marquis de Condorcet) **8:114**
On the Revolutions of the Celestial Orbs (Copernicus) 7:22
"open door" policy 9:8, 9:14
opium trade *8:17*, 8:68–9, 8:73
oracles
Chinese 2:42, 2:44, *2:44*
Greek 2:96, 2:97, 2:112, *2:137*, 2:161
Siwah 2:161
see also divination
Orange Free State, Boer republic 8:34
Order of Calatrava, military order 5:155
Order of the Knights of the Temple (Templars) 5:155, **5:155**
Order of Santiago *5:6*, 5:155, *5:155*
Ordoño II, king of León (914–924 CE) *4:158*
Ordos desert 2:32, *2:33*
Organization of African Unity (OAU) 10:57, **10:57**, 10:61
Organization for European Economic Cooperation (OEEC) 9:94, 9:96
Origen (c.185–c.254), Christian theologian 3:96, 3:117
origins of humankind 1:10–32
Orissa, conquered by Asoka 5:11
Orkhan (1288–1359), first sultan of Turkey (1326–1359) *4:119*, 4:120, *4:121*
Orkneys and Shetlands, colonization of by Norsemen 4:153
Ormazd, Zoroastrian creator god *4:11*
Ormuz 4:127, 6:129
Orpen, Sir William (1878–1931), British artist *8:159*
Orthodox Church
Bogomil heresy in 4:72
Catholic divergence from 4:52–4, 4:66–70, 5:154, 5:157
characteristics of 4:51–2
Iconoclast movement of 4:56, 4:63–6, **4:67**, 4:135, 4:161
icons of 4:63–6, *4:63*, *4:65*, **4:67**, *4:86*, *4:90*
in Russia 5:158
Slav conversion to 4:76–7, 4:87–8
theological disputations in 4:53–4, 4:56, 4:63–6, 4:118
Vladimir's conversion to 4:87
see also Christianity
Osaka 8:80, *8:84*
Osiris, Egyptian god 1:106, **1:112**, 1:114, *1:118*, 2:73
Osman I (1259–1326), Ottoman sultan (1299–1326) 4:119

Osmanli Turks 4:116
Osrhoene, Syrian kingdom 3:72
Ostade, Adriaen van (1610–1685), Dutch artist *7:15*
Ostrogoths, Germanic peoples 3:129, 3:132, 3:154–6, *3:156*
Arianism 3:155
Athalaric, king of the *3:158*
Ravenna, loss of to Justinian *3:159*
Rome, eviction from 3:161
Theodoric, king of the 3:154–6, *3:156*, 3:158, 3:160
see also barbarians; Goths; Visigoths
Otto I the Great (912–973 CE), Holy Roman Emperor *4:143*, 4:148–9, **4:149**
Otto II (955–983 CE), Holy Roman Emperor 4:148, 4:149
Otto III (980–1002), Holy Roman Emperor 4:148, 4:149
Ottokar I, king of Bohemia (ruled 1192–1193; 1197–1230) *4:92*
Ottoman dynasty (of Osmanli Turks) 4:119–20, *4:119*
Ottoman Empire 4:44, 4:122–3, 5:158, 8:52, 8:53, 8:57, 8:60, 8:64, *8:149*
Anglo-French influence 9:38–9
Bursa, capital of *4:119*
Caliphate, abolition of 9:44, *9:44*
constitution of 9:33–4, **9:34**
contraction of 6:96–7, *6:96*, **6:97**, 6:116, 6:119, **6:126**
Dardanelles campaign 9:38, *9:38*, **9:45**
decline of **8:119**, 8:141, 8:142, 9:43–4
disintegration of 7:122–3, 9:30
expansion of 6:84, 6:94, *6:94*
First World War and 9:30, 9:36–40
foreign intervention in 9:33–4
Italy, attack by 9:33, 9:35
literacy in 9:36
military organization of *4:119*
modernization in 9:33, **9:34**, 9:35
multiracial policy of 4:123
nationalism in 9:33–5, 9:36, 9:43
Russia, attack by 7:144
Safavid dynasty and 4:125
secret societies in 9:33, 9:36
Sinai, surrender of 9:36
territorial expansion of 4:120, 4:122, **4:122**
Young Turk movement in 9:33–5, *9:34*, **9:34**, *9:35*, 9:36, 9:43
see also Ottoman Turks; Turkey
Ottoman Turks 4:119, 6:39–40, 6:84, 6:86, **6:107**
and Constantinople, siege of 4:120
decline of 6:95–7, **6:97**
Hungary, occupation of *6:93*
Janissaries 4:120
Lepanto, defeat at 6:85
Russia, wars with 6:118–19
Russian-Polish alliance against 6:103
Timur Lang's defeat of 4:114, 4:120
Tunis, recapture of 6:85
Ottonian dynasty 4:147–50
Ottonian Empire 4:149–50, **4:149**
papacy, intervention in 4:148–9, 4:151, 4:161, 4:163
territorial expansion of 4:147–8
Ovid (Publius Ovidius Naso) (43 BCE–17 CE), Roman poet 3:40

Owens, Jesse (1913–1980), American athlete
    9:61
Oxford University 5:166, 7:10
Oxus River 4:14, 4:17, 4:26, 4:100, 4:107, 5:15
ozone depletion 9:158

P

Pacific Ocean
    first sighting by Europeans 6:139
    imperialism in 8:59–62
Paganism see Roman Empire and civilizastion
Pago Pago, capital of Samoa 8:61
Pahlavi, Mohammad Reza Shah (1919–1980),
    shah of Iran 10:121–2
Pakistan
    aid to Muslim rebels from 10:132
    and British Commonwealth 10:132
    creation by Partition 9:102
    famine in 9:103
    foreign policy of 10:22–3
    India, conflict with 10:20, 10:23
    Islamic state of 9:166, 10:21–2, 10:119,
        10:132
    Japan, treaty with 10:39
    military assistance from China 10:23
    military governments in 10:21–22, 10:21
    nuclear weapons in 10:176
    secession of East Pakistan (Bangladesh)
        10:20
    see also Islam
palaces 1:96, 1:99, 1:142
    Akrotiri 1:149
    Assyrian 1:172, 1:174, 1:176, 1:177
    Babylon 1:179
    Chinese 2:43
    Egyptian 1:106, 1:110
    Knossos 1:143, 1:147, 1:150
    Mari 1:92, 1:96
    Minoan Crete 1:143, 1:144, 1:146–7,
        1:148–50
    Mycenaean 2:129
    Nimrud 1:132
    Ninevah 1:134, 1:173
    Persian,
        Pasargadae 2:76
        Persepolis 2:75, 2:79, 2:80
Palaeolithic period 1:39–48
    cultural diversity 1:56
    human remains 8:125
    subdivisions of 1:39, 1:40
    tools 1:42
    weapons 1:41
    see also Upper Palaeolithic; Upper Palaeolithic
        art
Palaeologus dynasty, Byzantium 4:116–19,
    4:116
    John VI Cantacuzenus 4:115
Palaeozoic era 1:12
Palatine Hill 3:12, 3:45, 3:103
    sack of
        by Gauls (390 BCE) 3:18
        by Goths (410) 3:132, 3:135, 3:145–6
        by Vandals (455) 3:133
Palenque, Maya city 5:95
Palestine 1:35, 1:54, 1:125, 1:133, 1:167, 9:40,
    9:109–110
    Arab insurrection in 9:41
    British mandate in 9:40, 9:41, 9:108, 9:111

Palestine (cont.)
    British policy and 9:39, 9:110
    British withdrawal from 9:111
    crusaders' onslaught on 5:151–3, 5:154
    and Egypt 1:126
    intifada, the 9:111, 10:34
    Jewish immigration to 9:36, 9:41, 9:110
    Muslim conquest of 4:24, 4:25
    oil pipeline in 9:41
    origin of name of 1:161
    Ottoman rule of 9:36
    pan-Arab nationalism, focus of in 9:42
    partition in 9:110, 9:111
    refugee crisis in 9:110, 9:112
    Seljuk Turks, occupation of 4:100
Palestinian refugees 10:42, 10:49
    see also Israel; PLO
Palmyra 3:108
    Roman alliance with 3:112
Pan-African Congress 10:55
Panama Canal 8:30, 8:61, 8:63, 8:63, 8:138
Panama, Congress of states (1826) 8:26
Panama, Republic of 8:63, 8:63
Pan-American Congress (1889) 8:30
pan-Arab nationalism 9:31, 9:38–9, 9:42–3,
    10:42, 10:44, 10:49
Pangaea 1:10
Pantheon (Rome) 3:53, 3:68
papacy 3:173–6, 4:160–64, 9:169, 9:170
    authority of 4:163, 5:113–14, 5:116–17,
        8:123
    in Avignon 5:114–16
    Byzantine emperor and 4:135–6
    Catholic leadership in Counter-
        Reformation and 6:56
    China (Han dynasty), contacts with 5:42
    Church policy and 4:162
    claims of 5:106–7
    clash with French National Assembly 7:94
    conciliar movement and 5:116–17
    corruption of 5:115
    criticism of 6:45, 6:47
    curia (papal bureaucracy) 5:107, 5:113–14
    defence against lay powers 5:103–7
    Franciscans, support for 5:110
    Great Schism and 5:100, 5:115–16, 5:115
    and Henry VIII 6:52–4
    infallibility of 8:123
    Lateran treaties and 8:172, 8:172
    legalism and 5:113
    Lombards and 4:150
    Luther, dispute with 6:47
    and Mary Tudor 6:53–4
    Napoleon, concordat with 7:103–5
    opposition to 5:114–16
    Ottonian interventions in 4:148–9, 4:151,
        4:161, 4:163
    Pope Gregory I 3:174–6
    Pope Leo I 3:174
    reform and 5:116
    Society of Jesus dissolved by 6:73
    temporal power of 4:135, 8:122–3, 8:122
    worldliness of 5:113–14
    see also Christian missionary activity;
        Christianity; individual popes; popes; Roman
        Catholic Church
Papal States 4:135, 4:150–51, 6:84, 6:93
paper
    invention of 1:117, 5:55
    manufacture of 5:138–9, 5:171, 5:174–5
papyrus 1:67, 1:117–18, 1:140, 2:170, 4:169

papyrus boats 1:102
Paracelsus (1493–1541), Swiss physician and
    alchemist 7:16
Paraguay
    insurrection (1721–1735) 8:24
    military government 10:73
Paranthropus boisei 1:19, 1:20–21
Paranthropus robustus 1:20
parchment 2:170, 4:169
Paris 5:124, 5:135
    Bastille, storming of 7:91, 7:93
    cholera in 7:45
    commercial development in 6:20
    Commune (1871) 7:134–5, 7:135, 7:139–40,
        8:143
    demonstrations, popular in 7:95
    Eiffel Tower 7:71
    Frondes insurrection 6:67–8, 6:68
    growth in 7:60
    July Revolution (1830) 7:118, 7:120, 7:121,
        7:134
    June Days uprising in (1848) 7:125–6, 7:134,
        7:137
    Merovingian capital 3:152, 3:154
    monarchy overthrown by insurrection 7:94
    Notre-Dame Cathedral 5:108
    occupation by anti-Napoleonic Powers 7:107
    parlements in 6:67, 6:71
    population growth in 6:13–14
    strikes in 7:93
    university (Sorbonne) 5:166, 5:167, 5:169
    see also France; French Revolution
Paris Peace Conference 9:40, 9:42–3, 9:45
Parliament, English 6:28–9, 6:29, 6:65
    Crown and constitutional state 6:69–70,
        6:104
    Crown, quarrel with 6:63–4, 6:63
    Elizabeth I and 6:29, 6:54
    Henry VIII, support for 6:53
    House of Commons and 6:65, 6:69
    House of Lords and 6:29, 6:65
    in Reformation 6:54
    and Tudor monarchs 6:53–4
    see also Acts of Parliament
Parmenides (c.510–450 BCE), Greek philosopher
    2:142
Parni peoples (Parthians) 2:176
Parthenon, Athenian temple 2:82, 2:105, 2:130,
    2:151, 2:153
    sculptures of 2:128, 2:134
Parthia 2:174, 2:175, 4:10, 5:14, 5:15
    Ardashir I and 4:8
    cataphracts (heavy cavalry), use in 3:42
    Ctesiphon, capital city of 3:43, 3:108
    empire of 2:176–7
    Roman forces of 3:42–3, 3:44
    Rome and 3:107–8, 3:110
    Scythians in 4:15
    the Silk Road and 2:175–6
particle physics 9:140
Parvati, Hindu goddess 5:21
Pasargadae 2:76, 2:81
Pascal, Blaise (1623–1662), French
    mathematician 6:8
Pasiphae, legendary wife of Minos 1:143, 1:148
Pasteur, Louis (1822–1895), French chemist
    8:129, 8:130
Pathfinder Mars probe 10:173
Patna, capital of Gupta Empire 5:17
    capital of Maurya dynasty 5:10–11
Paul III (1468–1490), pope 6:171

Paul VI (1897–1978), pope 9:170
Paul of Tarsus (later St), Christian apostle 3:85,
    3:86, 3:86, 3:90–91, 3:117
    journeys of 3:87, 3:88
    letters of 3:87
    missionary teachings of 3:87, 3:88, 3:91,
        3:116
Pavlov, Ivan Petrovich (1849–1936), Russian
    physiologist 9:164, 9:165, 9:165
Pax Britannica 8:14
Pax Romana 3:43–6, 3:69
peace treaties
    Aix-la-Chapelle (1748) 6:161
    Augsburg (1555) 6:49, 6:85, 6:87
    Breda (1667) 6:159
    Karlowitz (1699) 6:96
    Kutchuk Kainarji (1774) 6:118
    Nijmegan (1678) 6:90
    Paris (1763) 6:157, 6:161
    Pyrenees (1659) 6:87
    Utrecht (1713–14) 6:91–3, 6:162
    Versailles (1919) 8:156–8, 8:158–9, 8:166,
        8:175, 9:52, 9:61, 9:63, 9:66–7
    Westphalia (1648) 6:87, 6:88, 6:88, 6:98
    see also treaties; wars
Pearl Harbor see United States of America
Peasant Family at Home (Le Nain) 6:11
peasants 3:29, 3:106, 3:114
    in China 10:27
    disappearance of 7:49, 7:52
    France, impoverished majority in 7:89, 7:89
    in Latin America 10:68
    poverty and exploitation of 8:70–74, 8:80,
        8:84–5, 8:103, 8:107–108
    in Vietnam 10:36
Peasants in the Tavern (David Teniers the
    Younger) 6:27
Pechenegs, Russian nomads 4:16, 4:72–3,
    4:84–5, 4:89–91
Peel, Sir Robert (1788–1850), English prime
    minister 7:68–9, 7:172–3
Peking (Beijing) 8:74, 8:75
    capital of Mongol China 5:58–9, 5:61,
        5:63
    Forbidden City 5:60
    Chinghis Khan's conquest of 4:105
    foreign legations beseiged at 8:76
    Japanese occupation of 9:25, 9:27
    national government in 9:11, 9:14
Peking man 2:32
Peking university
    activist students in 9:15
    Marxist study society of 9:17
    revolutionary reformers in 9:12–13
Pelagianism, Christian heresy 3:141
    Augustine's opposition to 3:144
Peloponnese, the 1:150, 2:92, 2:93, 2:114,
    2:122
    Macedon, government by 2:160
    Ottoman Turks, occupation of 4:122
Peloponnesian League 2:112
Peloponnesian War 2:120–23, 2:130, 2:133,
    2:147–8
penal reform 7:9, 7:33
penal systems 6:178
peninsulares 6:143, 8:24
Pennsylvania 6:155
    Quakers in 6:172
penology 7:9, 7:96
Pentateuch 3:74
    see also Bible, the; Judaism; Old Testament, the

Pepin the Short (714–768 CE), king of the Franks 4:135, **4:137**, 4:161, 4:162

Pergamum (Pergamon), kingdom of *2:146*, 2:165, **2:166**, *2:168*, 3:22, 3:27

library at 2:169–70

Pericles (c.490–429 BCE), Athenian statesman 2:82, **2:86**, 2:120–21, **2:129**, 2:130, **2:131**, 2:132, *2:133*, 2:136

funeral oration of **2:133**

Permian period **1:12**

Péron, Juan Domingo (1895–1974), president of Argentina 10:66

Perry, Matthew (1794–1858), United States naval officer 8:81

Persepolis *2:75*, 2:77, 2:79–81, *2:79*, *2:80*

Alexander, sack of 2:161

Persia 1:133, 2:75–81, 3:112, 3:125

Achaemenid dynasty 1:176–7, 2:76, 2:78, 2:81, **2:111**, 2:112, 2:167

Alexander the Great's defeat of **4:25**, 4:26

Athens, attack on *2:82*, 2:112

Babylon, invasion of 1:177

culture of 2:81

Cyrus the Great 2:76–8, *2:76*, **2:111**

Darius I 2:78–81, **2:111**

Darius III 2:161–3, *2:163*

decline of 2:156

fleets of 2:111–12, 2:114

gods of *4:8*

Greece, war with 2:111–16, 2:122–3

Greek architecture, influence of *2:75*

Il-khans in 4:112–14

Islamic conquest of *4:24*

Justinian and 3:160–61, 3:164

Levant and Asia Minor, destruction of 4:60

money in 4:109

persecution of Christians in 4:11–12

religion of 2:81

Rome, conflict with 4:11–13

royal tombs of 2:77

Russia, concessions to 7:144

Russia and Turkey, dismemberment of 4:128

Safavid dynasty of 4:97, 4:125–8

Sassanid dynasty 3:108–9, *3:111*

Syria, invasion of 3:109, **3:109**

Timur Lang's conquest of 4:114

see also Sassanid dynasty in Persia

trade in 3:109–10, **3:109**

see also Iran; Islam; Zoroastrianism

Persian Empire *2:75*, 2:76–81

decentralization under Darius I 2:79

resources of 2:77

satraps and 2:79, 2:161, 2:167, 2:169, 2:175–6

stability of 2:78

Susa, administrative centre of *2:78*

tolerance in 2:78, 2:81

Persian Gulf, oil discoveries 10:47–8

Persian khanate 4:107

Persian Wars, the 2:112–16, **2:129**

Herodotus' recording of 2:146–7

Peru 5:97–9

Chavin culture in *2:63*, 2:64

Spanish, conquest of *6:139*, *6:140–1*

expropriation of US-owned plantations by 10:72

insurrection in (1780) 8:24

Inca, civilization in 5:97–9

Peru (cont.)

military government in 10:73

mining of precious metals in *6:165*

nitrate deposits lost **8:26**, 8:29

Peshawar, Kushana capital 5:16

Peter (later St), apostle of Jesus 3:85, 3:90–91, 3:173

Peter I "the Great" (1672–1725), tsar of Russia 6:73, *6:74*, 6:105–13, *6:106*, *6:108*, 6:119

reforms of 6:105, 6:108–9

Russian territorial expansion and 6:106–7

westernization of Russia by 6:107–9

Peter II (1715–1730), tsar of Russia 6:114

Peter III (1728–1762), tsar of Russia 6:114, *6:115*

Peter the Hermit (c.1050–c.1115), First Crusade and *5:150*

Peterloo Massacre 7:170, *7:170*

Petrarch, Francesco (1304–1374), Italian writer *5:114*

pharaohs 1:106–7, *1:107*, 1:123, 1:124

see also Egypt

Pharisees 3:76, 3:80, 3:82–3, 3:85

Phidias (c.500–c.431 BCE), Greek sculptor *2:105*, 2:136, 2:153

Philadelphia 6:152

Philip I "the Handsome" (1478–1506), king of Castile *6:80*

Philip II (382–336 BCE), king of Macedon 2:156–9, *2:156–7*

defeat of Athens and Thebes by 2:159

Philip II (1165–1223), king of France *5:151*

Philip II (1527–1598), king of Spain *6:53*, *6:58*, 6:67, *6:85*, 6:86, 6:142

campaign against heresy by 6:54, *6:58*, 6:59, 6:60

Philip IV (1605–1665), king of Spain *6:72*, *6:87*

Philip V (1683–1746), king of Spain *6:73*, *6:92*

War of Spanish Succession and 6:91

Philippines

American paternalism in 8:104

British seizure of 6:161

cession of *8:62*, **8:91**

Japanese capture of 9:76

Japanese threat to *9:74*

Japan, treaty with 10:39

Spanish settlement in 6:129, 6:141

Philistine people 1:161, 1:168

Philosophical Transactions of the Royal Society 7:20

philosophy 2:173–5

centres of

Aristotle's Lyceum *2:145*, 2:170

Plato's Academy *2:143*, 2:145, 2:170

Ptolemy's Museum 2:170

Confucianism 2:47–51, **2:50**

cosmological speculations 2:140–41

Cynics 2:173–4

Epicurean school of 2:173–4

Greek philosophers, list of **2:143**

Indian 5:18, 5:22–3

Ionian school of 2:139–41

medieval scholasticism 5:168–9

rational thought 2:136–9

Stoicism 2:173–5

Taoism **2:50**, 2:51–2, *5:47*, 5:48, 5:59

Vedanta system of 5:21

see also individual philosophers

Phocis 2:157

Phoenicians 1:156–8, *1:158*

alphabet of the 1:140, 1:157

Phoenicians (cont.)

Carthage founded by 2:109, *2:109*, 2:177

colonization by 2:109

colonizers of the 1:157

currency of the 1:139

god of the *1:158*

Israel, conquered by the 1:168–9

necropolis at Puig de Molin *1:159*

script of the 2:79, 2:90

trade of the 1:156–8

Phrygia 2:100

Phrygian dynasty, Byzantium 4:63

Phrygian people 1:161, 1:175

physics 7:21, *7:21*, 7:23, 9:139–42

atomic structure 9:140

Newtonian 9:140–42

quantum mechanics 9:140–*42*

relativity theories (Einstein) 9:141–42

Picasso, Pablo (1881–1973), Spanish artist 9:65

Picts, replacement of by Norsemen 4:153

Pieck, Wilhelm (1876–1960), president of German Democratic Republic *10:8*

Pilate (Pontius Pilatus), Roman governor of Judaea (26–36 CE) 3:79, 3:89

Pilgrim Fathers 6:152

pilgrimage

to Jerusalem (Catholic) 4:70

to Jerusalem (Islamic) *4:40*

to Mecca (*hajj*) **4:22**

Pinochet, Augusto (1915–), military ruler of Chile 10:73

pinyin transcription system **2:45**

Piombino Apollo 2:90

piracy 6:163

in Caribbean 6:145, 6:148

by English 6:86, 6:158

Pirene 2:89

Pisa **4:77**, 4:151, 4:154

Council of (1409) 5:116

Pitati, Bonifacio de' (1487–1553), Italian artist *5:179*

Pius IX (1792–1878), pope 7:124, *7:124*

condemnation of liberalism *8:122*

Pizarro, Francisco (c.1475–1541), Spanish conquistador 6:139, *6:139*, 6:140–1

plague, bubonic 7:45

epidemics *5:140–41*, **6:10**, 6:14

Planck, Max (1858–1947), German physicist 9:141, *9:142–3*

plant geneticists 9:128

plastic materials 9:137, *9:138*

Plato (c.428–c.347 BCE), Greek philosopher 2:133, 2:137, *2:139*, 2:141, 2:143–4, *2:143*, 4:34, **8:164**

and Christianity 3:96, 3:117

and Pythagoras 2:141–2, 2:143

rational thought and 2:136

and Socrates 2:133, 2:143, *2:143*

writings of 2:144–5

Pliny the Younger (62–113 CE), Roman administrator 3:57, 4:167, 5:16

PLO (Palestine Liberation Organization) 10:48, *10:126*

coup by 10:153

Israel, peace pact with 10:134, *10:177*

in Lebanon 10:121, 10:131

nationalism and 10:49

Oslo agreement and 10:136

and Saddam Hussein 10:135

PLO (Palestine Liberation Organization) (cont)

terror campaign of 10:49–50

at UN General Assembly 10:121

see also Israel; Palestinians

ploughs and ploughing 1:58–9, 1:108, *2:34*, *2:66*, *5:93*

in Africa *5:85*

in Europe *5:134*, 5:137

see also agriculture; farming

Plutarch (Lucius Mestrius Plutarchus) (c.50–c.120), Roman biographer **3:31**

poetry see Greek literature

Poland 6:97–100, 6:116, 7:132, 8:155, 8:158, **8:165**, 8:166

agrarian society unchanged in 6:31

authoritarian régime in 8:174

class structure in 6:99

communist government in 10:9

collapse of 10:143

concessions of 10:142

repression of dissidents by 10:143

democratic coalition government of 10:143–4

despotism, failure of enlightened, in 6:73

EC application 10:151

economic decline of 10:143

elections in 10:143, 10:149

GDR, frontier with 10:15

government in 6:98–9

land ownership in 10:140

minorities, non-Polish 8:160

money economy in 6:35

Mongol defeat of 4:106

partial absorption of 9:82

partition of 6:119, *6:121*, *9:67*, 9:68

Podolia, loss to Turks 6:94

Polish Corridor 9:67

Prussia, conflict with 6:116

revolution against Habsburg rule *7:123*

revolutions supressed in 7:143

Roman Catholic Church 10:142

conversion to 4:85, 4:91–2

Russia and Soviet Union, relations with 6:98, 6:103, 6:106, 6:116, 6:119, 8:166, 9:92, 10:77

Slav origins of 4:85

Solidarity in 10:142–3, *10:142*

starvation in 7:126

territorial expansion of 4:92

Warsaw, capital city 6:99, *6:99*

police 7:133

in India 10:118

Napoleonic 7:110

in Russia 7:141, 7:143

in Soviet Union 10:14, *10:83*

Polish-Lithuanian kingdom 6:94, 6:97–100

political systems

authoritarianism 9:174

in Europe 8:173–4

military régimes (Latin America) 10:73

autocracy

in Byzantium 4:49–51, 4:56

of Justinian 3:161, 3:164

Mongol 4:110–11

in Russia 6:104–5, 6:109, 6:114–15, 8:135–6, 8:152, 8:155

autocratic terrorism (Nazi Germany) 9:63, 9:79

centralized feudalism (Japan) 5:78

Chinese 2:36, 5:46

city-states **4:77**, 4:151

political systems (cont.)
  conservative dictatorship (Hungary) 8:174
  constitutional statehood 6:69–70
  democracy 6:150, 7:84–5, 7:159, 7:170–2,
    10:141, 10:166–8, **10:167**
  despotism 6:104
    benevolent (Rome) 3:39–40
    democratic (Napoleon) 7:106
    enlightened 6:72–6, 6:137, 7:34, 7:98,
      7:100, 8:47, 8:93
    in Russia 5:157–8, *7:140*, 7:144, 8:169
  dictatorship
    disguised as constitutional monarchy
      (Turkey) 9:34
    in Mexico 10:64
    military dictatorship (France) 7:105
    in Rome 3:30, *3:32*
    in Russia 9:58–9
  divine kingship (Rome) 3:63–5, 3:113–15
  dynastic autocracy
    in Habsburg empire 7:124
    in Russia 7:141, 7:146
  emergency decree (Nazi Germany) 9:62, 9:63
  Fascism (Italy and Germany) 8:170–174
  federalism (United States) 7:84
  feudal anarchy (Japan) 5:71
  feudalism 4:170–77
    in Europe 5:120–1, *5:121*, 5:134, 5:141–4
  French National Assembly 7:90, 7:92,
    7:92–4, 7:94, 7:98
  Greek
    aristocracy 2:96–9, 2:104, 2:106
    democracy see democracy, Athenian
    monarchy in Sparta 2:96, 2:106
    oligarchy 2:104, 2:106, 2:122, 2:133,
      2:160
    politicians 2:132–3
    tyrants *2:104*, 2:105–6
  Hellenistic 2:170–73
  Indian 2:17
  international politics (United Nations) 9:86
  liberal democracy 9:173, *9:173*
  liberal parliamentism (Italy) 8:171
  meritocracy (China) 5:46
  military despotism (Russia) 7:140, 7:144
  monarchy 5:89, 5:121
    absolute 6:40–2, *6:41*, 6:54, 6:59, 6:67,
      6:68, 6:70–2
    constitutional 7:105, 7:119, 7:177, 8:137
    despotic monarchy (Rome) 3:101
    elected monarchy (Poland) 6:98–9
    monarchical absolutism (France) 7:83,
      7:88, 7:98
    in Sparta 2:96, 2:106
  oligarchies 6:70
    Greek 2:104, 2:106, 2:122, 2:133, 2:160
    municipal (Italy) 5:130
    Muslim (Pakistan) *10:21*
    republican (Brazil) *10:65*
    in Rome 3:14–17, 3:31
    theocratic 6:150
  one-party authoritarian régimes (Africa)
    10:56
  parliamentary assemblies 5:131–2
    in England *6:29*, 6:54
  Parliamentary monarchy (Great Britain)
    8:137
  popular authoritarian semi-fascist (Latin
    America) 10:66–7
  popular sovereignty 7:84, 7:98, 7:103, 7:110,
    7:118, 7:121

political systems (cont.)
  prefectorial system (Japan) 8:83
  proletarian dictatorship (USSR) **8:166**
  public opinion, power of 8:118
  republican city-states 5:130, *6:30*, 6:84
  republicanism
    in France 7:94–5, 7:97, 7:100, 7:124
    in United States 7:82–3, 7:153
  republics, England 6:64–6
  ruling hierarchies 6:29–33
  satrapy (Persia) 3:47
  sovereign states 6:79, 6:87
  terrorism 8:97, 8:109–10, 8:135–6
  tetrarchy (Rome)114–15
  theocracy (Geneva) 6:51
  theocratic oligarchy 6:150
  theocratic satrapy (Judah) 3:75
  totalitarian despotism
    Inca 5:98
    Russia 8:169
  two-party system (United States) 7:167–8
  see also government and administration
pollution 9:154, *9:154*, 9:156, *9:159*
Polo, Marco see Marco Polo
Pol Pot (1925–1998), Cambodian communist
  leader 10:95
Polybius (c.201–120 BCE), Roman historian
  3:26–7
Pompadour, Madame de, (1721–1764), mistress
  of Louis XV 6:36, 6:37
Pompeii 3:17, *3:57*, *3:58*, 3:67
  Boscoreale villa *3:51*, *3:56*, *3:105–6*
Pompey (Gnaeus Pompeius Magnus) (106–46
  BCE), Roman general *3:31*, *3:37*, *3:44*, 3:76
  Caesar's defeat of 3:34
Poor Clares, female branch of Franciscans
  5:110
Pope, Alexander (1688–1744), English poet, on
  Newton 7:24
popes
  Benedict XII **5:115**
  Boniface III 5:113–14, *5:113*
  Celestine V 5:113–14
  Clement V **5:115**
  Clement VI **5:115**
  Clement VII **5:115**
  Gregory I (the Great) *3:173*, 3:174–6, *3:174*,
    4:160, *4:161*
  Gregory VII **4:165**, 5:104, *5:104*, 5:105–7,
    5:105, 5:116
  Gregory IX **5:110**
  Gregory XI **5:115**
  Hadrian I 4:136
  Honorius 4:54–5
  Innocent III 5:107, 5:113
  Innocent VI **5:115**
  John XXIII 5:116
  Leo I 3:174
  Leo III 4:136, 4:138–9, *4:142*, 4:162
  Leo IX *5:102*, 5:103–4
  Martin V 5:116
  Nicholas I 4:162–4, *4:164*
  Stephen II 4:135, 4:161
  Urban II *5:6*, *5:103*, 5:107
  Urban VI 5:100, 5:115
  see also papacy; Roman Catholic Church
population and growth *10:158*, 10:159, 10:171
  in Africa 8:58, 10:53, 10:58
  Arabs and 10:123–4
  birth control and 8:106
  birth rates 6:12–13, **6:155**, *10:20*, 10:84

population and growth (cont.)
  in China 5:49–50, 5:66, 8:68, 10:32, 10:112
  death rates 8:106
  in Egypt 10:43
  in England 6:13
  emigration and 7:43
  in Europe 5:132–3, 5:140–2, *5:144*, **6:10**,
    6:11–14, **6:11**, **6:13**, 6:18, 6:27, 7:43–4,
    7:60–1, 8:22, 8:106
  imported crops, sustained by 6:173
  in France 6:14, 6:18, 7:89
  in Great Britain 7:44, 7:46, 7:58
  in India 8:93, 10:19–20, *10:20*, 10:116
  in Indo-China 8:101
  in Indonesia 8:103
  in Japan 10:113
  in Latin America 8:28, 10:73
  life expectancy and 7:44–5
  Malthusian theories of 7:42–4, 7:46–7
  medical progress, effects of 7:45
  mortality, declining 7:44–6
  of North American colonies 6:151, 6:152,
    6:153
  over-population, fears of 8:106–7
  in Russia 6:111, 7:142, 7:145
  social consequences of 7:46
  in South Africa 10:59
  in Southeast Asia **10:35**
  in United States 7:154, 7:157, 7:169, 10:84
  urbanization and 6:13–14, 7:46
  of West Indian colonies 6:146, 6:147
  population levels, military significance of 7:44,
    7:46
Port Arthur 9:24, 9:88, 10:30
Portrait of Gisze the Merchant (Holbein) 6:21
Portugal 5:128, 5:162–3, 6:92
  and China 6:125, 6:129, 6:132
    Macao 8:74, 10:112
  colonies
    in Africa and Asia 6:127–30, **6:128**, 8:57,
      8:59, 10:52, 10:55
    in the Americas **6:126**
    Angola, withdrawal from 10:60
    Mozambican independence *10:52*, 10:60
    and EC 10:106
  empire of 6:127–30
    Brazil taken from Dutch 6:142
    collapse of 6:130
    and Dutch Empire in East 6:130
    missionary activities in 6:129
    Portuguese East Africa 8:57
      forced labour in 8:59
    racial interbreeding in 6:142
  French invasion 8:24
  government of
    authoritarian régime 8:173–4
    enlightened despotism 6:73
    in exile (Rio de Janeiro) 8:24–5
  independence of (1822) 8:25
  in India
    food crops and tobacco introduced by 5:36
    missionaries at court of Akbar 5:28
    trading posts and 5:31, *5:31*, *5:35*, *5:36*
  in Japan 5:77, 5:79, *5:80*
    replacement by Dutch 6:132
  maritime exploration by 5:160–62
  shipbuilding and *6:124*, *6:127*
  slave trade and 6:23, 6:127, 6:169
  Spain
    acquisition by 6:59, 6:130
    revolution against 6:67

Portugal (cont.)
  trade
    Arab traders, conflict with 6:127
    with Benin 5:89
    monopoly of 6:129–30
    post at Macao 5:61, 6:129, 6:132,
      8:74
    routes and stations **6:126**, 6:127–9
    spice 6:127
    traders and trading ships 4:123, 4:127
  Zimbabwe and 5:90
Poseidonia *2:115*
postal services see communications
Postumus, Marcus Cassianius Latinius (d. 267),
  emperor in Gaul 3:103
potatoes 6:16, 6:166
Potocki family, Poland 6:99
Potosí silver deposits 6:141
Potsdam Conference (1945) 9:92
pottery
  Chinese 2:34, 2:36, 2:45, 2:54
  Egyptian 1:118
  Greek 2:90, 2:94, 2:98, 2:100–101, 2:105,
    2:112
    Athenian *2:114*, 2:117, 2:125, *2:131*
    Corinthian *2:103*, *2:106*, *2:125*
    types of **2:108**
  Indian 2:11
  Japanese, first developed in 1:59
  Minoan *1:145*, *1:148*
  Neolithic **1:55**, *1:56*, *1:62*, 1:67
  Sumerian 1:79, 1:88
  Urukian pots 1:79
Po valley 6:16, 6:84
poverty
  African Americans and 10:86–8
  in China 10:27, *10:27*
  in Europe 7:46, 7:133, 8:108–109, *8:110*
  gap rich and poor 10:164–5
    after First World War 8:164
  in France 7:89, *7:89*
  in Great Britain 7:175
  in India 10:19–20, 10:116, *10:162*
  in Soviet Union 10:14
  in United States 7:169–70
  urban societies and *10:162*
  see also unemployment
Prados, Diego de, Spanish explorer **6:177**
Praise of Folly, In (Erasmus) **5:172**
Praxiteles (4th century BCE), Greek sculptor
  2:153, *3:13*
Premysl, founder of first Bohemian dynasty
  4:92
press 8:118
  Arabic 9:36
  in Europe 8:54, 8:110
  in Japan 8:83
  and periodicals 7:14–15
Prester John (c.12th–13th century CE), legendary
  Christian king 4:102, **4:105**, 5:161
priestly class 1:71
  brahmans 2:15–17, 2:23–6, **5:19**
  Egyptian 1:115
  Hebrew 1:171
  Sumerian 1:85
Primary Chronicle, The, Russian historical text
  4:88
primates 1:14, 1:16, 1:18
  see also monkeys and apes
Primo de Rivera, Miguel (1870–1930), Spanish
  dictator 8:174

Prince, The (Machiavelli) **6:39**
Prince of Wales, HMS *9:73*
Principia Mathematica (Newton) 7:24
printing 5:174–5, 8:124
  the Bible 1:162, 5:172, 5:174–6
  Carolingian miniscule 5:176
  Chaucer and 5:174
  development in China *5:55*, **5:55**, 5:57
  diffusion of ideas and 5:175–6, 7:12, 7:13–15, 7:20
  in Europe 5:138, 5:172, 5:174–6, *6:48*, **6:48**
  evolution of *6:48*, **6:48**
  Luther's views and 6:47
  privateers 6:158, 6:163
Probus Orestes, Rufus Genadius, Roman consul *3:158*
Proconsul (*Dryopithecus* sp:) **1:16–17**
progress, concept of, developed in Europe 6:126–7
propaganda *8:118*, *8:140*, 8:150, 8:151, 9:42, *9:63*, *9:79*, *9:80*, *9:97*, *9:118*, *9:174*, 9:176
  and Austro-Hungarian armies 8:155
  in Nazi Germany *10:163*
  revolutionary 8:154, *8:163*, 8:167
  in Soviet Union 10:14, *10:14*
prophets
  Hebrew 1:68, 1:168, 1:170–71, 1:178, 3:73, 3:75
  Muhammad *see* Muhammad
Propylaea 2:82, 2:130
prosimians 1:14–15
Protestant Reformation 6:44–54, *6:46*, **6:48**, 6:55, 7:40
  Bible, translations of 7:14
  Catholic Church, authority undermined 7:30
  consequences of 6:51–2
  dissolution of the monasteries in England 6:53–4
  literacy in 7:14
  Martin Luther and 6:46–50, *6:46*, **6:46**
  in Switzerland *6:50*
  see also Counter-Reformation
Protestantism
  Anabaptists 6:50
  Calvinism 6:50–1, *6:50*, 6:150
  dissenting minorities within 6:65
  economic development, role in 6:33–4
  in England 6:52–5
  Lutheranism 6:49–51, *6:51*
  persecution of Protestants
    under Mary Tudor *6:53*
  Polish persecutions 6:98
  Puritanism 6:65–6
  in Spanish Netherlands 6:59–61
  see also Christianity
Provence 4:151
Prussia 6:116–18, 7:125
  administration in 6:74–5
  agrarian society unchanged in 6:31
  communist government of 10:15
  education in 7:14
  French Second Empire, destruction of 7:132
  German unification and 7:131
  Hohenzollern dynasty in 6:116
  landlords in 6:34
  Napoleonic reorganization of 7:108
  Poland, partition of 6:119
  serfdom in 6:74
  Silesia, conquest of 6:117
  standing army of 6:116
  Sweden, victories over 6:116

Prussia (cont.)
  taxation in 6:116
  territories in 7:106–8, *7:114*, **7:116**, 7:117
  wars
    Austria (1866) 7:131, **7:134**
    Denmark (1864) 7:131
    France (1792) 7:94
    Napoleonic France 7:105, 7:111
  see also Brandenburg; Europe; Germany
Pskov republic 5:158
psychology 9:162–5
  behaviourism 9:164–5, **9:165**
  psychoanalysis 9:51–2, 9:164, *9:164*
  see also Freud; Pavlov
Ptolemaic dynasty in Egypt 2:73, 2:164–5, **2:165**, 2:173
Ptolemy I "Soter" (c.367–283 BCE), king of Egypt 2:164, *2:164*, 2:170, 2:173
Ptolemy of Alexandria (2nd century CE), Egyptian astronomer 5:163–5, *5:170*
public health, improved sanitation 7:45
Puerto Rico, capture of 8:30, 8:62
Pugachev, Yemelian, Cossack leader of serf revolt *6:115*
Punch, patriotic cartoons *8:31*, *8:133*, *8:144*
Punic Wars 2:178, 3:18–23, *3:19*, **3:20**, 3:23, 3:28, *3:28*
Punjab, the **2:8**, 2:13–14, 2:17, 5:9, *5:14*, 8:46, *8:48*
  Alexander the Great's army in 2:161
  Babur's conquest of 5:25–6
  Islamic settlement in 5:24
Puritanism 6:65–6
  in British North American colonies 6:150
Pushkin, Alexander (1799–1837), Russian poet *7:143*
Pu-Yi (1906–1967), last Manchu emperor of China *see* K'ang Te
Pygmies 2:59
Pylos 1:151
pyramids 1:109–10, 1:114, 2:63
  at Giza *1:110–11*
  Mesoamerica *5:93*, *5:93*, **5:93**, 5:96
  at Saqqara 1:109
  see also Tower of Babel
Pyrrhus (c.318–272 BCE), king of Epirus 2:178, 3:18, *3:19*, *3:28*
Pythagoras (c.570–500 BCE), Greek mystical mathematician 2:141–2, *2:141*
  influence on astronomy 2:142
Pythagorean mysticism, revival of 2:173

Q

Qadesh, battle of *1:129*, **1:160**
quaestors 3:14–15
Quakers 6:172
quantum mechanics 9:140–422, *9:142*
Quebec
  British, capture of *6:150*
  as French settlement 6:149
Quebec Act (1774) 7:75–6
Quetzalcoatl, Aztec god *5:93*, 5:97
quipus, Inca coded records 5:98–9
Quirós, Pedro Fernández de, Portuguese navigator **6:177**
Qumran 3:80, *3:80*, 3:81

Quraysh, Bedouin tribe 4:18, 4:20, 4:24
  opposition to Muhammad 4:23, 4:28
  patriarchal caliphs from 4:24, 4:28

R

Rabia Daurani, wife of Aurungzebe *5:34*
Rabin, Yitzhak (1922–1996), Israeli prime minister 10:136, *10:177*
racial consciousness, curb on state power 9:177
racial groups established 1:46
Radegunda, Queen, wife of Chlotar I *3:153*
radio 9:137, 9:161
radio-carbon dating **1:32**, 1:70
Radischev, Alexander Nikolaievich (1749–1802), Russian political exile 6:115
railways 7:54–5, 7:56–7, *7:136*, 7:137
  in Africa 8:53
  agricultural produce distributed by 7:52–3, *7:53*, 7:54
  in Canada and Australia 8:32, *8:32*, 8:37
  communication and 7:133
  in Great Britain 7:59
  Indian network of *8:18*, 8:47, 8:92
  industrial development and 7:56, 8:107
  isolation reduced 8:18
  in Japan 8:83
  and migration 8:22
  in Russia 8:143
  in United States *7:155*
    transcontinental **7:168**, *7:169*
  in war 7:129, *7:144*
  see also canals; steam engines
rainforests, tropical *9:157*, **9:157**
Rajasthan 5:28
Rajas' Travels in India (Rousselet) **8:95**
Rama, Hindu god **2:20**, *2:21*, 5:13
Ramayana, Indian epic 2:18, **2:20**, *2:21*, 5:13
Ramón Berenguer I, Count of Barcelona (1024–1276) *4:158*
Ramses II, king of Egypt (1279–1213 BCE) *1:75*, **1:105**, *1:114*, *1:117*, *1:128–9*, 1:160
Ramses III, king of Egypt (c.1200–1168 BCE) 1:129
Ramses XI, king of Egypt (12th century BCE) 1:129
Ranthambor, conquest of 5:28
Rape of Europa, The (François Boucher) *5:101*
Raphael (1483–1520), Italian artist *7:17*
Rastrelli, Bartolomeo, architect *6:113*
Ravenna 3:135, *3:146*, **3:163**, 3:176, 4:62, 4:142
  churches of *4:49*, *4:51*, *4:58*, *4:67*
  as gift to St Peter 4:135
  imperial exarch of 4:160
  Justinian and *3:159*
  Lombard, conquest of 4:161
  mosaics of *3:81*, *3:138*, *3:161*, *3:163*
  Theodoric and *3:154*, *3:156*, 3:160
Reagan, Ronald (1911–), United States president 10:130–1, *10:138*
Recared I, king of Visigoths (586–601 CE) **3:157**
Recesvinto, king of the Visigoths (653–672 CE) *3:176*
Recueil général des anciennes lois françaises (Isambert) **6:171**
red ochre 1:42
Red Turban secret society 5:60

Redwald, king of East Anglia (599–625 CE) 4:152
Reflections on the Revolution in France (Burke) 7:100
Reform Acts (1832, 1867, 1872) *7:171*, 7:172–3
Reformation *see* Protestant Reformation
refugees
  in Africa *9:126*
  from East to West Germany 10:78, *10:79*
  Jewish *9:109*
  Palestine camps 9:110, *9:110*, 9:112
  Palestinian 10:42, 10:49
  Rhodesian war *10:60*
  Second World War *9:48*, 9:81, *9:90*
  Vietnam War *10:91*
Re-Harakhty, Egyptian god *1:130*
Reign of Terror *see* French Revolution
Reims Cathedral *5:108*
relativity theory 9:141–2, *9:141*
religion
  Arab polytheism 4:19
  atheism 7:37, 7:62
  Aztec 5:97
  Babylonian 1:97–8, 1:176–7
  Bogomil heresy 4:72
  Brahmanical 5:10, 5:18, 5:21
  Buddhism *see* Buddhism
  Byzantine theological disputations 4:53–4, 4:56, 4:63–6
  Chinese
    ancestor worship in 2:41
    family roles in 2:41, 2:42
    nature gods in 2:42
    political forms, influence on 2:42
    see also Confucianiam; Taoism
  Christianity *see* Christianity
  Church of England 7:10
  Confucianism *see* Confucianism
  declining belief 9:49, 9:165–6, 9:169
  in Eastern Empire 3:166–8
  ecumenism 9:169, *9:170*
  Egyptian *see under* Egypt
  Enlightenment, scepticism of 7:28–30, 7:37
  Etruscan **3:10**
  evangelism in cities 7:62
  diversity, expression of 1:142
  fertility figures 1:148
  Greek *see* Greek religion
  Hebrew *see* Hebrews
  heresy 4:72, 6:44–5, 6:50–1, 6:53–4, *6:58*, 6:60, 7:8, 7:10, 7:25, 7:36
  Hinduism *see* Hinduism
  Iconoclasm 4:63–6, *4:67*, 4:135, 4:161
  Inca 5:98
  in India 5:10–13, *5:12*, 5:14, 5:16, 5:28, 5:32
  Aryan 2:15–16
  Buddhism *see* Buddhism
  Hinduism *see* Hinduism
  Hindu-Muslim conflicts 6:135, 6:138, **6:138**, 8:96, 8:97–101, *9:100*, 9:102, 9:168, *10:116*, 10:117
  Hindu-Muslim assimilation 5:30
  Jainism *see* Jainism
  monasticism 2:25, 2:27
  Vedic 2:15–16, 2:23–4
  Islam *see* Islam
  Lutheranism 6:49–51, *6:51*
  Manichaeism *see* Manichaeism
  Marxism as secular religion 7:139
  massacres, driven by 9:168

religion (cont.)
 Maya 5:93–4, *5:94*, 5:95
 Minoan 1:148, *1:150–51*
 missionary activities *see* Christian missionary activity; missionary activities
 Mithraism *3:65–7*, **3:68**, 3:93, *3:121*
 Mongol 4:110
 monotheistic 1:164, 4:18, 4:21, 4:23, 4:31
 morality and 1:171
 mystery cults, ancient 3:66, *3:67*, **3:68**, 3:93–5
 myth and mysticism in **2:23**
 origins 1:37, 1:44, 1:67, 1:71
 Orthodox Christianity *see* Orthodox Church
 Orthodox Church *6:100*, 6:115
 persecution and 7:36, **9:168**
 Persian 2:81
 pluralism institutionalized 6:50
 and politics 1:85
 Protestant Reformation *see* Protestant Reformation
 Puritanism 6:65, 6:150
 Quakers 6:172
 Russian Orthodoxy *9:166*
  opposition to 6:104, 6:115
 Ryobu-Shinto 5:71
 science and 7:21–2, 7:24–6
 science, impact of 9:162
 Shintoism *see* Shintoism
 Sikhism 6:135
 Sumerian 1:79, 1:82–5, 1:97–8
 Taoism *see* Taoism
 Unitarianism 6:65, 6:70
 universities, control of 7:10
 in urban populations 7:63
 violence and hatred rooted in 9:168, *9:169*
 World Council of Churches 9:169
 Zoroastrianism 2:81, 4:10
 see also Christianity; Islam; Roman Catholicism; Roman empire and civilisation; Shi'ites; Sunnites
religious discrimination 7:10, 7:173
religious orders, devoted to teaching 7:14
religious tolerance 7:36, *7:37*, 7:98
 of Asoka 5:12
 in China 5:57
 in English colonies in North America 6:152
 as Hohenzollern policy 6:116
 of Moghul rulers 5:28, 5:32
 of Ottoman Turks 6:95
 in Prussia 6:73
 in Spain *5:170*
 in United Provinces 6:61
 by William the Silent *6:61*
Rembrandt (Hermensz van Rijn) (1606–1669), Dutch artist *6:10*
Renaissance, the 5:172–4
 Catholicism and *7:8*
 pessimism of 7:27–8
 science in *7:6*, 7:16–17
Renan, Ernest (1823–1892), French scholar 8:124
 Life of Jesus 8:124
 What is a Nation? **8:124**
Repin, Ilya (1844–1930), Russian artist 7:146–7
Republic, the (Plato) 2:144–5, **2:144**
republicanism 7:82–3, 7:94–5, 7:97, 7:100, 7:153
 see also conservatism

resources, natural
 consumption of 9:115, 9:130–131
 energy **9:132**, *9:133*, 9:156–7
 food 9:124–5, **9:124**, 9:156–7
 population and 9:156–7
Restoration, the (Great Britain) 6:66, *6:66*
Revisionist Marxists 8:111–12
revolution
 army, use of 7:133–5, *7:135*
 British reluctance to adopt 7:175–6
 in Marxist theory 7:138–40
 new concept of 7:72–3, 7:101, 7:116–17
 radical movements of (1848) 7:123–5
revolutions
 American *see* American Revolution
 in China, *see* Chinese Revolution
 in France, *see* French Revolution
 in Italy (1898, 1914) 8:110
 in Russia (1905) 8:110
Reymerswaele, Marinus van, Dutch artist *6:20*, *6:44*
Rhine River
 barbarian threat to 3:110, 3:129
 Franks and 3:111
 as frontier of empire 3:42, 3:125
 Vandals and Alans, crossing by 3:133
Rhodes 2:157
 Sassanid, capture of 4:12
Rhodesia 8:59, 10:55
 as Zimbabwe 10:61
 economic sanctions in 10:59
 secession from Commonwealth 10:59
 South African, pressure on 10:60
 see also Zimbabwe (Rhodesia)
Ribbentrop, Joachim von (1893–1946), Nazi foreign minister 9:67, **9:67**
rice 5:10, 5:50, 8:84–5, 8:101
 as cash crop 5:80–81
 cultivation of *5:64*
 price fluctuations of 5:80
 varieties of 5:56, 5:81
 yields of 9:129
Richard I the Lionheart (1157–1199), king of England *4:103*, *5:151*
Richelieu, Armand de (1585–1642), French cardinal and statesman 6:66–7, *6:67*, 6:70–1, 6:87
Rig-Veda, Indian religious text 2:15–16, **2:23**, 2:25, **5:19**
Rimush, king of Akkad *1:90*
Ritchie, John, English artist *7:172*
road-building
 in the eastern Mediterranean 2:86
 in the Persian Empire 2:79
 in the Roman Empire *3:47*, **3:55**
Roanoke settlements 6:148, 6:158
Robespierre, Maximilien de (1758–1794), Jacobin leader *7:94–5*
Roboam, king of Judah (c.930–c.914 BCE) **1:168**
robots, industrial use of 9:134, 9:136
rock art *2:57*, *2:60*
 African *1:8*, *1:42*, 1:44
 Spanish *1:51*
 see also cave paintings
Roggeveen, Jacob, Dutch navigator **6:177**
Rollo, first duke of Normandy (c.911–c.925) 4:84, 4:146, 4:158
Roman army 3:9, 3:17–18, *3:18*, **3:33**, 3:40, 3:69–70

Roman army (cont.)
 barbarian mercenaries **3:126**, 3:129, 3:132, 3:134–5
 citizenship earned by service in 3:29, **3:33**
 conscription into 3:17–18, 3:28–9, **3:33**, 3:114
 construction labour, as source of 3:51–4
 emperors chosen by 3:41, 3:70, 3:101, 3:113
 Germanic tribal defeat of 3:42
 growth of in later empire 3:107–8, 3:114
 Herod's Temple, destruction of by **3:78**
 legionary standards in 3:29, 3:43
 military camps in **3:59**, **3:111**
 Mithraism *3:65*, 3:66
 Parthian defeat of 3:42–3
 in politics 3:29
 Praetorian Guard **3:33**, 3:38, 3:70, *3:71*, 3:101
  disbanded by Constantine 3:119
 property qualifications abolished 3:29, **3:33**
 reorganization of
  under Aurelian 3:112–13
  under Constantine 3:119
  under Diocletian 3:114
 soldiers' pay in *3:107*
 strength of **3:33**, 3:70
  decline of 3:128–9
 tetrarchy and 3:114
 veterans of *3:34*, 3:39
 volunteers in 3:70
Roman Catholic Church 6:33, 9:169–70
 anti-Marxism and 8:171
 anti-papal prejudice of 8:123
 Arian barbarians and 3:141
 authority questioned 8:123–4
 bishops, role of 3:169–70, 3:174
 in Canada (Quebec Act) 7:75
 censorship and 7:10, 7:15, 7:25
 chivalry, support of 5:143
 conversions to
  Clovis, king of the Franks **3:152**, 3:153
  Recared, king of the Visigoths **3:157**
  Visigoths in Spain 3:156, **3:157**, 3:176
 Counter-Reformation *see* Counter-Reformation
 cultural monopoly of 4:167
 culture, decreasing domination of 5:174
 Donatists and 3:143
 ecclesiastical reforms 5:103–4, 5:107
 economics of 4:168–9
 education, loss of domination in 8:123
 in Europe 5:102–3, 5:117–19
 in France 7:99
 friars and 5:109–12, 5:166
 in Habsburg empire 6:74–5
 impact of 4:167–8
 Inquisition and 5:111
 insecurity of 4:159–60
 intolerance of heretics 5:111–12
 in Lithuania 5:157
 missionary activity 3:176, 6:171, **6:172**, 8:123
 Muslims and 5:31
 nationalisation of lands 7:92, 7:94
 and native populations 6:143–4, *6:143*, 6:171
 Orthodox Church, divergence of 4:52–4, 4:66–70, 4:85, 5:154, 5:157
 papacy and 3:173–4, 5:103–8, 5:111
 political importance of 3:153
 and progress, hostility to 8:122
 Reformation and 7:30

Roman Catholic Church (cont.)
 and sexuality, hostility toward 5:146–7
 South American colonies, domination by 6:143
 in Spanish colonies 6:145
 St Augustine baptized in 3:143
 tax immunities of 6:44
 taxation and 5:132
 transubstantiation, theory of 5:108
 worldliness of 5:113–14
 see also Christian missionary activity; Christianity; Church and State; clergy; monasticism; papacy; popes
Roman emperors
 Antoninus Pius (136–161 CE) 3:41
 Arcadius (383–408 CE) *3:134*
 Augustus (27 BCE–14 CE) *see* Augustus
 Aurelian (270–275 CE) *3:107*, 3:113
 Caracalla (211–217 CE) *3:103*, 3:104, *3:104*
 Claudius (41–54 CE) 3:42, **3:54**, *3:64*
 Commodus (180–192 CE) 3:41, 3:101, *3:102*
 Constantine I (306–337 CE) *see* Constantine I
 Constantius (305–306 CE) 3:118
 Decius (249–251 CE) 3:117–18
 Diocletian (284–305 CE) *3:14*, 3:113–15, *3:114*, 3:118
 Domitian (81–96 CE) 3:41, **3:45**
 Gaius (Caligula) (37–41 CE) 3:41
 Galerius (305–311 CE) 3:118, *3:124*
 Hadrian (117–138 CE) 3:41, *3:43*, *3:53*, 3:68, 3:90
 Honorius (395–423 CE) *3:134*
 Julian "the Apostate" (361–363 CE) 3:135–6, *3:135*
 Justinian I (527–562 CE) *see* Justinian I
 Marcus Aurelius Antoninus (161–180 CE) **3:33**, 3:41, *3:41*
 Maximinus (235–238 CE) 3:103
 Nero (54–68 CE) 3:40
 Nerva (96–98 CE) 3:41
 Romulus Augustulus (475–476 CE) 3:134, *3:147*
 Septimius Severus (193–211 CE) 3:101, 3:103–4, *3:104*, *3:110*
 Theodosius I (379–395 CE) *3:136*, 3:137–40, *3:137*
 Tiberius (14–37 CE) *3:6*, *3:39*, 3:40, *3:45*, **3:45**
 Titus (79–81 CE) *3:69*
 Trajan (98–117 CE) 3:41–3, 3:68
 Valerian (253–260 CE) 3:109, 3:118
 Vespasian (69–79 CE) *3:40*, 3:41, **3:41**
 Vitellius (69 CE) *3:40*
Roman Empire and civilization 2:87, **2:129**, *2:138*, *2:177*, *3:6*, 3:8, 3:12, **3:35**, 3:125
 amphitheatres in 3:58–9, *3:61*
 barbarian incursions into 3:107–12, 3:129–33, *3:130*
 Christianity, reaction to 3:87–9
 citizenship
  army service and 3:29, **3:33**
  extension of 3:16, 3:28, 3:30, 3:47
  influence of 3:16
  in republic 3:14–16, 3:28
 coinage in 3:107
 corruption in 3:104, 3:114, 3:135, 3:165
 cosmopolitan character of 3:47–8, *3:49*
 daily life in *3:16*, *3:58*, **3:112**
 differentiation between West and East **3:125**, 3:126

Roman Empire and civilization (cont.)
  Eastern Empire
    architectural heritage of 3:164
    art of *3:163*, **3:163**
    Church and State in 3:126
    citizens of 3:165–6
    Justinian, emperor *see* Justinian
    religions of 3:166–8
    Western Church and 3:168–9
    see also Byzantine Empire
  economy of *see* economic developments
  education in 3:51, *3:51*
  emperors *see* Roman emperors
  frontiers of 3:107–11, 3:129–33
  Greek and Etruscan influences in 3:12, *3:13*,
    3:26–7, 3:48–51, **3:52**
  growth of 3:17–24, 3:27, **3:35**, 3:41–3
  ideological crisis in 3:114–15
  imperial administration of 3:24–5, 3:27,
    3:101–3
    Constantine's reforms of 3:119
    systems of 3:113–14, **3:125**
  imperial cult in 3:63–5
  imperial succession to
    adoption 3:41
    hereditary principle 3:41, 3:101
  inflation in *3:107*, 3:135
  internal unrest in 3:66–8, 3:101–3
  Jewish nationalism, response to 3:89
  Justinian's attempts to restore **3:157**,
    3:160–64, **3:160**
  law in 3:27, **3:54**
  literature in 3:48–51, **3:50**
  political and cultural disintegration in 3:101
  provinces of 3:22, 3:24–5
    Africa *see* Africa
    Asia Minor 3:22, 3:27, 3:125–6
    Britain (Britannia) 3:42, 3:125, 3:150–2
    Cisalpine Gaul 3:27
    Egypt 3:38, 3:123, 3:126
    Gaul *see* Gaul
    governors of 3:24–5
    Judaea 3:76, 3:79
    Mauretania 3:42
    Moesia 3:111
    Sicily and Sardinia 3:19, 3:22
    Spain 3:21–2
    Syria *see* Syria
    Transalpine Gaul 3:27
  provincial cities of 3:58, **3:59**
  public entertainments in 3:58–9, **3:60**, *3:92*,
    3:94, *3:137*
  religions of
    Christianity 3:119–23
    civic authorities responsible for 3:62, **3:68**
    external influences on 3:65–6
    gods of 3:63, *3:65*, **3:68**
    imperial cult (deification of emperor)
      3:63–5, *3:64*, 3:68, 3:113–15
    mystery cults 3:66, *3:67*, **3:68**
    pagan cults
      restoration by Julian 3:135–6
      worship forbidden by Theodosius
        3:136–7
    sun-god cult 3:120–21
    superstitions 3:63, 3:65, 3:92, 3:140–1
    temples 3:62, *3:62–3*
    see also religions
  Republican period 2:70
    Aegean hegemony 3:22
    agrarian reform in 3:29–30

Roman Empire and civilization, Republican
  period (cont.)
    Carthage, destruction of *2:110*, 3:19, 3:23
    citizenship of 3:14–16, 3:28–30, **3:33**, 3:47
    conscription and 3:17–18, 3:28
    constitution of 3:12–17, 3:25
    corruption in 3:25, 3:31–2
    decline of 3:12–14, 3:27–36
    dictatorship in 3:30
    end of 3:32–6
    establishment of (509 BCE) **3:9**, 3:12
    foreign policy of **3:10**, 3:17
    Greek politics and 3:21–22
    growing strength of 2:177–8
    Hellenization of 3:25–6
    naval warfare in 3:19, *3:21*
    plebeians (*plebs*) in 3:15–17, 3:30
    political structure of 3:12–17, 3:28, 3:31
    social foundations of 3:15–17
    territorial expansion of **3:10**, 3:17–23,
      3:22, *3:23*
    Tribunes of the People in 3:16, 3:29
    votes for sale in 3:28
  road network of *3:47*, **3:55**
  Romano-British civilization 3:150–52
  sale of offices in 3:135, 3:165
  social divisions of 3:55–7
  taxation *see* taxation
  technical skills in 3:54–5
  town-planning in 3:51, 3:54, 3:58, **3:59**
  trade in 3:69, *3:70*, 3:109–10, **3:109**,
    3:128
  urban daily life in 3:58, **3:112**
  villas *see* villas
  wealth 3:24–5, *3:24*, 3:28–9, 3:57–8
  Western Empire (4th–5th century CE)
    collapse of state apparatus in 3:127–35
    division of Church and State in 3:126–7
Romanesque architecture **4:165**
Romania 7:129–30, **7:129**, 8:119, 8:160, 9:82,
  9:92
  Comecon and 10:96
  communist government in 10:9
    collapse of *10:148*
  in First World War 8:147
  Magyar minority in 8:160
  revolution in 10:149
  royal family of *8:160*
Romanov dynasty in Russia 6:103, 6:106,
  6:112
Romanticism 7:38–40, 7:100, *7:142*
Rome, city of *3:30*, 3:58
  architectural ostentation in 3:54–5
  Caracalla Baths, the 3:59, **3:59**
  Colosseum, the *3:94*
  daily life in *3:30*, 3:58, **3:112**
  fortification of 3:107, *3:107*
  Forum, the *3:6*, *3:36*, **3:54**
    Curia Julia *3:14*
    Rostrum, the *3:15*
    Severus Memorial Arch, the *3:110*
    Trajan's Markets *3:112*
  mystic rituals banned in *3:67*
  Ostrogoths expelled from 3:161
Rome, see of 3:173–4
Romulus Augustulus, last Western Roman
  emperor (475–476 CE) 3:134, *3:147*
Romulus and Remus, legendary founders of
  Rome 3:9, *3:9*
Röntgen, Wilhelm (1845–1923), German
  physicist 9:140

Roosevelt, Franklin Delano (1882–1945), United
  States president 9:55–6, *9:55*, 9:73, 9:75,
  9:78, 9:83, 9:92, 9:102, 9:176, 10:67
  Great Britain, support for 9:73
  New Deal and 9:56, 9:89
  Tennessee Valley Authority and *9:56*
  at Yalta Conference *9:81*
Roosevelt, Theodore (1858–1919), United States
  president 8:63
Rosas, Juan Manuel de, Argentine dictator
  (1835–1852) *8:11*
Rosetta stone 1:117
Rostrum (Roman Forum) *3:15*
Rotterdam 6:89
Rousseau, Jean Jacques (1712–1778), Swiss
  philosopher 7:38, *7:38*, 10:162
Rowlandson, Thomas (1756–1827), British artist
  7:65
Roxana (d.311 BCE), Bactrian wife of Alexander
  the Great 2:162–4
Rum, Turkish sultanate of 4:72, 4:100, *4:101*,
  4:119
  Mongols, defeat of 4:106
Rurik (d.879), prince of Russia 4:83, **4:89**
Rurik dynasty in Russia 6:103
Rushdie, Salman (1947–), British writer *9:168*
Russia (to 1917) 4:119
  Afghanistan and 8:55
  agrarian society unchanged in 6:31
  agriculture in 7:52–3, 7:145, 8:136
    primitive 6:111–12
  Alaska sold to United States 8:43
  Alexander II **7:129**
  Austria-Hungary, rivalry with 8:141
  authoritarian bureaucracy, tradition of 7:141
  autocratic government of 8:135–6
  Baltic, access to 6:105–6
  Bolshevik revolution in 8:152–5
    see also Russian Revolution
  Bolsheviks 8:112
  boyars in *6:100*, *6:103*, 6:104–5, *6:108*,
    6:109
  bureaucracy in 6:102, 6:104, 6:108
  Catherine II 7:34–5
  censorship in 7:143
  cereal exports from 6:112
  Chinese territory, cession of 8:73
  Christianity, conversion to 4:84–7, *4:85*, *4:87*
  Church subordinated to lay authority in
    6:104
  class structure in *6:103*, 6:104–5, 6:109,
    6:116
  conservative despotism in 6:73
  Crimea, annexation of 6:119
  Decembrist movement in 7:141
  economy 6:110–13
  education in 6:109
  expansion into Siberia 6:101–2, **6:107**
  famine in 7:46, 8:152
  foreign policy of 7:144, 8:141–2
  France, alliance with 8:143
  Germany, containment of 9:53–5
  and Hungarian revolution 7:125, 7:130
  ideological unity in (Official Nationality)
    7:142–3
  industrial workers living conditions *7:61*
  industrialization in 6:111–13, 8:15
  intellectuals in *7:142*, 7:143
  Isfahan and 4:127
  Istanbul (Constantinople), claims on 9:37,
    9:43

Russia (to 1917) (cont.)
  Japanese defeat of 8:89, 8:96, 8:110, 8:138,
    9:8, **9:24**
  literacy in 6:109, 6:115
  Manchu dynasty and 5:63
  military power of 6:109, 6:115, 6:119, 7:144
  mining industry in 6:26, 6:112
  minorities in 8:119
  mobilization of (1914) 8:146
  modernization of 6:73, 7:145, 7:147–8,
    9:171
  money economy, slow development of 6:35,
    6:113
  national identity developing in 6:100–3
  Nicholas I **7:129**, 7:140–3, *7:140*
  nobility in *6:103*, 6:104–5, 6:109, 6:115,
    7:142
  North America, expansion in 7:144
  origins of 4:81, 4:83
  peasant oppression in 6:112, 6:115
  Peter the Great, expansion under 6:106–7,
    6:107
  Poland, alliance with 6:103
  Poland, partition of 6:119
  Polish peace treaty 8:166
  Polish rebellion and 7:122
  population growth in 7:142, 7:145
  railways in 8:88, 8:143
  rebellions in 6:115
  reforms 7:147–8
    of Peter the Great 6:105–6
  revolutionary movement in 8:109–10
    1905 revolution 8:110, 8:135
    see also Russian Revolution
  St Petersburg, capital city of *6:105*, 6:107,
    6:108, *6:109*, *6:113*, 6:114
  science in 6:108
  secret police in 7:141, 7:143
  serfdom in 6:28, 6:34–5, 6:105, 6:109–11,
    6:113, 6:115, 7:145–6, 7:146, 7:149
    abolition of 7:52, 7:146–7
  state in 5:157–8
  Sweden, conflicts with 6:103, 6:106,
    6:113
  territorial acquisitions of **7:116**
  territorial expansion of 8:43
  trade 4:83–4, 6:108, 6:112–13
    with China 8:74
    with Korea 8:88
  treaty of Nerchinsk 6:102
  tsar, abdication of 8:152
  Volga valley, control of **6:107**
  wars
    Crimean 7:128–30, *7:128–9*, **7:129**, *7:144*,
      7:145
    Napoleonic 7:105
    with Sweden 6:103, 6:106, *6:113*
    with Tatars 6:101
    with Turks 6:103, 6:118–19, 7:123
  westernization in 6:107–9, *6:109*
  wheat trade in 7:53
  xenophobia in 6:108
  see also Russian Revolution; Soviet Union
    (USSR)
Russia (Russian Federation) 10:152
  Chechnya war *9:171*
  economy of 10:147
  modernization in 9:171
  price controls abandoned in 10:152
  see also Commonwealth of Independent
    States

Russian Revolution   **8:146**, 8:152–5, 8:164–5, **8:164**
Rutherford, Ernest (1871–1937), New Zealand scientist   9:140, 9:142
Ryobu-Shinto   5:71

S

sacrifice   5:93, *5:98*
  animal   5:21
  human   2:36–7, 2:36, 5:95–7
  Sumerian   1:83, 1:85, *1:89*
sacrificial rites
  in China   2:36, 2:43
  Vedic   2:24–5
  Zoroastrian   2:81
sadaqa (alms-giving)   **4:22**
Sadasiva, Hindu god   5:21
Saddam Hussein *see* Hussein, Saddam
Sadducees   3:80, 3:83
Safavid dynasty in Persia   4:125–8
Sagan, Carl (1934–96), United States writer   **9:146**
Sahara desert   *1:8*, 1:35, *1:53*, 2:57–8, 5:85–6, 5:88, 8:57
  cave paintings in   **2:56**
  climate changes in   **2:58**
  racial groups in   2:58–9
  rock art in   *2:60*
  vegetation in   2:58, 2:60
St Helena, Bonaparte exiled to   7:111–12
St Lucia   8:43
saints *see* individual names
Saint-Simon, Claude de (1760–1825), French socialist thinker   7:137, *7:138*
St Sophia, Constantinople   4:48, **4:51**, 4:70, 4:80, 4:84, 4:120, *4:123*
  construction ordered by Justinian I   **4:51**, *4:53*
  desecration by crusaders   4:75
  Islamic alterations to   *4:124*
  mosaics in   *4:50*, *4:73*
Sakhalin   10:37, 10:115
Sakharov, Andrei (1921–1989), dissident Soviet physicist   *10:83*
Saladin (Salah al-Din al-Ayyub) (1137–1193), Sultan of Egypt and Syria   4:38, 4:75, *4:103*, 5:151
  battle of the Horns of Hattin and   *4:102*
  in Egypt   4:102
  recapture of Jerusalem by   4:103
salat (prayers)   **4:22**
Salazar, Antonio de Oliveira (1889–1970), Portuguese prime minister   *8:175*
Salmanazar III, king of Assyria (858–824 BCE)   *1:169*
Salt, Sir Titus (1803–1876), English industrialist   *7:68*
Salvation Army   7:62, 7:63
Samanid dynasty, Abbasid caliphate   4:97
  conversion of Seljuk Turks to Islam   4:99, **4:100**
Samaria, capital of Israel (northern kingdom)   **1:168**, *1:170*, 1:172
Samarkand   4:14, **4:25**
  Babur's conquest of   5:25
  Mongol sack of   4:105, **4:105**
  Neanderthal burial site   1:37
Samnite peoples   *3:18*
Samoa, administration of   *8:61*

Samuel, Hebrew prophet   1:168, 1:170–71
San Francisco Charter   **9:85**
San Lorenzo, Olmec ceremonial centre   2:62
San people (Bushmen)   *1:29*, *1:63*, *2:59*, *5:85*
Santiago de Compostela, shrine, taken by Al-Mansur   4:159
Santo Domingo   8:24
Saqqara pyramids   1:109
Sarai, Tatar capital   5:157
Sarajevo   *8:145*
Sarawak   10:25
  see also Malaysia
sarcophagi   *1:113*, *1:131*, *1:151*
  Christian   3:83–4, 3:89–90, 3:95, *3:117*
  of Constantina   *3:120*
  Etruscan   *3:10*
  Ludovisi   *3:130*
  of Scipio family   *3:22*
Sardinia   6:93, 7:124–5
  Austria, war with (1859)   7:130–1
  Genoa, absorption of   7:108, 7:117
  unification of Italy and   7:131
Sardis, former capital of Lydia   2:112
Sargon I, king of Akkad (2334–2279 BCE)   1:90, *1:91*, 2:11
Sargon II, king of Assyria (721–705 BCE)   1:174, **1:174**, *1:177*
Sarnath, Buddhist site   5:11, **5:20**
Sarraut, Albert, governor of French Indo-China   *8:105*
Sassanid dynasty in Persia   4:8–13, *4:8*, *4:12–3*
  Achaemenid Empire, re-creation of   3:108–9, **3:109**
  Ardashir I, founder of   3:108, 4:8
  Jerusalem, sacking of   4:12
  Khusrau I   **4:9**, *4:10*, 4:12, 4:140, *4:140*
  Khusrau II   *4:10*, 4:12–3, *4:13*
  Rome and   3:108–10
  Shapur I   *4:12*
  Syria and Egypt, invasion of   4:12
Sassanid Empire
  Arab conquest of   **4:9**, 4:18, **4:25**, **4:44**
  Byzantine conflict   4:8, **4:9**
  collapse of   4:13, 4:17–18
  map of   **4:9**
  Mesopotamia and   4:25
The Satanic Verses (Rushdie)   *9:168*
satrapies   2:167, 2:169
  and kingdom of Parthia   2:175–6
satraps
  Darius III, murder of   2:161
  establishment under Darius I   2:79
  Seleucid government and   2:167
Saudi Arabia   9:41
  Arab League in   9:110
  oil in   10:48,10:50
  and Saddam Hussein   10:135
Saul (d.c.1010 BCE), king of Israel   1:168
savannah   *1:15*, *1:18*
Savonarola, Girolamo (1452–1498), Italian reformer   5:117
Savoy, duchy of, ceded by Sardinia to France   7:131
Savoy dynasty   6:93
sawm (fasting)   **4:22**
Saxons, Germanic peoples   3:24, 3:129, 3:150, 4:135, 4:147
  Charlemagne's conversion of   4:137–8
  in England   *4:152*

Scandinavia   9:60
  Lutheranism   6:51
  see also Norsemen
Schiaparelli, Giovanni (1835–1910), Italian astronomer   **10:173**
schistosomiasis   1:119
Schliemann, Heinrich   *1:152–3*, **1:155**
Schoenberg, Arnold (1874–1951), composer   **9:50**
The School of Athens (Raphael)   *7:17*
Schopenhauer, Arthur (1788–1860), German philosopher   **9:50**
Schrödinger, Erwin (1887–1961), Austrian physicist   9:142
science
  benefits of   7:27
  Biblical interpretation, impact on   8:124–5
  in education   8:128
  evolution, theory of   8:125, **8:125**, 8:126
  geology   8:124–6
  institutes of science and technology   8:128
  medieval   7:16–17, *7:16*
  mythology of   8:126, 8:130–131
  philosophical implications of   8:127, 8:130–132, **8:131**
  prestige of   8:126
  progress in   8:127, 9:50, 9:129–59, 9:137–8, 9:154–8, 9:161
  and religion   7:21–2, 7:24–6, 8:124–5
  in Russia   6:108
  scientific revolution   7:15–24
  society, effects on   8:126–7, 8:129
  warfare, effects on   8:139
  see also biological sciences; Greek science; medicine; physics; space science
Scipio Aemilianus Africanus, Publius Cornelius (185–129 BCE), Roman general   3:19
Scipio Africanus Major, Publius Cornelius (236–184 BCE), Roman general   *3:20*
Scotland
  Calvinism in   6:51
  and England   6:64, 6:91
  Norse settlements in   4:153
  socio-economic stagnation in   6:34
  see also Great Britain
Scott, William Bell (1811–1890), British artist   7:66
scripts
  Canaan   1:167
  Carolingian minuscule   4:142, 4:169
  cuneiform   **1:70**, 1:80, **1:80**, 1:85, 1:97, 1:140
  Cyrillic   4:79–80, 4:88
  Greek   2:90
  Hebrew   1:167
  hieratic   1:140
  hieroglyphic   **1:70**, 1:100, *1:117*, 1:140, **1:141**, 1:150, 2:63–4, 5:84, 5:92–4, **5:94**, *5:95*
  Linear A and Linear B   **1:141**, **1:147**, 1:150
  of Minoan Crete   1:140, 1:150
  Phoenician   1:140, 1:157, 2:90
  Turkish   4:109
  see also writing
sculpture   *2:18*
  Assyrian   1:156–7, 1:176–7
  Benin bronzes   5:85, 5:90–91
  bronze-working, Later Han dynasty   5:42
  Buddhist   2:26, 2:29, 5:15–17, 5:20–21, 5:23
  Ch'an period, China   5:47
  Cycladic   *1:144*
  Egyptian   1:126

sculpture (cont.)
  Etruscan   *3:8–10*
  Greek   *3:13*, 3:26
    see also Greek art
  Hindu   2:24, 5:17
  Hittite   *1:160–61*
  Japan   5:70, 5:72, 5:77
  Minoan   *1:150*
  at Mohenjo-Daro   *2:10*, 2:12, 2:14, 2:29
  Olmec   2:62, 2:63
  Palaeolithic   *1:44*, **1:45**
  Persian   2:78, 2:80
  Roman   3:27, 3:51
    Augustus, emperor   *3:39–40*, 3:65
    Boethius   *3:155*
    Claudius, emperor   3:64
    Commodus, emperor   3:102
    Constantine, emperor   3:121
    Greek influence on   *3:13*, 3:26
    Hermes, Greek god   *3:13*
    Julian the Apostate, emperor   *3:135*
    Julius Caesar   3:32, 3:37
    Ludovisi sarcophagus   *3:130*
    Marcus Aurelius, emperor   *3:41*
    Marius, general   *3:31*
    Nero, emperor   *3:91*
    sarcophagi   3:83–4, 3:89–90, 3:95, *3:117*
    Stilicho, general   *3:134*
    Sulla, general   *3:32*
    Vespasian, emperor   *3:40*
    votive statues   *3:12*
  Sassanid   *3:111*
  stone-carving in Maurya period   5:17
  see also bronze statuary
Scythia   2:112
Scythians   2:76, 2:79, 4:14–15, *4:14*, 4:78
  Huns and   4:15
  India, invasion of   5:15
  in Iran   1:175
  in Russia   1:176
sea peoples ("Peoples of the Sea")   1:127–8, 1:133, 1:161–2, 2:74
SEATO (Southeast Asia Treaty Organization)   *10:40*
Sebastopol   7:128, *7:128–9*
Second Socialist International *see* Socialist International
Second World War   **8:86**, 8:139, 9:64, 9:68–83
  America and Russia in   9:87
  atomic bombs in   9:78, **9:78**, 9:79
  Far East campaigns of   9:76–9
  German declaration of war   9:73–4
  German invasion of Russia ("Barbarossa")   9:72–3
  Japan   9:74, 9:75
    surrender of   **9:78**, 9:79
  maps of   **9:69**, **9:77**
  moral dimension   9:79–80
  neutral countries in   **9:69**, 9:75
  Normandy, Allied invasion of   **9:77**, 9:78, 9:82–3
  North Africa in   9:75–7
  Pacific campaign (1942–1945)   10:37
  refugees   9:48, 9:81, *9:90*
  submarine warfare   9:76, 9:78
  see also air warfare; battles; individual countries; suffrage, female
secret societies   7:117, 7:141, 9:11, **9:24**, 9:33, 9:36

Security Council, United Nations organization
9:85–6, **9:85**, *9:86*, 9:87, 9:107, **10:11**,
10:13
China in 10:93
veto, power 9:86, 9:93–4
Seleucia, Seleucid capital 2:167
Seleucid dynasty 2:165, **2:165**, 3:21, 3:75, *3:75*,
3:121, 5:9
absolutism and 2:167
Egypt, Ptolemaic 2:175
Hellenistic and oriental civilization under
2:167
Iran, loss of *2:174*
Syria, confinement to 2:176
weakness, eastern 2:175
Seleucus (c.325–281 BCE), Macedonian general,
founder of Seleucid dynasty 2:165
Selim I (1467–1520), sultan of Turkey
6:95
Seljuk Turks *4:34*, *4:73*, 4:99, 4:100–102
see also Oghuz Turks; Ottoman Turks; Turkish
peoples
Semitic peoples 1:74, 1:78, 1:133, 1:156,
1:162–4, 1:167, 1:173
see also Hebrews; Hyksos
Senate (Roman) 3:16, 3:24–5, 3:30, 3:32, 3:34,
3:54
conflict between emperor and 3:103
Gracchi brothers and 3:29
membership of 3:14–15, 3:47, *3:54*
power of 3:40, 3:46, 3:103
republican forms of 3:39, 3:101
Senegal 5:86–7, **8:55**, 8:57, 10:52
Septimania 4:146
conquest by Franks 4:136
Serbia 4:78, **7:129**, 8:119, **8:119**, 8:142, 8:148,
8:158–9, 9:30
Byzantine Empire, attack on 4:116
Ottoman Turks, conquest of 4:120–21
Russian support of 8:142, 8:145
serfdom 5:134, 5:141
abolition of *7:37*, 7:50–52, 7:146–7
in Eastern Europe 6:16, 6:28, 6:34–5, 6:38,
6:74, 6:109–11
flight from 6:102, 6:111
legal restrictions on serfs 6:110–11, 6:115
in Poland 6:98
in Roman Empire 3:106
in Russia 6:102, 6:109–11, 6:113, 6:115
in Spanish colonies 6:142
Seven Wonders of the Ancient World **2:174**
Severus, Lucius Septimius (146–211 CE), Roman
emperor 3:101, 3:103–4, *3:104*, *3:110*
Mesopotamia, penetration into 3:108
palace of **3:45**, *3:103*
worship of Egyptian gods under 3:65–6
Seville 5:128, *6:23*
sexual discrimination 1:31, 1:48
in economic roles 1:21
Sforza family 6:85
Shah Jahan (1592–1666), Moghul emperor
5:32–5, *5:33*, *5:37*
shahada **4:22**
Shakespeare, William (1564–1616), English
poet and playwright 6:81
Shamash, Babylonian god **1:95**
Shang dynasty 2:39, 2:40, 2:45, 2:53, 2:54
Chou dynasty and 2:37, 2:42–3
cultural influences of 2:36–7
domain of 2:36
language in 2:44

Shanghai *8:68–9*, *9:16*, *9:18*, *9:22*, 9:26, *9:104*
Japanese, bombardment *9:28*
Japanese invasion of 9:25
Shansi, goal of Long March 9:26–7, **9:26**
Shantung 9:14, **9:24**
Shapur I, Sassanid king of Persia (241–272 CE)
4:12
Sharrumkin, king of Akkadia *see* Sargon I
Shi'a, party of the Shi'ites 4:32
Shibanov, Mikhail, Russian artist *6:110*
Shidehara, Kijuro (1872–1951), Japanese
Minister for Foreign Affairs **9:24**
Shih-Huang-ti, Ch'in (Qin) First Emperor
(221–210 BCE) *2:52*, *2:55*, *5:39*
Shi'ites, Islamic sect 4:28, 4:32–3
Abbasid caliphate and 4:43
Abu-al-Abbas and 4:32
Buwayhid dynasty of 4:100
Fatimid caliphate and 4:43, *4:43*
Safavid dynasty of Persia and 4:125, 4:127–8
Umayyad caliphate and 4:30
Shintoism 5:71–2, **5:71**, 8:99
Amaterasu, sun goddess *5:68*, **5:71**
shipbuilding 6:23, 6:162–3, *6:163*
colonial expansion and 6:153, 6:166
European development *6:124*, 6:125–6, *6:125*
merchant ships 6:162–3
warships 6:125–6, *6:125*, 6:162–3
shipping
Dutch 6:22, 6:163, 6:166
eastern Mediterranean 2:85, *2:85*, *2:87*
Egyptian *1:73*, 1:102, *1:102*, 1:137
French 6:163
in Great Britain 7:59
Minoan 1:145
Norse 4:153
Phoenician *1:157*
Portuguese 4:123, 4:127, *6:124*, *6:127*
refrigerated 8:29
steam driven 7:53, 7:56, *7:152*, *7:155*, 8:22
submarine warfare 8:150–152
in war 7:129
see also naval power
Shiva, Hindu god 2:21–3, **2:23**, *2:24*, 5:20,
5:20
Shivagi, Mahratta leader 5:34
shogunates
Kamakura 5:74–7, *5:76*
Muramachi 5:77
Tokugawa 5:77–8, 5:80–2, 8:79, 8:84
shoguns (military dictators) *5:72*, *5:72–3*, *5:75*,
5:78
Shriners, secret fraternity 1:112
shudras (untouchable/labourer caste) 2:16, **5:19**
Siam (Thailand)
autonomy of 8:53, 8:59–60, **8:91**, 8:100
French missionaries to 6:132
Portuguese trading privileges in 6:130
see also Thailand
Siberia
Russian expansion into 6:101–2, 8:43
serfs escape to 6:102, 6:111
Sicilian Expedition 2:122, 2:131, 2:136, 2:177
Sicily 5:170, 6:82, 6:84
Arab conquest of 4:151
Greek settlement in 2:109, *2:120*, 2:140,
2:177
Norman conquest of 5:151
Roman conquest of 3:19, 3:21
Sidon, Phoenician city 1:157
siege-craft *1:132*, 1:133, *1:136*, *1:170*, 1:175

Siena, Council of (1423–1424) 5:116
Sierra Leone, refuge for freed slaves 6:170
Sikhs 10:117, *10:118*
Sikh empire 6:135
silk and silk trade 5:39, 5:42, 5:52, 5:171
Silk Road 2:175–6, 4:39, 4:56
silver
Asian demand for 6:129, *6:165*
as coinage 2:100, **2:103**
Europe, influx to 6:82, 6:85, 6:141, 6:153,
6:165
ingots as currency 1:138
Laurium mines 2:130
from Spain 1:157
Sinai 1:129, **9:40**
copper mines in 1:125
dispute in 1:133
Egypt, surrender to 9:36
Israelites in 1:166
Sinan (Ottoman architect) *4:123*
Sind 2:13
British, annexation of 8:46
Singapore 10:26, 10:39
economic growth in 10:113, **10:113**
Japanese capture of 9:97
Singh, Gulab, Maharajah 8:92
Singh, Ranjit, Maharajah 8:48
Sinkiang 10:30
Sinn Fein (Irish nationalist party) 10:101–103
Sino-Tibetan languages **2:45**
Siquem, capital of Israel (northern kingdom)
1:168
Siwah oracle 2:161
Slav peoples 2:66, 3:160, **3:160**, 3:164, 4:58,
4:61, 4:76–81, 9:72
in the Balkans 4:12, 4:78
in Bohemia and Moravia 4:93
Bulgars *see* Bulgars
Byzantium, raids on 4:79
Charlemagne, conflict with 4:138, 5:157
civilization of 4:77–80
in Croatia and Serbia 4:93
Greek influence on 4:52
nationalism 7:124
origins of 4:78
Orthodox Christianity, conversion to 4:76–7,
4:80, 4:85
in Poland 4:85
in Russia 4:81
"slavery" and 4:169
survival of 4:78
Teutons, cultural conflict with 4:138, 5:157
topography and culture of 4:76–8
slave trade
abolition of 8:12
in Latin America *8:11*
in South Africa 8:33
British supply Spanish colonies 6:160, 6:162
contribution to growth of trade 6:165, 6:169
Britain, domination by **6:147**
Europeans, acceptance by 6:170
in Nazi Germany 8:12
Portugal and 6:23, 6:127, 6:169
West Indies and 6:147–8
slavery 2:97–9, *2:99*, *2:108*, 2:125, 6:23–4,
6:24, 6:127, 6:146, **6:147**
Arab *5:87*
Babylonian 1:95–6
on Caribbean sugar plantations 6:146–7
Egyptian 1:120, *5:87*
estate workers 3:28–9, 3:61

slavery (cont.)
in feudal society 4:173
France, laws relating to **6:171**
freedom *3:61*
helots and 2:107–8, 2:118
in India 5:11
under Islam 4:45
Italian merchants and 5:135
as labour for building 3:51, *3:52*
as labour for imported crops 6:24, *6:24*,
6:142, *6:145*, **6:155**, 6:173
ministri 3:65
in North American colonies 6:151
Portuguese and 5:177
rebellions 6:170
revolts, in Rome 3:66–8
in Roman society 3:16, 3:28, 3:57, 3:61
in Russia 4:91
in Seljuk armies 4:101
Slavs and 4:169
in Spanish colonies 6:142, *6:145*
Stoics, condemnation by 2:174
in United States 7:73, 7:81, 7:157–67
1850 Compromise 7:162
abolition of 7:52, 7:64, 7:65, 7:147,
7:164–5, *7:166*, 8:12
anti-slavery movement 7:158, 7:159,
7:161–2, *7:163*
and cotton-growing
7:158–9, *7:160*
Kansas dispute 7:162
Missouri Compromise (1820) 7:160, **7:161**
North-South balance of states and 7:160,
7:161
social consequences of abolition 7:167,
7:167
and southern economy
7:81, 7:158
see also Civil War, American; serfdom
Slovakia 8:119
Slovenia, independence from
Yugoslavia 10:151, *10:160*
smallpox, vaccination against *7:45*
Smith, Adam (1723–1790), Scottish economist
7:28, 7:33, 7:42, *7:43*, 7:66, 8:16
Smolensk 6:103
Smuts, Jan Christian (1870–1950), South African
prime minister 10:16, 10:59
Smyrna 1:154
persecution of Christians 3:93
So-Ami (16th century CE), Japanese artist *5:75*
Sobketpe, tomb of *1:124*
social services and welfare,
child allowances 7:46
Poor Laws (GB) 7:173
socialism 7:135–40, 7:176, 8:111–13
economic and social egalitarianism 7:136,
7:137
historical inevitability, theory of 7:138–9
Marx and 7:138–40
Second Socialist International 8:111–12
parliamentary system, use of 8:112
see also communism; Marxism
societies 7:10–11, 7:176
Freemasons 7:11, *7:11*
learned 7:10, 7:20–21
secret 7:117, 7:141
society
Greek 2:96–9, 2:128–9
limitless improvement, belief in 10:166,
10:169–70

society (cont.)
  modernization of 10:17, 10:162, 10:165,
    10:167, 10:169–70
  motor car industry in 9:134–6
  population control in 9:122–3
  religion in 9:168–9
  scientific progress, impact of 9:156,
    9:162–5
  traditional ways of life 10:161–2, *10:161*,
    10:169, 10:176
    in Asia 10:17–18, 10:114
    in India *10:17, 10:18*, 10:118, *10:119*
sociology 8:131–2, **8:131**
Socotra 6:129
Socrates (470–399 BCE), Athenian philosopher
    2:133, 2:136–7, *2:139*
solar observatories 2:68
Solomon (c.974–c.937 BCE), king of Israel
    1:157, 1:169, 5:85
  death of **1:168**, 1:171
  navy of 1:169
  and Temple 1:157, *1:166*, 1:170
  see also Solomon's Temple
Solomon's Temple 1:157, *1:166*, 1:170,
    1:172
  first Temple 3:73, **3:78**
  second Temple 3:75, *3:75*
  third Temple 3:69, **3:78**, 3:89
  see also Jerusalem; Solomon
Solon (c.638–558 BCE), Athenian legislator
    2:105, *2:108*
Solutrean culture *1:42*
Somalia 8:57
Song of Roland, The 5:122, 5:154
Songs of the Virgin Mary, The (Alfonso X)
    5:177
Sophocles (495–406 BCE), Greek tragedian
    2:148, 2:149, 2:151, 2:153
Sorbon, Robert de (1201–1274), founder of
    Maison de la Sorbonne, Paris university
    5:167
Soseki, Natsume, Japanese novelist **8:83**
South Africa 8:33–7, 10:55, 10:58–64
  apartheid system in 10:58–9, *10:58*, 10:61,
    10:61, 10:62–3
  Boer Wars *8:35–6*
  British territory in 8:34
  constitution (1983) 10:62
  constitution (1993) 10:64
  constitution, draft 8:36–7
  diamonds discovered in 8:34, 8:37, *8:37*
  economic growth *10:59*
  government in 8:34
  industrialization of 8:35, 8:37
  mineral production in 8:37
  Namibia and 10:62
  and native populations 8:38–9
  natural resources in 8:28–9
  nuclear weapons and 10:176
  population growth in *10:59*
  sanctions 10:62
  UN General Assembly and 10:61
South America
  civilizations of 5:97–9
  Portuguese, discovery of *5:162, 5:164*
  see also Americas, the
South Carolina **6:155**
Southeast Asia 8:99–103
  agriculture in 1:53
  Burma *8:45*, 8:59, *8:74*, **8:91**, 8:100, *8:100*,
    8:104

Southeast Asia (cont.)
  colonization of 6:129, 6:131
  decolonization in 9:106–108
  Dutch trade in 6:132
  French Indo-China 8:100–101
  French presence in Siam 6:132
  local traditions, corrosion of 8:99–101
  Malaya 8:44, 8:59, **8:91**, 8:100
  nationalist movements in 9:97
  Portuguese trading privileges in 6:130
  Siam 6:132, 8:53, 8:59–60, **8:91**, 8:100
Southern Rhodesia see Rhodesia;
    Zimbabwe
South Korea 10:13, 10:25
  anti-Japanese nationalism in 10:115
  automobile industry in 10:115
  economic growth in 10:112–13, **10:113**
South Sea Bubble see England
South Vietnam
  American support for 10:34, *10:36*,
    10:89–90, 10:94
  Vietcong 10:36, *10:89, 10:92*
South Yemen 10:119
Soviet Union (USSR) (1917–1939)
  agriculture in 8:169
  Arab communists, support for 9:42
  Civil War in *8:155*, 8:167
  famine in 8:167, *8:167*, 8:169
  foreign policy of 9:65, 9:67
  formation of 8:153
  industrialization in 8:169
  and Kuomintang 9:22–3, 9:25
  Mongolia 9:20
  Persia and 9:45
  propaganda in 9:42, 9:58–9
  Spanish republic, support for 9:65, 9:67
  Treaty of Versailles, absence from 8:158,
    8:161
  see also Lenin; Russian Revolution; Stalin and
    following entries
Soviet Union (USSR) (1939–45)
  Baltic States, conquest of 9:72
  Berlin, advance to 9:78
  Finland, attack on 9:72
  German invasion of 9:72–3
  German-Soviet Pact of Non-Agression
    9:67–8, *9:67*, **9:67**, **9:69**
    secret protocol of **9:67**
  Japan, declaration of war on 9:79
  Manchuria, invasion of 9:105–106
  Stalingrad, siege of 9:77
  see also Second World War
Soviet Union (USSR) (1945–1990)
  Afghanistan and **10:12**, 10:124, *10:127*,
    10:131, 10:138, 10:146
  agriculture in *10:81*
  Albania and 10:96
  anti-semitism in 10:47
  arms expenditure of 10:128, 10:137, **10:137**
  blockade of west Berlin by 10:10–11,
    10:10
  and China 10:29–31, 10:40
  Cold War and 9:96–7, *9:97*
  collapse of 10:146–7, 10:152–3
  Comecon and 9:96, **10:12**, *10:76*, 10:96
  Cominform and 10:77
  Communist Party demolished in 10:152
  corruption in 10:32
  Cuba and 10:70–71, *10:71*
  Cuba, missile sites in 10:70–71, *10:71*
  Czechoslovakia and 10:96, *10:97*

Soviet Union (USSR) (1945–1990) (cont.)
  diplomacy 10:8
  disintegration of 9:173, *9:179*
  dissent in 10:83, *10:83*, 10:130
  east European policies of 10:140–42
  eastern Europe, absorption of 9:82, 9:88
  economy of 10:14–16, 10:81–2
    arms expenditure and 10:128, 10:137
    collapse of *10:144–5*, 10:146
    market economy, transition to 10:144
  education in 10:81–2
  Egypt, support for 10:50, 10:77
  foreign policies of 9:92, 9:93–4
  German war "reparations" to 9:92
  glasnost (openness) in *10:6*, 10:137
    public opinion polls and 10:144
  Helsinki agreement and 10:130, 10:141
  liberalization of 10:80–81
  living conditions since 1945 10:14
  Marshall Plan rejected by 9:95
  Mongolia and 9:88
  naval base in Aden 10:119
  Nuclear Non-Proliferation Treaty 10:175–6
  nuclear tests **10:13**, 10:14
  nuclear weapons, development of 9:90–91
  perestroika (restructuring) *10:6*, 10:137
  politics and trade 10:15–16
  population control 9:122
  pro-Arab policy 10:47
  rapprochement with United States 10:129–30,
    10:129
  republics in **10:146**
    claim autonomy 10:144
    declare independence 10:146–7, **10:146**
  Romania and 10:96
  Security Council UN 9:85
  social services 10:82
  space program 9:146–9, *9:147*, **9:151**, 9:152,
    10:82
  spheres of influence of 9:88–90, 9:98
  Suez invasion, reaction to 10:76–7
  territories regained by **8:165**
  trading, internal 10:140
  United States, relations with 9:86–7, 9:89–91,
    9:92, 10:129–30, *10:129*
  see also Commonwealth of Independent States;
    Russia (Russian Federation); Stalin
space science and exploration 9:146–53, **9:146**,
    9:151, 10:95, 10:172–5
  early developments 9:146–7
  Mars 9:152–3, *10:173*, **10:173**
  moon landings 9:148–52, *9:150*, 10:172–3
  radio astronomy *9:139*
  Russian-American rivalry 9:146, *9:148*,
    9:152
  safety 10:172–3
  satellites
    Sputnik *9:146*, 9:147–8
    Vostok *9:147*
  space shuttles *9:114*, 9:152, *9:152, 9:155*,
    9:156, *10:174, 10:179*
  see also scientific progress
Spain 5:162–3, 6:92
  abdication of dynasty 8:24
  American Revolution and 7:78
  aquisition of territories 7:154, **7:156**
  Arab conquest of **4:25**
  Armada against England *6:62*, 6:86, 6:158,
    6:158
  authoritarian régime in 8:173–4
  Bourbon monarchy in 6:91

Spain (cont.)
  Catholic monarchy in 6:57–9
  Civil War (1936–39) in 9:64–5, 9:67
  colonization
    in Americas **6:126**, 6:139–46
    in Canary Islands **6:128**
  disorder in 8:110
  EC, entry into *10:106*
  El-Andalus and 4:41–3, **4:42**
  enlightened despotism in 6:73
  Enlightenment in 7:33–4
  gold, from Americas to 6:27
  Jamaica, loss of 6:160
  military orders in 5:155
  military supremacy ended 6:87
  mortality in 7:44
  navigation and *5:162, 5:163*
  Norse raids in 4:154
  political entities of **4:43**
  reconquest of 4:102, *5:127–8*, 5:142, 5:151,
    5:154, **5:155**
  reforms of imperial system in 8:23
  regionalism in 6:68
  religious unity of 6:58–9
  as Roman province 3:21–2, 3:163
  seapower, end of 8:24
  Spanish March 4:138, 4:158
  taxation in 6:67
  as trading nation 6:34
  Umayyad rule of 4:41–3, **4:42**
  as Vandal state 3:133, 3:156
  viceroyalties in South America 8:23
  as Visigoth kingdom 3:156, **3:157**, 3:163,
    3:176
  wars
    with Britain and France 8:24
    with United States 8:30, 8:55, 8:62
    War of Spanish Succession 6:91, 6:93,
      6:160, 6:161
  see also Philip II; wars
Spanish America see Latin America
Spanish Empire 6:141–46
  Caribbean islands 6:139, 6:141
  class structure in 6:142–3
  diseases in 6:140, 6:143
  economy of 6:141–2, 6:147, 6:158
  education in 6:144
  Mexico (New Spain) 6:139–40
  native populations
    abuse of 6:168
    Church, protection of 6:143–4, *6:143*,
      6:170
    decline in numbers of 6:143
    in Peru *6:139*, 6:140–1, *6:140*
  royal councils *6:140*, 6:141
  slavery in 6:142, *6:145*, 6:160, 6:162
  viceroys in *6:140*, 6:141
Sparta 1:153, 2:96, 2:101, 2:106–8, *2:107*,
    2:115, 2:119, **2:121**, 2:144
  Athens, coalition against 2:120
  Athens, rivalry with 2:118
  confederation opposed to 2:123
  conservative culture of 2:100, 2:106
  government of 2:106–7
  helots in 2:107–8, 2:118
  kings, hereditary 2:106
  League of Corinth 2:159
  Leuctra, defeat at 2:123
  Peloponnesian League against Persia 2:112
  Peloponnesian War and 2:122
  Persia, war with 2:122

Sparta (cont.)
  topography of 2:103
  women, status in 2:126
Spectator, British journal 7:14–15
Spencer, Herbert (1820–1903), English
  philosopher 8:131
spice trade 6:128
  Dutch control of 6:131–3, *6:132*,
    6:133
  Portuguese manipulation of 6:127
The Spirit of Laws (Montesquieu) 7:33
sport
  boxing 1:142
  bull-leaping 1:142, *1:143*, 1:148
Sputnik satellites *see* space science
Sri Lanka *see* Ceylon
Stalin, Joseph (1879–1953), Soviet leader
  8:164, 8:168–70, *8:168–9*, 9:22, 9:72, 9:83,
    9:90–91, 9:102, **10:12**, *10:14*
  agriculture, collectivization of 8:169
  de-Stalinization policy 10:80–81
  death 10:14–16, 10:29, 10:32
  European policies 9:92, 9:94–5
  Germany, alliance with 9:67–8, *9:67*, **9:67**
  industrialization and 8:169
  invasion of Europe 9:78
  Marxist philosophy inverted by 8:168–9
  Middle East policies of 9:110–11
  purges of political dissidents 9:58–9,
    9:58
  Yalta Conference *9:81*
  see also Soviet Union
Stalingrad, battle of 9:77
Stamp Act (1765) **7:72**, 7:74–5, *7:74*
standing stones 2:68, 2:69
  see also megalithic monuments
state power
  increase of 7:115–16, 9:170–171, 9:174–6
  restraints on 9:176–8
statistical evidence
  application to life insurance 6:22
  growth of 6:9–11
steam engines 7:49, 7:56–7, 7:59
steamships 8:22, 8:107
Steinheim man 1:34
Step Pyramid 1:109
Stephen (later St), apostle and first Christian
  martyr 3:85, 3:90
Stephen II, pope (752–757 CE) 4:135
Stephenson, George (1781–1848), British
  engineer *7:54*
Stevens, John, chief engineer of United States
  Isthmian Canal Commission **8:63**
Stilicho, Flavius (d.408), Roman general of
  Vandal descent *3:134*
stirrups *1:134*, 1:135, 4:16, 4:175
Stoicism 3:41, 3:51
Stone Age cultures 1:39–40, 1:46, 1:48, 2:20,
  2:59
stone tools *see* tools, stone
stone-working 2:64, 2:68
Stonehenge 2:68–9
Storrs, Ronald, Arab specialist **9:40**
Stowe, Harriet Beecher (1811–1896), American
  author *7:162*
Stuart dynasty in England and Scotland 6:63,
  6:90–91
  rejection of 6:69
  restoration of 6:66
  sea-power, maintenance of 6:160, 6:162
stupas *2:6*, *2:29*

Suárez, Adolfo (1933–), Spanish prime minister
  10:141
Sudan 1:161, 5:85–6, 5:88
  as Fourth World country *10:164*
  Mahdi's revolt 8:14, *8:15*, *8:57*
  militant Islamic fundamentalist régime in
    10:132–3
Sudetenland, seized by Germany 9:66, *9:66*
Suetonius Tranquillus, Roman historian *3:42*
Suez canal 8:18, *8:19*, **8:19**, 9:31–2, *9:33*
  British protection of 9:32, *9:33*, 9:37, 9:42,
    9:108
  nationalization by Nasser 10:45
  protection by British troops 8:57
  shipping costs, effect on 8:51
Suez crisis
  Anglo-French invasion and 10:46
  cease-fire 10:46
  Israeli invasion and 10:45
  Soviet reaction to 10:76–7
suffrage, female 8:104, 8:116–18, *8:137*, 8:177
suffrage, universal adult male 8:113
suffragettes 8:116–18, *8:117*, 8:137
Suffren, Pierre de, French admiral 8:47
sugar 6:145–7, *6:146*, 6:159
  Cuba 10:69
  economic importance of 6:145
  imported into Europe 6:166
Sukarno, Achmed (1902–1970), president of
  Indonesia 9:107, 10:24–5, *10:25*,
    10:80
Suleiman "the Magnificent" (1494–1566), sultan
  of Turkey 4:123, 6:93
Sulla, Lucius Cornelius (138–78 BCE), Roman
  general and politician 3:30–31, *3:32*, 3:42,
    3:146
Sumatra 10:24
Sumer 1:78–92, **2:72**
  agriculture in 1:89
  art of *1:82*, 1:85–6, 1:91, *1:101*
  building on massive scale in 1:88
  cities of 1:79, 1:81–3, 1:88
  city-states of 1:89
  cult centres of 1:79
  daily life *1:82*, 1:86, *1:87*, *1:97*
  death and afterlife in 1:85
  earliest civilization in 1:78–92
  Egypt, influence on 1:100–101
  Elamites conquer 1:92
  gods of *1:84*, *1:84*
  history of 1:89–92
  marriage in 1:86–7
  palaces of 1:90
  pottery in 1:79
  religion in 1:79, 1:82–5, 1:97–8
  ships of 1:77
  technology in 1:87–8
  temples of 1:83, 1:91, 1:140
  trade, international 1:88–9
  war wagons (chariots) *1:91*, 1:133–4
  women and law in 1:86, 1:87, 1:95
  writing, invention of 1:79–80
  ziggurats 1:84, 1:88, 1:91
Summa Theologica (Thomas Aquinas) 5:169,
  5:169
A Summer's Day in Hyde Park (Ritchie)
  7:172
Sung dynasty 5:51–2, 5:57
  art 5:55
  economic improvement under 5:55
  industrialization under 5:55–6

Sunnites, Islamic sect 4:28
  Afghans 4:128
  Ottoman Turks 4:125
  Seljuk Turks 4:100
Sun Stone, Aztec solar calendar 5:97
Sun Yat-sen (1866–1925), Chinese revolutionary
  leader 8:76–9, *8:77*, 8:101, 9:11, 9:14,
    9:15, **9:21**, *9:105*
  collectivist views of 9:19
  death of 9:20–22, **9:21**
superstition 2:136–7, 7:8–9, *7:9*
  in Greek medicine **2:142**
  Greek speculations and 2:141
Surinam 6:159
Surrealism school of art **9:50**, 9:51
Susa 2:78
Sutlej River **2:8**
suttee, self-immolation of Indian women 5:21,
  5:30
Sutton Hoo burial ground *4:152*
Sviatoslav, prince of Russia (962–972 CE)
  4:84–5
Swabians 4:147
Swanscombe man 1:34
Sweden 6:87–8
  expansion into Europe 6:98, *6:98*
  industrialization in 6:26
  North America, settlements in 6:148
  Poland, attacks on 6:98
  power of 6:106, 6:115, 6:119
  Prussian, defeat of 6:116
  Russia, conflicts with 6:103, 6:106, 6:116
  Stockholm, capital city *6:106*
Switzerland 6:72
  Calvinism in 6:50–1, *6:50*
  Reformation introduced to *6:50*
Symmachus, Quintus Aurelius (c.340–c.402),
  Roman aristocrat 3:140
synagogues 3:74–5, 3:77
  Dura-Europos 3:73, *3:121*
Syracuse 3:19, 3:21
Syracuse, Corinthian colony 2:109, *2:120*,
  2:121, **2:169**, *2:176*
  Carthage, war with 2:177–8
  Corcyra and 2:178
  Rome, as threat to 2:178
  Sicilian Expedition, target of 2:177
Syria 3:72, *3:75*, 4:62, 10:136
  in Alexandrine Empire 2:161
  anti-American policy of 10:47
  Arab League in 9:110
  Ba'ath régime in 10:48, 10:50
  Christianity in 3:118, 3:123, 3:126, 3:166–7
  communal monasticism in 3:170
  conquered by
    Arabs 4:24–5, **4:25**
    Assyria 1:173
    Islam *4:24*
    Ottoman Turks 4:122, 6:95
  crusaders' onslaught on 5:151–4
  Egypt and *1:124*, *1:126*, 10:121
  France and 8:53, 9:36–8, 9:40, 9:42–3, 9:108
  Huns in 3:134
  independence of 6:97, 9:108
  Krak des Chevaliers, crusader castle in 5:153
  Kurdish revolt in 9:41
  Mamelukes in 4:103, 4:112–13
  Minoan connexions with 1:145
  Monophysites 3:168
  nationalism in 9:40–41
  Ottoman rule 9:36

Syria (cont.)
  Persia, invasion of 3:109, **3:109**
  as Roman province 3:79
  Saddam Hussein, opposition to 10:135
  Sassanid, invasion of **4:9**, 4:12
  Second World War and 9:75–6
  in Seleucid Empire 2:165
  Seljuk Turks, occupation of 4:100, 4:102
  Six Day War and 10:48–9
  Umayyad caliphate and 4:24, 4:28–30
  in United Arab Republic 10:46
  Yom Kippur war 10:50, *10:50*
  see also Egypt; Israel; Levant; Palestinians;
    PLO
Szechwan, overcome by Ch'in 5:40

T

Tabriz 4:125
Tabula Claudina 3:54
Tacitus, Publius Cornelius (c.56–c.120), Roman
  historian **3:41**, **3:132**
Taharqa, king of Egypt (690–664 BCE) *2:74*
Tahiti *6:177*, 6:178
Taiping movement, land distribution scheme
  8:72, **8:72**
Taiping rebellion (1850–1864) 8:71–3
Taiwan 9:106, 10:26, 10:112, 10:115
  economic growth in 10:112–13, **10:113**
  withdrawal of United States forces from
    10:110
  see also China; Formosa (Taiwan); Japan
Taj Mahal 5:32, *5:37*
Tale of Genji, The (Lady Murasaki) 5:76
Tamberlane *see* Timur Lang
Tamir River 4:17
T'ang dynasty 5:39, *5:43*
  Ch'an school of Buddhism under *5:47*
  civil servants and 5:44
  clan influence and 5:43
  collapse of 4:98
  Confucian civil service and *5:44–6*
  culture of 5:52–5, 5:76
  decline of 5:51, 5:55
  demographic shift and 5:50
  family and state 5:43
  government and administration of 5:43–4
  Japan and 5:70
  military rebellions under 5:51
  population pressure during 5:49–50
Tanganyika 8:57
Tantrism, semi-magical cult 5:23
Taoism **2:50**, 2:51–2, *5:47*, 5:48, 5:59
Taranto, emirate of 4:151
Tariq (d. c.720), Berber commander 4:25
Tasman, Abel (1603–1659), Dutch navigator
  6:177
Tasmania (Van Diemen's Land) **6:177**, *6:179*
Tatars (Mongolian tribe) 4:104, 4:119, *5:42*,
  5:157
  Ivan the Terrible's defeated of 6:101, *6:101*,
    6:106, 6:118
  Moscow, attack on 5:158
taxation 6:43–4, *6:44*
  on Arab land 4:34
  Byzantine 4:57
  in China 5:45, 5:49, *5:59*
    Buddhist monasteries and 5:60
    Constantine, reformation by 3:119

taxation (cont.)
in English North American colonies 6:153
in Europe
papacy and 5:132
rebellion and 5:141
representative assemblies and 5:132
by French 6:66–7, 6:71
in Great Britain
on trade to fund warships 6:163
for war with Scotland 6:64
in India
under Akbar 5:28–30
Maurya 5:14
poll-tax on non-Muslims 5:28, 5:34
under Shah Jahan 5:33–4
under Shivagi 5:34
in Islamic countries 4:31, 4:34
in Japan 5:73
Mongols and 4:109
Muslim 4:28
Persian 4:10
rebellions caused by 6:66–7
in the Roman Empire 3:24–5, 3:27, 3:38,
3:46, 3:68–9, 3:79, 3:104–7, 3:114, 3:127–8,
3:133, 3:135
Shah Abbas and 4:127
see also economic developments
tea 6:133–5, 6:153, 6:166, 6:173
technology 4:170, 7:19
agriculture 6:16, 7:49–50, 7:49, 7:169
in China 5:26, 5:40–41, 5:55–7, 5:55, 5:56
domestic appliances 8:116
early civilizations and 1:69
Egyptian 1:102, 1:109, 1:110–11, 1:118
Egyptian Neolithic 1:102
in Europe 5:136–9
cartography 5:160, 5:16–2, 5:163–44,
5:163
magnetic compasses 5:160
ship design 5:159–61
fire, use of 1:27
flying-machines 8:127, 8:128, 8:129
food processing and storage 8:116
guns 6:125–6, 6:163
horse population, impact on 8:129
industry 6:25–6
maritime 1:137
motor vehicles 8:18, 8:107, 8:127, 8:129, 8:130
Neanderthal humans 1:36
Palaeolithic artifacts 1:31, 1:36–7, 1:41
in printing 7:14–15
progress of 9:161
radio 8:127, 8:129
shipbuilding 6:125–6, 6:125, 6:127, 6:163
signalling 6:163
smelting techniques 7:55, 7:59
space exploration and 9:147–52, 9:148,
9:149–50, 9:151
steam engines and 7:49, 7:56–7, 7:59
Sumerian 1:87–8
tools and weapons 1:18, 1:20–21, 1:31, 1:41,
6:125
see also engineering
telegraph 7:59, 8:18
telescopes 7:19, 7:19, 7:23
television 9:137, 9:150, 9:161
temples 5:17
Adinatha (Ranakpur, Rajasthan) 5:12
Buddhist, Ajanta caves 2:26–7
Chinese 2:45
Egyptian 1:106, 1:110

temples, Egyptian (cont.)
at Abu Simbel 1:112, 1:128–9
at Filac 1:64
Hatshepsut's mortuary temple 1:116, 1:126
in Jerusalem (Solomon) 1:157, 1:166,
1:170
at Karnak 1:75
of Marduk 1:176–7
of Sobketpe 1:124
Sumerian 1:79, 1:83, 1:86–7, 1:91
Ggantija 2:71
Greek 2:120, 2:152
of Apollo 2:137, 2:151
of Athene 2:82, 2:89
of Concord 2:109
Erechtheum 2:130
of Hephaestus 2:118
of Olympian Zeus 2:172
Parthenon 2:82, 2:105, 2:128, 2:130,
2:134, 2:151, 2:153
of Poseidon 2:115, 2:160
in Gupta period 5:17
Maltese 2:69, 2:71
in Mesoamerica 5:93, 5:93, 5:94, 5:96
to the Palmyran gods (Dura-Europos) 3:75
Roman
of Hadrian (Ephesus) 3:62
of Hercules Victor (Rome) 3:63
of Vesta (Rome) 3:63
see also Solomon's Temple
Tengri, Mongol sky god 4:110
Teniers the Elder, David (1582–1649) 7:16
Teniers the Younger, David (1610–1690) 6:27
Tenochtitlán, Aztec capital 5:96
Teotihuacán, first Mesoamerican city 5:93
terrorism and assassinations 10:49–50, 10:73,
10:74, 10:102–103, 10:102, 10:138, 10:175
anarchists and 8:110, 8:112
assassination of Franz Ferdinand 8:145
in Bosnia 8:142
Indian nationalism and 8:97
in Russia 8:109–10
Tertiary period 1:14
Tertullian (c.152–222 CE), Christian churchman
3:141, 4:167, 5:171
Texan republic 7:156
textile production 5:56
Thailand
economic growth in 10:113
treaty with Japan 10:39
see also Siam (Thailand)
Thales of Miletus (c.620–c.555 BCE), Greek
philosopher 2:140, 3:146
Thatcher, Margaret (1925–), British prime
minister 10:103–5, 10:103
theatre
Greek 2:88, 2:138, 2:148, 2:149, 2:176
theatrical traditions 2:148–51, 2:148
Thebes, capital of New Kingdom (Egypt) 1:106,
1:120, 1:123, 1:125, 1:127
sack by Ashurbanipal 2:75
school for scribes 1:108
Thebes (Greece) 2:123, 2:157
destruction by Alexander 2:159–60
Themistocles (c.514–449 BCE), Athenian
statesman 2:132–3
Theodelinda, queen of the Lombards 3:175
Theodora, Byzantine empress (c.500–548 CE)
4:49
Theodoric (455–526 CE), Ostrogothic king
3:154–6, 3:156, 3:158, 3:160

Theodosius I (c.346–395 CE), Roman emperor in
East 3:136, 3:137–40, 3:137
St Ambrose and 3:137–40
Thera 1:149
Akrotiri settlement of 1:137
volcanic eruption in 1:144
Thermopylae Pass 2:159
battle for 2:114, 2:115
Theseus, legendary Athenian hero 1:143
Thesis on Public Education (Gaspar de
Jovellanos) 7:32
Thespis (6th century BCE), Greek actor 2:149
Thessaloniki, besieged by Bulgars 4:78
Thessaly 2:159
The Third Class Carriage (Daumier) 7:136
Third World Nations 10:22–3
Thirty Years' War 6:66, 6:86–8, 6:86, 6:98,
6:116
Thomas á Kempis (c.1380–1471), Christian
mystic 5:112
Thomson, Sir Joseph John (1856–1940), British
physicist 9:140
Thor, Norse god 4:82–3, 4:83, 4:156–7
Thotmes III, king of Egypt (c.1500–c.1446 BCE)
1:126–7
Thrace 2:66, 2:112, 2:159, 4:62, 4:116
annexation by Darius I 2:111
Bulgars in 3:164
colonization by Greek farmers 2:93
ravage by Visigoths 3:132
Thucydides (c.460–400 BCE), Greek historian
2:122, 2:122, 2:123, 2:133, 2:133, 2:147–8
Thuringians, Germanic peoples 3:129
Tiahuanaco, Peru 1:69
Tiananmen Square incident 10:155–6, 10:155,
10:157
Tiberius, Claudius Nero (42 BCE–37 CE), Roman
emperor 3:6, 3:39, 3:40
palace of 3:45, 3:45
Tibet 5:60–1
British, invasion of 8:13, 8:60
Chinese invasion of 10:28, 10:29
K'ang-hsi, occupation of 5:63, 5:66
Tiflis 4:128
Tiglathpileser III, king of Assyria (744–727 BCE)
1:172, 1:174
Tigris River 1:72, 1:76–7, 1:78, 1:83, 1:94,
1:173, 1:174
Til Barsib 1:172
Timbuctoo 5:86
Timur Lang (c.1336–1405), Mongol emperor
4:106, 4:114
Delhi and 5:24
Isfahan and 5:25
tin
from Anatolia 1:136
from Britain 1:157
in Europe 2:67, 2:86
Tito, Josip Broz (1892–1980), president of
Yugoslavia 10:22, 10:23, 10:77
Titus Flavius Vespasianus (39–81 CE), Roman
emperor 3:69
tobacco
in Caribbean 6:145, 6:146–7
economic importance of 6:146–7
import into Europe 6:166
in North America 6:150, 6:152, 6:155
as staple crop 6:147, 6:150
Tocqueville, Alexis de (1809–1859), French
political analyst 7:158, 7:159
Tokugawa shogunate 8:79, 8:82, 8:84

Toledo 5:127, 5:170
Visigoth capital in Spain 3:157, 3:176
see also Visigoths
Tolstoy, Leo (1828–1910), Russian writer 8:109
Toltec peoples 5:95
tombs
of Agamemnon, king of Mycenae 1:153
of Cyrus the Great 2:76, 2:81
of Darius I 2:79
Egyptian 1:115, 1:117, 1:119, 1:122, 1:122,
1:123, 1:125, 1:128
megalithic 2:67–9
Mycenaen 1:140, 1:155
of Persian kings 2:77
of the Shang dynasty 2:37, 2:53, 2:54
at Ur 1:89
in the Valley of the Kings 1:110, 1:117
Tonga, kingdom of, British protectorate 8:10
Tonkin, kingdom, French Indo-China 8:102,
9:107
tools 1:18, 1:20–21, 1:31, 1:54, 1:109, 1:135,
1:135
agricultural 1:52, 1:54, 1:58–9
copper 2:11, 2:66
Ethiopian 1:21
harpoons 1:41, 1:42
of Homo sapiens 1:41
iron 1:58–9, 2:15, 2:44, 2:62
in Jordan valley 1:21
needles 1:41, 1:59
Neolithic defined by 1:51, 1:52
Palaeolithic 1:42
stone 1:27, 1:39–41, 1:51, 1:52, 1:54, 1:89
flint 1:36, 1:41, 1:42
hand-axes 1:23, 1:26, 1:26
obsidian 1:54
Tordesillas, treaty of 5:162
Torres, Luis Vaez de, Spanish explorer 6:177
Toulouse 5:140
Visigoth kingdom in Gaul 3:132–3, 3:156,
3:157, 3:158
tourism 10:161, 10:169
Tower of Babel 1:84
see also pyramids
towns and cities
early development in Mesopotamia 1:77
Europe 6:13–14, 6:13, 6:19, 6:32–3
growing independence of 5:144
and trade 5:134, 5:144
immunities of 6:44
see also individual towns and cities
trade 3:69, 3:70, 3:128, 4:34, 4:43, 4:70, 4:127
banking services 5:130, 5:135, 5:139, 6:13,
6:20, 9:127–8, 9:128
barter 2:125
capitalist market economy 10:15–16
Caribbean 6:146–8
in China 2:46, 8:16, 8:51, 8:73, 8:74
Ch'ang-an, trading centre 5:52
between China and Europe 8:67–8, 8:73
in Mongol China 5:59
coffee 6:133, 6:145, 6:153, 6:166, 6:173
with colonial empires 6:22–3, 6:22–3
commercial fairs 5:136, 5:136
commodity transfers 1:138, 1:140
communist political intervention in 10:15–16
complexities of 1:135–7, 1:146, 1:158
consumer markets 7:46, 7:58
cotton 6:173
decline in 4:169
Dutch domination of 6:22, 6:130–3

trade (cont.)
East India Company monopoly 8:46
Egyptian 1:103–4, 1:125–6, *1:139*
England
Anglo-American expansion 8:16
Anglo-Indian expansion 8:51–2
with Persia 4:127
wool and cloth 5:126, 5:135
in Europe 5:134–6, 5:135, *5:136*, 5:137,
5:140, 8:14–18
British foreign policy, encouraged by 8:44
between east and west Europe 10:130
eastern Mediterranean 2:85–6, *2:87*, **2:92**,
2:93
expansion, impetus to 6:122–4
French competition with Britain 6:161
Mediterranean revival of 5:130–31
Spanish and Portuguese 5:162–3
fish 6:22–3
free movement of 8:14, 8:44
free trade doctrine 8:16–17, 8:137
in Germany 8:175–6
Greek 2:98, 2:100, 2:125
Harappan 2:12–13
in India 5:16, 5:31–2, 5:35–6
infrastructures of 8:18
in Italy 5:135–6
in Japan 5:75, 5:79–80, *5:80*, 8:81–2, *8:81*,
8:84, 8:87, 9:9–10, 9:23
in Kiev Rus 4:87
local economies, effects on 8:18
in Maurya empire 5:14
marketing changes *9:160–61*
metals 1:135–6
Minoan 1:145–6, 1:152
money and barter 1:138–40, **1:138**
Mongol protection of 4:109
Mycenaean 1:152
in North America 6:150, 6:152
opium *8:17*, 8:68–9, 8:73
Portuguese 6:127–30
re-export 6:130, 6:166
between Rome and Persia 3:109–10, **3:109**
routes *see* trade routes
in Russia 5:66, 6:108, 6:112–13, 8:74, 8:88
sea-borne 1:137
Spanish Empire 6:142, 6:145–6
spices *see* spice trade
sugar 6:145–7, *6:146*, 6:166, 6:173
Sumerian 1:88–9
tariff barriers demolished 8:16–17
tariff barriers, post-war 8:175, 8:177–8
tea 6:133–5, *6:153*, 6:166, 6:173
tobacco **6:155**, *6:166*
in Caribbean *6:145*, 6:146–7
in North America 6:150, 6:152, **6:155**
United States 7:152, 7:154, 9:88–9, **9:88**
urban growth and 5:134, 5:144, **6:13**
Venice and 5:130
wars in defence of 6:20
without money 1:56, 1:139–40
worldwide
economic integration of 8:17–18
growth of **6:126**, **6:141**, 6:153, 6:165–6,
9:127–8
see also slave trade; trade wars; transport
trade routes *2:136*, 4:9, 4:14, 4:19, **4:20**, 5:52
Central Asia, access to **6:107**, 6:176–7
to East 4:123
in Europe 5:135, **5:136**
European domination of 6:122–4

trade routes (cont.)
of Kiev Rus **4:89**
Mahayana Buddhism and 5:22
in Mesoamerica *5:93*
Mongol 4:109–10
Silk Road 4:39, 4:56
trade unionism 8:111, *8:111*
in France 7:98
in Great Britain 7:176
trade wars 6:158–61
Anglo-Dutch 6:20, 6:159–60
Trafalgar, battle of 7:105
Trajan (Marcus Ulpius Trajanus) (c.52–117 CE),
Roman emperor 3:41, 3:42, 3:68
conquest of Ctesiphon (Parthian capital) by
3:43
Trans-Jordan
Arab League in 9:110
British mandate in 9:40
Islamic conquest of *4:24*
independence of 9:41
oil pipeline in 9:41
Transoxiana 4:97–8, 4:114
Chinghis Khan and 4:105–6
Seljuks and 4:99, 4:102
transport and travel 6:22–3, *6:156*, 7:53, *8:18*,
8:22–3, 9:136–7
aeroplanes 9:137
agricultural produce and *7:53*
asses and donkeys 1:136
Berlin airlift 10:10–11, *10:10*
in British India 8:47
camels *1:136*
canals 7:55
caravans 1:136–7
carts 1:136, *2:14*
Celtic 2:66
chariots 2:14, 2:58, *2:65*
costs of *7:53*
improvements to **6:10**
industrial development and 8:107
military 2:36, 2:46
in Mongol Empire 4:109
motor cars 9:133–5
railways *see* railways
river transport in Russia 6:102, 6:112
Roman 3:30, *3:113*
slave-ships 6:24, 6:165, *6:169*
space flight 10:172–3
speed, increase of 7:56–7
standardization of *10:170*
steamships 7:53, 7:56, *7:152*, *7:155*
trans-oceanic 7:54, 7:56
by water *1:102*, 1:137, *3:90*
see also chariots
Transvaal 5:85, 8:34, *8:35*
annexation of 8:34
fire, early use of 1:27
gold discovered in 8:35
government of 8:36
industrialization of 8:35, 8:37
treaties
Anglo-Irish (1921) *8:162*
Brest-Litovsk *8:154*
Ghent (1814) *7:153*
Lateran (1929) *8:172*
Locarno (1925) *9:52*
Maastricht (1991) *10:107*
Madrid (1985) *10:106*
North Atlantic 10:11, **10:11**
Nuclear Non-Proliferation (1968) 10:175–6

treaties (cont.)
Oregon (1846) 7:153–4, **7:156**
Paris (1783) 7:78, 7:152, 7:156
Paris (1856) **7:129**
Rome (1957) 10:99, 10:107
Sino-Soviet (1950) 10:28
Versailles (1919) 8:156–8, *8:158*–9, 8:166,
8:175, 9:52, 9:61, 9:63, 9:66, 9:67
Vienna (1815) *7:114*, **7:116**, *7:117*, 7:122–3,
7:134
Washington (1988) *10:138*
Westphalia 6:87, *6:87*, 6:88, **6:88**
see also peace treaties
Trebizond 4:58, *4:72*, 4:109
as ally of Byzantium **4:51**, 4:116
Ottoman Turks, conquest of 4:121
The Tree of Liberty (Gillray) *7:100*
Trent, Council of 6:55, *6:56*, 6:57, 6:59, 6:171
Triassic period **1:14**
trilobites *1:13*
Trincomalee, Ceylon (Sri Lanka) 8:43
Trinidad 8:24
Triple Alliance (1882) 8:143
Tripoli
Italian invasion of 9:33, 9:35
Latin county of 4:102
Tripolitania, taken by Italians 8:57, 8:64
triremes, Greek **2:113**
Trojan wars **1:155**
Trotsky, Leon Davidovich (1879–1940), Russian
revolutionary *8:154*, 8:168, *9:58*
Troy 1:160–61
excavations at **1:155**
fall of 1:152, **1:155**
trade with Mycenae 1:152
Treasury of Atreus *1:153*
Troyes, Council of **5:155**
Truman, Harry S. (1884–1972), United States
president 10:85
American policy changes 9:92, 9:94–5, 9:111
Korean War and 10:13
Truman Doctrine 9:94–6
Tsolikovsky, Konstantin (1857–1935), Russian
scientist 9:147
Tuaregs 2:58, *5:86*
Tudor dynasty in England 6:52–4, 6:62, 6:81
dissolution of the monasteries 6:53–4
state jurisdiction, growth of 6:42
Henry VIII's break with Catholicism 6:52–3
rebellions 6:42
Tunis
conquest by Charles V *6:84*
French protectorate 8:52, 8:57
independence of 6:97
recapture by Turks 6:85
Tunisia
emirate of 4:41
caliphate *4:43*
independence of 10:45
Turkestan 4:107
invasion of 5:41
Turkey *9:30*, 9:43
American missiles in 10:79
Arab revolt in 8:149
Armenians, massacre of *8:119*
cession of Bessarabia to Russia 7:122
Dardanelles campaign and 8:148
in First World War 8:146, *9:37*
Indian pan-Islamic movement and 8:99
Italy, war with 8:134
Massacre of Chios *7:122*

Turkey (cont.)
modernization in 9:44
nationalism in 9:33–6, 9:43–4
Republic proclaimed by Mustafa Kemal **9:45**
Russian threat to 9:88
Serbian revolt in 7:122
territories surrendered by 9:44
Treaty of Versailles and 8:158
United States aid to 9:95
woman's emancipation in 9:44–5
see also Ottoman empire
Turkish peoples 4:97–101
art of writing and 4:98
of first Turkish Empire 4:17, 4:98
Ghaznavid dynasty in Iran 4:99–100
iron-workers 4:16, **4:17**
of second Turkish Empire 4:100
siege of Constantinople and 4:17
see also Black Sheep Turks; Oghuz Turks;
Ottoman Turks; Seljuk Turks
Turner, Joseph (1775–1851), English Romantic
artist *7:41*
Tuscany 5:135
Tutankhamon, king of Egypt (c.1360–1350 BCE)
1:107, 1:128, *1:142*
Tuthmosis (Thutmose), king of Egypt
(1479–1425 BCE) **1:105**
The Twelve Caesars (Suetonius) *3:42*
Twelve Years' Truce 6:87
Tyre, Phoenician city 1:156–7, 1:169
destruction by Alexander 2:161
Tyrol 6:82

U

Uganda 8:57
Ukraine **8:165**, 10:147, 10:152
acknowledgment of Turkish suzerainty 6:94
army 10:147
Cossack peoples 6:98, 6:100, 6:106
Russian takeover of 6:116
Ulbricht, Walter (1893–1973), East German
politician *10:76*
Umar, second caliph (634–644 CE) *4:24*
Umayyad caliphate 4:24, 4:26, 4:28–32, *4:29*
Africa and **4:42**, **4:43**, **4:43**
army of 4:28
Charlemagne and 4:140
Constantinople *4:57*
end of 4:32, *4:33*
sea power of 4:43
Spain and 4:41–3
see also Abbasid caliphate; Islam; Islamic
civilization; Islamic science
Uncle Tom's Cabin (Harriet Beecher Stowe)
7:162
unemployment *7:63*
in Europe 7:133
in France 7:120, 7:123, 7:126
in Great Britain 7:46
in Poland 7:126
see also poverty
Unitarianism 6:65, 6:70
France, threat to 6:70
United Arab Republic 10:46
United Kingdom *see* Great Britain
United Nations Organization (UNO) 9:80,
9:84–6, *9:84*, **9:85**, 9:87, 9:97, 9:176–7
Arafat, Yasser speech *10:126*

United Nations Organization (UNO) (cont.)
 Argentina, condemnation of   10:104
 Economic and Social Council (UNESCO)
  9:85
 Commission of Human Rights   10:61
 Declaration of Human Rights   10:165–6,
  10:165
 General Assembly of   10:61, 10:78, 10:121,
  10:126
 Gulf War and   10:135
 Israel, condemnation of   10:49, 10:61
 Kashmir plebiscite   10:20
 Palestine problem, mediation of   9:111
 Saddam Hussein, condemnation of   10:124
 Security Council   **10:11**, 10:13, 10:20, 10:135
 Soviet Union, condemnation of   10:78
 Suez cease-fire and   10:46
 Yugoslavia, peace-keeping force in   *10:150*,
  10:151
 Zionism denounced   10:121
United Provinces   6:30, 6:61, 6:72, 6:92, 6:119
 and native populations   6:168
 colonial territories of   6:157
 Dutch United East India Company   6:131,
  6:131
 Grand Alliance   6:91
 see also Low Countries; Netherlands
United States of Africa   10:57
United States of America
 agriculture in   7:47, 7:52, 7:158, 7:169
 Alliance for Progress   10:71–2, 10:73
 Apollo moon-landing project   9:148–52,
  9:150
 Arab-Israeli settlement and   10:136
 Articles of Confederation   7:81
 Canada, frontier with   7:153–4
 cities in   10:88, 10:95
 Civil Rights Campaign of   10:86–8, **10:87**
 Civil War *see* American Civil War
 Cold War and   9:96–7, *9:97*
 constitution of
  abolitionist amendment in   *7:166*
  bicameral legislature   7:83
  democracy and   7:84–5
  historic significance of   7:81–5
  English constitutional theory, influence of
   7:83–4
  judicial interpretation of   7:158
  republican   7:82–3
  signing of   *7:81*
 Constitutional Convention (1787)   7:80–81
 cotton-growing in   7:52, 7:158
 Cuba, links with   10:69
 demobilization of   9:88, 9:90
 Democratic Party   7:162, 7:163, **7:164**,
  7:167–8, 9:55–6, *9:55*, 10:85
 Dumbarton Oaks meeting   9:85
 economy of   7:168–70, **7:168**, 8:16, 8:61,
  8:149, *8:177*, 9:89, 9:127, 10:85, 10:95
 Falklands war and   10:104
 federal government, power of   9:56
 federalism in   7:84
 food production and distribution in   7:52–3
 foreign aid   10:68
 foreign policy   7:153, 10:85
  in Asia   9:14, 9:23, 9:28, 10:23–4, 10:34,
   10:37–40, 10:93
  in China   9:106, 10:28, 10:110, 10:93
  covert operations   10:68
  in Europe   9:55–6, 9:94–5, 10:11
  in Latin America   10:67–8

United States of America, foreign policy (cont.)
  pro-Zionist   9:111
  in Vietnam   10:89
 German declaration of war on   9:73–4
 German rearmament and   10:98
 Good Neighbor policy of   10:67–8
 Great Depression in   9:49, *9:54–5*, 9:89
 Greece and Turkey, aid for   9:95
 immigration into   7:169, *8:21–2, 8:23*,
  8:138–9, *8:138*, 10:84
 industrialization   7:58–9, 8:138, 8:149
 Iranian hostage crisis   10:124, *10:125*, 10:131
 isolationism of   7:153, 8:163, 9:55–6, 9:75,
  9:86, 9:95, 10:11, 10:94
 Japan, embargo on   9:74–5
 Japanese trade and   8:81
 Latin America, opposition in   10:69, 10:71–3
 League of Nations, absence from   8:161
 Lend-Lease Act   9:73, 9:82, 9:90
 Libya, bombing of   10:138, *10:138*
 Louisiana Purchase (1803)   7:154, **7:156**,
  7:159–60, **7:161**
 Manhattan Project   **9:78**
 Marshall Plan **9:94**
 Mexican territory, acquisition of   7:156,
  7:156, 7:159, 7:162
 military bases overseas   9:88
 Mississippi River
  commercial transport and   *7:155*
  freedom of navigation   7:154
  as western frontier   7:78
 Monroe doctrine   7:155–6, 10:70
 nationalist feelings   8:139
 NATO and   10:11
 natural resources   8:138
 naval bases
  Hawaii (Pearl Harbor)   8:62, *9:74, 9:75*
  Samoa   8:61
 Neutrality Proclamation of (1793)   7:153
 New Deal   9:56, 9:89
 New Orleans   *7:153, 7:154–5, 7:157*
 Nuclear Non-Proliferation Treaty and
  10:175–6
 nuclear weapons   10:79–80, 10:121
 Pacific campaign, World War II   10:37, *10:37*
 Pacific states, relations with   10:39
 Panama Canal and   8:63
 Pearl Harbor, attack on   *9:74, 9:75*
 political evolution   7:158–9
 population growth   7:154, 7:157, 7:169,
  10:84
 poverty   7:169–70
 power   10:90–91
 racial prejudice and segregation   7:167, *10:86*,
  10:87–8
 Republican Party   7:162, 7:163, **7:164**,
  7:167–8, 9:55–6, *9:55*, 10:85
 science, funding by government   *10:85*
 Security Council and   9:85
 similarities to United Kingdom   7:150–2
 slavery *see* slavery, United States
 South American investments   10:65
 Soviet Union and   9:86–7, 10:129–30, *10:129*
 Soviet Union, balance of power with   10:76
 space programme of   9:147–52, *9:150*, **9:151**,
  9:152, 9:155
 Spanish-American war   8:30, 8:55, 8:62,
  8:138
 Spanish territory, acquisition of   7:154, **7:156**
 stock market crash   *8:177*
 Suez crisis cease-fire and   10:46

United States of America (cont.)
 Sukarno, support for   10:24–5
 Supreme Court   7:84
 tariff protection   8:61, 8:177
 Tennessee Valley Authority   *9:56*
 territorial expansion   7:154–7, **7:156**, 8:61–2
 Texas, annexation of   7:156, **7:156**
 Treaty of Versailles and   8:156, *8:158*
 two-party system in   7:167–8
 Vietnam War, domestic effects of   10:90,
  10:91, 10:92
 see also Vietnam War
 Wall Street crash (1929)   **9:54**
 welfare state in   10:85
 withdrawal of missiles from Turkey   10:79
 World War I and   8:151–2, *8:152*, 9:39
 World War II, role in   9:76–7
 see also Second World War
 see also American Civil War; American
  Revolution; black Americans; imperialism,
  American; individual presidents; North
  American colonies; Roosevelt, Franklin Delano
 universities   5:166–7, *7:12*
  Aristotle's Lyceum   2:145, 2:170
  Chinese political activism in   9:12–13, 9:15
  clerical control of   7:10
  medieval foundations of   **5:128**, 5:166, *5:167*
  Plato's Academy   2:143, 2:145, 2:170
  science departments of   8:128
  see also education; individual universities
 Untouchables (*shudras*)   2:16, **5:19**
 Upanishads   **2:20**, **2:23**, 2:24–5, **2:25**, 2:27
 Upper Palaeolithic   1:39, 1:40, 1:52, 1:60
  art   1:42–6, *1:61*
  buildings   1:48
  racial groupings   1:46–8
  worldwide diffusion of peoples   1:46, 1:48
 Ur   1:163–4, *1:68, 1:79, 1:82, 1:87, 1:88–91,
  1:91–2, 1:94, 1:95*
 Urban II (c.1042–1099), pope   *5:6, 5:103*, 5:107
 Urban VI (1318–1389), pope   *5:100*
 urban decline   3:106–107, 3:135
 urbanization   1:71, 1:77–8, *1:142*, 2:81, *4:170,
  7:13, 7:46, 7:54, 7:60–4, 7:60*
  in Africa   10:53
  in Europe   6:13–14, *6:13*, 6:19
  in Japan   10:113–14, *10:114, 10:172*
  poverty and   *10:162*
  see also cities; industrialization
 Ur Nammu, king of Ur (c.2112–c.2095 BCE)
  1:78, 1:85, 1:91
 Urubamba River   *5:99*
 Uruguay
  food production and distribution in   7:52–3
  human rights violations   10:73
 Uruk (Erech)   *1:77–8, 1:79, 1:81*, **1:81**, 1:82
 USSR (Union of Soviet Socialist Republics) *see*
  Soviet Union
 Uthman, son-in-law of Muhammad, third caliph
  (644–656 CE)   *4:24*
 Utnapishtim   **1:81**

V

 vaccination   *7:45*
 vaishyas (farmers and merchants caste)   2:16,
  2:17, **5:19**
 Valdemar IV (1320–1375), king of Denmark
  5:145

 Valencia   5:128
 Valens (c.328–378 CE), Eastern emperor   3:111,
  3:132, *3:133*
 Valerian (Publius Licinius Valerianus), Roman
  emperor (253–60 CE)   3:109
  persecution of Christians by   3:118
  Persian murder of   3:118
  Sassanid defeat of   *4:12*
 Valois dynasty in France   6:80–81
 Vandals, Germanic peoples   *3:128*, 3:129,
  3:132–4, 3:152
  Belisarius, defeat by   3:161
  North African conquest of   *3:128*, 3:133
  Rome, sack of   (455)   3:133
 Vanguard satellites   9:148
 Varanasi, sacred city   **5:20**
 Varangians (Norsemen)   4:81–4, **4:89**, 4:153
 Vargas, Getúlio (1883–1954), president of Brazil
  10:65
 Varuna, Vedic god   2:15, *2:16*
 Vedanta, philosophical system of   5:21
 Vedas   **2:23**
 vegetables   1:108, 2:63
 Velázquez, Diego (1599–1660), artist
  6:122
 Venezuela   6:139, 10:66
  European settlements in   6:145–6
  naval blockade of   8:30
  oil in   8:29
 Venice   4:73–6, **4:74, 4:77**, 4:116–17, 4:119,
  4:151, 5:130–1, 5:135, *5:139*, 159, *5:179*,
  6:84
  Aegean islands and   4:115–16
  ambassadors of   6:78
  Austrian absorption of   7:108, 7:117
  Byzantium and   4:140
  commerce, diplomatic defence of
   6:158
  commercial empire   4:75, 5:131, 5:135
  Constantinople and   **4:74**, 4:75, 5:153
  doge   6:30
  Fourth Crusade and   **4:74**, 4:75, 5:153
  independence from Austria   7:127
  industry in   5:139
  maritime techniques of   6:95
  naval power of   4:74
  Turks, resistance to   6:94
 Verdun, Treaty of   4:145–6
 Vermeer, Jan (1632–1675), Dutch artist
  6:34
 Vernet, Claude-Joseph (1714–1789), French
  artist   *7:53*
 Vernet, Emile, French artist   *8:52*
 Vernet, Horace (1789–1863), French artist
  7:121
 Versailles, Palace of   6:71, 6:89, *6:90*
 Versailles, Treaty of (1919)   8:156–8, *8:158–9*,
  8:166, 9:52, 9:61, 9:63, 9:66–7
  Germany, economic effects on   8:175
  weaknesses of   8:162–3
 Verwoerd, Hendrik (1901–1966), prime minister
  of South Africa   *10:58*
 Vesalius, Andreas (1514–1564), Belgian
  anatomist   7:16–17
 Vespasian (Titus Flavius Vespasianus) (9–79 CE),
  Roman emperor   3:40, *3:40*, **3:41**
 Vespucci, Amerigo (1454–1512), Italian
  navigator   5:163, *5:164*
 Vesta, Roman household goddess   *3:63*, **3:68**
 Victor Emmanuel II (1820–1878), king of Italy
  7:131

Victoria (1819–1901), queen of Great Britain
  and Ireland, empress of India 7:173, 7:176,
  7:177, 8:44, 8:91, 8:137
  anaesthetics, use of 8:130
  Boer war, views on 8:36
  at Colonial and Indian Exhibition 8:41
Vienna 6:118
  Ottoman sieges of 4:122, 4:122
  Turkish seizure of 6:93, 6:94, 6:95, 6:96,
    6:99
Vietcong 10:36, 10:89, 10:92
Viet Minh communist party 9:107
Vietnam 5:59
  China, relations with 10:93
  Comecon, member of 10:98
  decolonization of 9:107–108
  emperor of Annam (Bao Dai) 9:107–8
  French rule 8:100
    nationalism in 8:101
    universities in 8:101–103
    rebellion against 9:23, 9:108
  north–south partition in 10:34
  see also Annam; Indochina; North Vietnam;
    South Vietnam; Vietnam war
Vietnam War 10:12, 10:34–6, 10:89–91, 10:95,
  10:115
  bombing raids on North Vietnam
    10:90
  cease-fire in 10:91, 10:95
  peace talks 10:93
  refugees in 10:91
  Tet offensive 10:92
  United States domestic outcry against 10:90,
    10:90
  United States support for South Vietnam
    10:34–6, 10:89–90
Vikings see Norsemen
Viking space probes 10:173
Villanovan people and culture 2:70, 3:11
villas 3:16, 3:49, 3:57, 3:60, 3:104
  Boscoreale, Pompeii 3:51, 3:56, 3:105,
    :106
  Villa of the Mysteries, Pompeii 3:67
A Vindication of the Rights of Women
  (Wollstonecraft) 8:114
vines 1:144
Vinland 4:154
Virgil (Publius Vergilius Maro) (70–19 BCE),
  Roman poet 3:48, 3:50, 5:171
Virginia 6:148–50, 6:155, 6:168
Vishnu, Hindu god 2:20, 2:23–4, 2:23, 2:24–5,
  5:13, 5:20
Visigoths, Germanic peoples 3:129–33, 3:133,
  3:157
  in Aquitaine 3:152, 3:158
  Christianity, conversion to 3:176
  Franks, conquest by 3:153
  kingdom of (Spain) 3:132, 3:156, 3:163
  kingdom of (Toulouse, Gaul) 3:132–3, 3:156,
    3:157, 3:158
  Vandals and 3:133
The Visit (Vermeer) 6:34
Vitellius, Aulus, Roman emperor (69) 3:40,
  3:41
Vladimir I, St (c.956–1015), Christian prince of
  Russia 4:85–7, 4:89
  conversion to Christianity 4:85, 4:87
  marriage to Byzantine princess Anna 4:85,
    4:87
Vladivostok 7:144, 8:73, 8:88
  Russians, founding by 8:43

Voltaire (François-Marie Arnouet) (1694–1778),
  French writer 6:33, 6:35, 7:27, 7:28, 7:33,
  7:34, 7:35, 7:36–8
Vostok satellites see Space program
Votes for women see female suffrage

W

Wade-Giles transcription system 2:45
Walesa, Lech (1947–), Polish leader and
  president 10:142, 10:143, 10:149
Wallachia 7:129
Wallis Islands 6:177
Wallis, Samuel (1728–1795), English navigator
  6:177, 6:177
Wanderer over the Sea of Clouds, The (Friedrich)
  7:39
Wang Ch'eng, Chou capital 2:45
Warad-Sin, king of Larsa (c.1835–c.1823 BCE)
  1:93
warfare 8:121–2, 8:139, 8:140, 8:149
  see also air warfare
Warring States period, China 2:38–40, 2:46–7,
  5:39–40
wars
  Afghanistan 10:12
  American Independence (1773–1783)
    7:78
  Anglo-American (1812–1814) 7:153
  Anglo-Dutch (1652–1654) 6:88–9, 6:159,
    6:163
  Anglo-Dutch (1665–1667) 6:159–60
  Anglo-French 6:70
  Anglo-French (1793–1802) 7:95, 7:105,
    7:153
  Arab-Israeli War of Independence (1948–1949)
    9:110, 9:111, 10:43
  of the Austrian Succession (1740–1748)
    6:117, 6:161
  Balkan (1912–1913) 8:119, 8:145, 9:34,
    9:35, 9:37
  Boer War (1899–1902) 8:34, 8:35–6, 10:59
  China-India (1962) 10:28–9, 10:29
  China-Vietnam frontier war (1979) 10:95
  civil wars
    Afghanistan (1979–1989) 10:43
    Chile (1891) 8:28
    Congo 10:55
    English (1642–1651) 6:63–4, 6:64, 6:65–6
    Lebanon (1975–1989) 10:43
    Nigeria 10:56
    Roman 3:30, 3:34, 3:38, 3:40, 3:101
    Russia (1918–1922) 8:155, 8:166–7, 8:167
    Spain (1936–39) 9:64–5, 9:67
    United States (1861–1865) 7:163–6, 7:164,
      8:121, 8:140, 8:149
  Crimean War (1853–1856) 7:128–30,
    7:128–9, 7:129, 7:144, 7:145
  Dutch Revolt (Eighty Years' War) 6:59–61,
    6:85–6, 6:130, 6:158
  England and Scotland 6:64, 6:88
  Falklands (1982) 10:104–5, 10:104
  First World War see First World War
  Franco-Prussian (1870) 7:132, 7:147
  Great Northern (1700–1721) 6:106
  Gulf (1991) 9:116, 9:116, 10:43, 10:134–5,
    10:134, 10:135
  Habsburg-Bourbon 6:84, 6:87
  Habsburg-Valois 6:84–5, 6:87

wars (cont.)
  of Independence (1810–22) 8:24, 8:26–7,
    8:61
  India-Pakistan (1965; 1971) 10:20, 10:23
  Iran-Iraq (1980–1989) 9:167, 10:43, 10:121,
    10:127, 10:131, 10:133–4
  Italy-Turkey (1911) 8:134
  Java (1825–1830) 8:103
  of Jenkins' Ear (1739) 6:161
  Judean (66–74 CE) 3:78, 3:88
  Korean (1950–1953) 10:12, 10:13–14, 10:13,
    10:26, 10:39
  of the League of Augsburg (King William's
    War) 6:91, 6:160
  Mexico-United States (1846–1848) 7:156
  Napoleonic (1804–1815) 7:102, 7:105,
    7:108, 7:111, 8:43, 8:52–3, 8:55
  Opium (1839–1842) 8:16, 8:68
  Pacific (1878–1883) 8:26, 8:29
  Peloponnesian see Peloponnesian War
  Persian 2:112–16, 2:129, 2:146
  Polish-Russian (1918–1921) 8:166
  Prussia-Austria (1866) 7:131
  Prussia-Denmark (1864) 7:131
  Punic 2:178
    First (264–241 BCE) 3:18–19, 3:20
    Second (218–201 BCE) 3:19–21, 3:20, 3:20,
      3:23, 3:28
    Third (149–146 BCE) 3:23
  of Religion 6:54–5, 6:54, 6:55
  of the Roses (1455–85) 5:131, 6:81
  Russia-Turkey (1827–1829) 7:123, 7:144
  Russo-Japanese (1904–1905) 8:86, 8:88–9,
    8:89, 8:96, 8:110
  Russo-Persian (1826–1828) 8:43
  Second World War see Second World War
  Seven Years' War (1756–1763) 6:136, 6:138,
    6:150, 6:157, 6:161
  Sikh (1846) 8:92
  Sino-Japanese (1894–1895) 8:74–5, 8:86,
    8:87
  Sino-Japanese (1937–1945) 9:27–9, 9:28–9,
    9:104
  Six-Day (1967) 8:19, 9:111, 10:48–9, 10:49
  Social War (90 BCE) 3:30
  Spanish-American (1898) 8:30, 8:55, 8:62
  of the Spanish Succession (1701–1714) 6:91,
    6:92, 6:93, 6:160
  Thirty Years' War (1618–1648) 6:66, 6:86–8,
    6:86, 6:98, 6:98, 6:116, 6:157
  Triple Alliance (1864–1870) 8:26
  Trojan 2:120
  Vietnam (1964–1973) 10:12, 10:34–6,
    10:89–91, 10:89, 10:92, 10:121
  World War I see First World War
  World War II see Second World War
  Yom Kippur War (1973) 9:111, 9:116, 10:50,
    10:50
  see also battles; Cold War; peace treaties; trade
    wars
Warsaw 6:99, 6:99
Warsaw Conference (1884) 8:143
Warsaw, Grand Duchy of 7:109, 7:116
Warsaw Pact 9:96, 10:15, 10:16, 10:96, 10:98
  forces crush Czechoslovakian liberalization
    10:96, 10:97, 10:140, 10:143
  Hungarian withdrawal from 10:78
Washington, George (1732–1799), United States
  president 7:78, 7:79–80, 7:81, 7:82–3, 7:90
  Farewell Address 7:153, 7:155, 7:157–8
Waterloo, battle of 7:105

Watt, James (1736–1819), Scottish engineer
  7:56
Wealth of Nations (Adam Smith) 7:28,
  7:42
weapons 1:135, 1:135, 1:140, 9:139
  airships 8:150
  armour 1:155
  artillery 6:95, 6:125, 6:162–3, 8:148
  axes, bronze 1:58
  barbed wire 8:139, 8:147
  bow and arrows 1:51
  bronze 2:14, 2:46
  cannon 4:120, 5:61, 5:120
  catapults 2:157
  composite bow
    Akkadian 1:91
    Kassite 1:134
  copper 2:66
  crossbows 5:41, 5:120
  Egyptian 1:125
  electronic guidance systems 9:116
  European superiority 8:13–14, 8:15
  firearms 5:26, 5:77, 5:79, 5:92, 6:25
  flame-throwers 8:150
  Greek fire 4:56, 4:57, 4:61, 4:84
  gunpowder 5:55, 5:65
  inter-continental rockets 10:79–80
  iron 1:135, 1:168, 1:175, 2:44, 2:46, 2:62,
    5:40
  in Israel 1:168
  long pikes (sarissa) 2:157, 2:159
  machine-guns 8:139, 8:147, 8:150
  Moghul army, guns in 5:26
  nobility and 2:41
  nuclear see nuclear weapons
  Palaeolithic 1:30, 1:39, 1:41
  poison gas 8:122, 8:150, 8:151
  ritual and 2:36–7
  scale of production 8:121, 8:149
  spearheads 1:52
  submarines 8:150–152
  tanks 8:139, 8:148, 8:150
  see also arms and armour; atomic bomb;
    military techniques; shipbuilding
The Wedding Feast (Pieter Brueghel the Elder)
  6:18
weights and measures
  metric 7:98, 7:110
  standardization of
    in China 5:44
    in Japan 5:81
Weimar Republic 9:53
welfare state 9:175
Wends 4:138, 4:148
Wessex, Anglo-Saxon kingdom of 4:155–6
West Bengal (Hindu) 8:97
West Germany see German Federal
  Republic
West India Company, Dutch 6:146, 6:160
West Indies
  British acquisitions in 6:159–62, 8:24
  discovery of 6:139
  English and French settlements in 6:146
  Spanish settlements in 6:139, 6:141–2
  see also Caribbean islands
Western Empire
  collapse of 3:127–34, 3:135
  separation from the East 3:113, 3:126–7
Westphalia, Treaty of 6:87, 6:88
What is Enlightenment? (Kant) 7:26
wheat 9:128–9

wheeled transport *2:65*
  Celts and 2:66
  Harappan culture and *2:14*
wheels *5:85, 5:94, 5:96*
  development of 1:71
    in Egypt 1:118
    hooped with iron 1:135
    in Sumer 1:88–9
Whitby, Synod of 4:155
White Horde khanate 4:107, 4:112
White Sheep Turks 4:125
Wilhelm I (1797–1888), king of Prussia and
  emperor of Germany *7:133*, **7:134**,
  8:143
Wilhelm II (1854–1941), emperor (Kaiser) of
  Germany *8:120*, *8:143*, *8:147*
  abdication of 8:156
William I the Conqueror (1027–1087), king of
  England 5:123, 5:147
William II, duke of Normandy (1035–1087)
  4:177
William III "of Orange" (1650–1702), king of
  Great Britain (1689–1702) 6:69–70, *6:70*,
  6:90–1, 6:160, 6:164
William of Roebruck (13th century CE),
  Franciscan friar 4:112
William "the Silent" (1533–1584), prince of
  Orange 6:60, *6:61*, 6:85
Willibrord, St (658–739 CE), Anglo-Saxon
  missionary 4:164
Wilson, Thomas Woodrow (1856–1924),
  president of the United States 8:156, *8:158*,
  8:160–61, *8:161*, 8:163, 9:39, 9:55
  and Bolsheviks 8:162
wine *3:69*, *3:70*, *3:113*
witchcraft *7:8*, *7:9*
The Witches' Coven (Goya) 7:9
Witte, Emmanuel de (1617–1692),
  Dutch artist *6:164*
Wittel, Gaspar van (1653–1736), Dutch artist
  7:9
Wolfe, James (1727–1759), British general
  6:150
women
  birth control and 8:106, 8:115–16
  campaign for vote *8:113*, 8:114, 8:116–18,
  8:117
  divorce and *4:44*
  economic liberation of 10:168
  education of 8:115
  emancipation of 10:167–8, *10:168*
  employment of 8:149
  as factory workers 7:67
  feminist movement 8:114–18, *8:114*, **8:114**
  and Islam *4:44*, 4:45
  Islamic fundamentalism and *10:122*, 10:123
  life expectancy of 5:147, 6:12
  oestrus, loss of 1:24–5
  manual labour and *5:146*, *5:147*
  monastic orders and *5:146*, 5:147
  opportunities for 7:128, *8:113*, 8:115, *8:121*
  salons, intellectual expression in 6:35–6, *6:35*
  status of *2:125*, 2:126–7, *2:126*
    in China 5:52–4, *5:54*, 10:33
    in Egypt 1:122–4
    in Europe 5:143, 5:146–7, 6:35–6, 6:51
    in India 5:21, 9:123, **9:123**
    Sumerian 1:86–7, 1:95
    in Taiping movement 8:72
  technology and 8:116
  as vegetable gatherers 1:48

The Women of Troy (Euripides) **2:126**
wool and wool trade 1:144, 2:125, 5:126,
  5:135, 6:25–7, 8:37
Woolf, Virginia (1882–1941), English writer
  9:50
World Bank 9:127–8, *9:128*
World War I *see* First World War
World War II *see* Second World War
World Zionist Congress 9:36, 9:110
Worms, Council of 5:102
Worms, Diet of (1521) 6:49
Wright, Joseph (1734–1797), English artist
  7:21, *7:25*
writing **1:70**, *1:71*, 1:140, **1:141**
  accounting and 1:140
  calligraphy 2:44
  Chinese pictographs 2:44, **2:45**, 5:70
  cuneiform **1:70**, 1:80, *1:80*, 1:117
  earliest form of 1:80
  in Egypt 1:103
  Etruscan 2:70, *3:10*
  Ganges valley civilization and 2:18
  Harappan 2:13–14
  hieroglyphics
    Egyptian **1:70**, 1:100, *1:117*, 5:84
    Mesoamerican 2:63–4, 5:92–4, **5:94**, *5:95*
  invention in Sumer 1:79–80, **1:80**
  Lydian 2:100
  materials
    clay tablets *see entry under* clay tablets
    paper *see* paper
    papyrus 1:117–18, 1:140
    parchment 1:117, 2:170, 4:169
    reed stalks 1:80
  in the Persian Empire 2:79
  Phoenician alphabet 2:79, 2:90
  quipus 5:98–9
  Semitic 1:117
  Turkish 4:98, 4:109
  see also scripts
Wu-Wei, excavation of bronze horses 5:42, *5:42*
Wyclif, John (c.1320–1384), English Church
  reformer 5:117

X

x-ray *see* Röntgen, Wilhelm
Xavier, St Francis, (1506–1552), Jesuit
  missionary 5:77, *5:78*
Xenophon (c.430–c.354 BCE), Greek historian
  2:156
Xerxes I, king of Persia (485–465 BCE) 2:77,
  2:80
Ximenes de Cisneros, Francisco (1436–1517),
  Spanish cardinal 6:47, *6:57*

Y

Yahweh, god of the Hebrews 1:164, 1:167,
  1:171
  covenant with Israelites 1:164
  creative power 1:164–6
  and Moses 1:166, *1:167*
  temple of Solomon 1:157, 1:170
Yalta Conference *9:81*, **9:82**, **9:85**, **9:92**
Yang Kuang, Sui emperor (1605–1617) *5:62*
Yangtze River **2:31**, 2:32

Yangtze River valley 2:40
Yaroslav I the Wise, prince of Kiev Rus
  (1019–1054) *4:87*, 4:88–9, *4:93*
Yathrib (Medina), Muhammad's flight to 4:23,
  4:23
Yellow River (Hwang-Ho) 2:31–4, **2:31**, *2:33*
Yellow River valley 2:31–2, 2:34, 2:36, 2:39
Yeltsin, Boris (1931–1999), president of Russian
  Federation 10:152
Yen Fu (1854–1921), Chinese scholar **8:76**
Yen Li-Pen (7th century CE), T'ang emperor 5:53
yoga **2:23**, 2:27
Yorimoto, Japanese *shogun* (1147–1199) 5:72,
  5:73
Yoruba tribe (Benin), bronze sculptures of *5:85*
Yoshida, Shigeru (1878–1967), Japanese prime
  minister 10:40
Young Turk movement 9:33–5, *9:34–5*, *9:37*
Ypres *5:135*, *5:140*
Yuan Shih-k'ai (1859–1916), president of China
  8:78, **8:78**, 8:79, *9:11*, 9:14
Yucatán *5:93*, *5:95*
Yueh-chih people 4:15
Yugoslavia 8:142, 8:158, 10:23
  Albania, invasion of **8:161**
  Bandung Conference 10:22–3, **10:22**, *10:44*
  Cominform, expulsion from 10:77
  communist state of 9:88, 9:93
  federal state, dissolution of *10:150*, 10:151,
  10:161
  economy of *10:139*
  German capture of 9:72
  loans from United States and IMF *10:23*
Yunan dynasty *see* Mongol China
Yung-lo (1360–1424), Ming Chinese emperor
  5:60

Z

Zaire *see* Congo (Zaire)
zakat (alms-giving) **4:22**
Zanzibar 5:89
Zealots, Jewish sect 3:80, 3:89
  Simon and 3:83
Zen Buddhism, Japan 5:77
Zeno (c.340–265 BCE), Greek philosopher
  2:171, 2:174
Zeppelins *see* air warfare
Zeus, Greek god 1:148, **2:94**, *2:95*, *2:154*
Zhao Ziyang (1919–), Chinese politician
  10:154
ziggurats *1:78*, *1:83*, *1:84*, *1:85*, *1:88*, 1:91
Zimbabwe (ancient) *5:85*, 5:89–91
  buildings in 5:90–1
Zimbabwe 10:53, 10:60–61
  see also Rhodesia
Zionism 9:36, *9:36*
  Balfour Declaration 9:39, **9:39**, 9:109
  extremists of 9:111–12
  Russian support for 9:111
  World Zionist Congress 9:36, 9:110
Zoroaster 2:81
Zoroastrianism 3:66, 3:109, 4:10, 4:12, 4:18,
  4:38
  see also Persia
Zulu people, South Africa *8:33*, *8:34*, 8:39
  British defeat of 8:57
Zwingli, Huldreich (1484–1531), Swiss
  Protestant theologian *6:50*